Bible Studies
for the Preparation
of the Bride

A STUDY OF THE SONG OF SOLOMON

BY
BOB & ROSE WEINER

"Eat, O friends, and drink; drink deeply, O lovers!"
Song of Solomon 5:1

MARANATHA PUBLICATIONS
P.O. Box 1799
Gainesville, FL 32601

Cover Photograph
by Jerry Sieve

Bible Studies
For the Preparation of the Bride

Table of Contents

Scripture references in *Bible Studies for the Preparation of the Bride* are designed for use with the *New American Standard Version* unless otherwise noted.

BIBLE STUDIES FOR THE PREPARATION OF THE BRIDE

A STUDY OF THE SONG OF SOLOMON

INTRODUCTION

He who has My commandments and keeps them,
it is he who loves Me;
And he who loves Me shall be loved by My
Father, and I will love him,
And will disclose and reveal Myself to him. —
John 14:21

I call you friends — that I may make Myself
known to you. —
John 15:14-15

In these scriptures lie the heartbeat of Jesus our Savior, for within them is revealed the desire on the part of Jesus to make Himself known to those who love Him and obey Him — those whom He calls *His friends*. Jesus is seeking those with whom He can share His *heart*, His *purpose*, and His *plans*. He earnestly desires those with whom He can enter into a mature relationship — those that He will share His *life*, His *power*, and His *throne*. In short, He is seeking a *Bride* — those who will become *one Spirit* with Him. He is *not* looking for someone who is concerned with his own life and blessing or even for one who is determined to do great things for God. Rather, He is looking for those who *desire* to enter into intimate union with Him. This was God's thought in originally creating Adam, giving him dominion over all the works of God's hands. Through sin, Adam lost this place of fellowship. Today, Jesus is *seeking* those who would desire to re-enter that which Adam had only just begun to experience. But the Lord will not cast His pearls before swine or give what is holy to the dogs.

The truths of God are very precious. They are holy and precious pearls. They are thoughts and wisdom which come from the *very depths* of His being. These things He gives only as He knows that the one who is seeking is a *trusted friend* and *companion*. To share precious truth with the scoffers and mockers will cause them to turn and react violently. This brings a very deep grief to the Spirit of God. Consequently, the Lord must be *convinced* of our *diligence* in *seeking Him*, thus revealing the sincerity of our heart. As in the natural, man will share and reveal his most intimate thoughts with only those of whom he is convinced love him; so it is with God for we are made in His image. When He finds an earnest and diligent seeker, He will reveal to him His secrets, make known to him His covenant, and with this person He will share His life.

Such a person is the Shulamite maiden of the Song of Solomon. She is a diligent seeker after the heart of God. She is one like Paul, who with everything she has, is pressing in to the excellency of knowing Christ Jesus her Lord. The Song of Solomon is a love song between Jesus and His Bride—Solomon being a type of the Lord Jesus Christ. The Song of Solomon is written in figurative and symbolic language. It, in its entirety is an allegory made up of many parables. An allegory is a story in which people, things and happenings have a hidden or symbolic meaning. A parable is like an allegory but is much shorter in context. The Bible is full of both allegories and parables from Genesis to Revelation. Jesus constantly taught the multitudes in parables.

His disciples asked Him, "Why do you
speak to them in parables?"
He answered them, "To you it has been
granted to know the mysteries of the
Kingdom of heaven,
But to them, it has not been granted." —
Matt. 13:10-11

Again He said, "I will open My mouth in
parables;
I will utter things **hidden** *since the*
foundation of the world."-
Matt. 13:35

In His parables are found the *hidden* things of the Kingdom of God.

When His disciples pulled Jesus away from the multitude, they were saying, "Explain to us the parable of the field." It is here, in the thirteenth chapter of Matthew that Jesus reveals the Biblical method for parable interpretation. It is on the basis of this principle that this study of the Song of Solomon was written. Consequently we will examine what Jesus had to say concerning this.

As Jesus began to explain to His disciples who were His friends and trusted companions, He said,

The one who **sows** *the* **good seed** *is the*
Son of Man, *the* **field** *is the* **world**;
As for the **good seed**, *these are the* **sons**
of the **Kingdom**;
And the **tares** *are the sons of the* **evil one**;
The **enemy** *who sowed them is the* **devil**,
The **harvest** *is the* **end of the age**;
And the **reapers** *are the* **angels**.
Therefore, just as the tares are gathered
up and burned with fire, so shall it be
at the end of the age.
The Son of Man will send forth His angels,
And gather out of His Kingdom all stumbling
blocks and those who commit lawlessness.
Then the righteous will shine forth as
the sun in the Kingdom of their Father.
He who has ears to hear let him hear. —
Matt. 13:37-41, 43

In the explanation that Jesus gave of this parable, He took natural things and gave them a spiritual meaning—the *field* is the *world*, the *good seed* are *the sons of the Kingdom*, the *enemy* is the *devil*, and so on. We find then, from the teachings of Jesus, that parables are interpreted by applying a spiritual meaning to the people, things and happenings spoken about, and then giving the story a spiritual application. Now the question is, how can we determine the spiritual meaning of the people, things and happenings spoken about? Again we find the answer to this in the Book of Books, the Bible.

The Bible is a dictionary, defining and interpreting itself. We find these Biblical explanations by using a Bible Concordance as we look up all the scriptures using that particular word or thing, and compare those scriptures. The definition will either be plainly spelled out or can be concluded by revelation from the Spirit of God. The first method is more obvious, while the second is more hidden and obscure, requiring more patience, more diligence and more meditation to search it out. Let us take an example of a more obvious definition. In reading a passage with reference to the *cedars of Lebanon*, we find the definition by using the method above in Psalm 92:12-14.

The righteous man will flourish like a
palm tree,
He will grow like a cedar of Lebanon,
Planted in the house of the Lord.
They will flourish in the courts of our
God.
They will still yield fruit in old age;
They shall be full of sap and very green. —
Psalm 92:12-14

We find from this passage that the definition of the *cedar of Lebanon* is the *righteous man*. We find within this passage that the *palm tree* also represents the *righteous man*. This passage paints for us a very graphic picture of the righteous man — a picture much more explicit and descriptive than the mere word *righteous* can depict.

As we continue to investigate this passage further we find the following scriptures written about Lebanon.

*It will blossom profusely and rejoice
with rejoicing and shouts of joy.
The glory of Lebanon will be given to it,
The majesty of Carmel and Sharon.
They will see the glory of the Lord,
The majesty of our God. —
Isa. 35:2*

*The glory of Lebanon will come to you,
The juniper, the box tree, and the
cypress together,
To beautify the place of My sanctuary;
And I shall make the place of My feet
glorious. —
Isa. 60:13*

From these scriptures we find that *Lebanon* represents a place of glory, even the *glory of the Lord*.

If the *righteous man* is said to be as a *cedar in Lebanon* then we can deduct that the righteous man is the *glory of the Lord*. This goes along with the teachings of the New Testament that depict the Bride of Christ as God's crown and His glory.

The Song of Solomon, God's greatest and most intimate allegory, paints a word picture for us of the desire and love between Jesus and His Bride that is vivid and glorious, extending far beyond mere words. And this, in essence, is the beauty of all God's allegories and parables; we find hidden there beautiful word pictures that portray with great meaning and deep feeling words that otherwise seem dry and uninteresting, the understanding of which is sometimes hard to grasp.

Jesus likened the Kingdom of God unto hidden treasures and precious pearls. Proverbs 2:3-5 says:

*For if you cry for discernment,
Lift up your voice for understanding;
If you seek her as silver,
And search for her as for hidden
treasures;
Then you will discern the fear of
the Lord,
And discover the knowledge of God.*

To find hidden treasures you must dig very deep, search in many places and be very committed to not giving up until you find what you are searching for. Jesus likened the hearers and doers of the Word as those who *dug deep*, and built their house on the Rock. In Job 28 we find a beautiful word picture of a man mining for silver, gold, and precious stones. Verse ten says, "He hews out channels through the rocks," that "his eye sees anything precious," and "what is hidden he brings out to the light." The passage concludes with this *key* found in verse 20:

*Where, then, does wisdom come from?
And where is the place of understanding?
Thus it is hidden from the eyes of all
living and concealed from the birds of
the sky.*

As we read the Word daily, we receive the bread with which to feed our spirit; but down underneath its surface, down deep in the Word, is found the precious gems of God's hidden wisdom.

For those definitions and meanings that are less obvious and more obscure and hidden, Ecclesiastes says this:

I tested all this with wisdom and I said,
"I will be wise," but it was far from me.
What has been is remote and exceedingly
mysterious, who can discover it?
I directed my mind to know, to investigate,
To seek wisdom and an explanation...
Behold I have discovered this, says the
preacher,
"adding one thing to another to find an
explanation."—
Ecc. 7:23-25, 27

In this method of Biblical interpretation the student must be careful to look up all scriptures using that particular word, write them down, and compare one with the other. To make an incomplete investigation might result in an incomplete or inaccurate definition. Because of the length of this method of investigation, we have not included an example of this type of word study here, but we have included an example of it at the end of this study for your observation. The word study is on *lighting* with the apparent conclusions at the end. It is important to note that this method takes much diligence, prayer, meditation and waiting upon the Spirit of the Lord to bring *revelation knowledge*. It cannot be figured out or discovered with the natural mind, for the meanings are hidden, veiled and only to be revealed to *trusted companions*. As Paul tells us:

We speak God's wisdom in a mystery,
The hidden wisdom,
Which God predestined before the ages
to our glory...
Things which eye has not seen
And ear has not heard,
And which have not entered the heart
of man,
All that God has prepared for those who
love Him.
For to us God revealed them through the
Spirit,
For the Spirit searches all things,
even the depths of God...
Even so the thoughts of God no one
knows except the Spirit of God.
Now we have received, not the Spirit of
the world,
But the Spirit who is from God,
That we might **know** *the things*
freely given to us by God,
Which things we also speak,
Not in words taught by the human wisdom,
But in those taught by the Spirit,
Combining and comparing spiritual
thoughts with Spiritual words.
But a natural man does **not accept** *the*
things of the Spirit of God;

For they are foolishness to him,
And he **cannot understand** *them,*
Because they are spiritually discerned. —
I Cor. 2:7, 9-14

When the Spirit of God gives the revelation and interpretation of a thing, it will be accompanied by an inner witness of the Holy Spirit and will bring great light, life and spiritual edification.

As we dig deep into God's Word, mining for the silver, gold and precious stones found there, God's glorious nature will be wrought within us. As we discover the precious promises of God's Word, we become partakers of the divine nature, escape the corruption that is in the world through lust, and become transformed into God's image from glory to glory. Truly the acquisition of wisdom is far above the acquisition of gold, silver or precious stones.

And all of us, as with unveiled face,
Because we continue to behold in the
Word of God,
As in a mirror, the glory of the Lord,
Are constantly being transfigured into
His very own image,
In ever increasing splendor,
From one degree of glory to another.
For this comes from the Lord who is
the Spirit. —
II Cor. 3:18 Amplified Version

Along with the Bible, God has inspired many men to compile reference books and resource books which are classics, enhancing and shedding light upon the Word of God. We would like to give reference to those books which we used as resource for compiling these studies. We recommend these books for the library of any serious student of God's Word.

Young's Analytical Concordance of the Bible, United Society for Christian Literature

Unger's Bible Dictionary, Moody Press

Preaching from the Types and Metaphors of the Bible by Keach, Kregel Publications

Number in Scripture by Bullinger, Kregel Publications

Manners and Customs of the Bible by Freeman, Logos

The text of these studies and the answers were written in accordance with the New American Standard translation of the Bible. Other texts, when quoted, were given reference. Certain passages were quoted from the Amplified Bible to enhance their meaning. The reading of the Amplified Bible itself is not suitable for use in the study of the Song of Solomon, as it is in great error in suggesting that the Song is a love suit between an anonymous shepherd lad and the Shulamite maiden which King Solomon tries to breach, thus losing the hidden and symbolic meaning of the entire Song.

In conclusion, we would like to give reference to the writings of Mrs. Jessie Penn-Lewis (*Thy Hidden Ones*), and of Watchman Nee (*Song of Songs*), for their inspiring work done on the Song of Solomon and the inspiration that the writings of both of these great saints of God had in compiling of these studies.

Finally, we would like to give all the praise and glory to God for the wonderful gift of His Holy Spirit which brings the Spirit of wisdom and revelation in the knowledge of Him. For His revelation and enlightenment we give Him thanks, for without it the understanding of this great allegory of the Song of Solomon would have been hidden and veiled from us also. We thank God for the privilege of mining for the precious gems that are found here — truly pearls of great price. We thank Him for the privilege of the revealed secrets of His great and matchless love for us. Our prayer for you, the readers and students of this work, is that the Lord of Glory may grant unto you:

...the Spirit of wisdom and of revelation
in the knowledge of Him,
That the eyes of your heart may be
enlightened,
So that you know what is the hope of His
calling,
What are the riches of the glory of His
inheritance in the saints
And what is the surpassing greatness of
His power toward us who believe. —
Eph. 1:17-18

And may God by His grace draw you in ever
increasing pursuit and desire of that
"One whose goings forth are from long ago
from the days of eternity." —
Micah 5:2

NOTES

STUDY 1

A SONG OF LOVE—
A SONG OF DESIRE

The Song of Solomon is the *love song* between the Messiah and His Bride. It is the *Song of Songs*. It is the *Song of Songs* in the same manner that the most holy place in the tabernacle is called the *Holy of Holies*. It is the *Song of Songs* in the same manner that Jesus is the *King of Kings and the Lord of Lords*.

In contrast, the preceding book, Ecclesiastes, is an exposition of the *vanity of vanities*. In Ecclesiastes we find that *all things* under the sun are sought for—the wrong things in the wrong way. In the Song we find that *one* thing is pursued: a relationship with the King which, in its consummation, tells us that satisfaction cannot be obtained through knowledge alone. The Song speaks of rest from wandering and tells us that man can reach satisfaction only through love.

In the Song of Songs, the King is set forth before us as a type of the Lord Jesus Christ in all the triumphant life of His resurrection and ascension. The Shulamite maiden is set forth as a type of the believer who longs for a fuller experience of Jesus. The maiden's experience represents that of the individual believer. The Song describes the beginning of deeper seekings after the Lord until such longings are realized in the *fullest* friendship.

The book's heartbeat speaks of spiritual communion. It is a book for the heart. The Song deals with the path of the believer who is actively pursuing the Lord. The book is addressed toward those who desire and long for a fuller experience of Christ. In the Song, the King speaks of the Shulamite maiden in this manner:

> *There are sixty queens, and eighty*
> *concubines, and virgins without*
> *number;*
> *But my dove, my undefiled and perfect*
> *one,*
> *Stands alone above them all,*
> *She is the only one of her mother,*
> *She is the choice one of her who bore*
> *her.*
> *The daughters saw her,*
> *called her blessed and happy,*
> *Yes, the queens and the concubines,*
> *They praised her.—*
> *Song of Solomon 6:8-9 Amplified Version*

The concubines and queens represent those believers who have varying degrees of relationship with the Lord. The maidens or virgins, in this particular passage, represent the children of grace who are born again but have developed no intimate fellowship with the Lord. But the dove, the undefiled one, the Shulamite maiden, represents those believers who have sought after the Lord (not for His mighty acts or for His conquering of the enemy) but for an appreciation and love for Him as a Person and a desire to be close to His heart. The believers who fully satisfy the Lord's heart are those who are regarded as the *only daughter*. This company of believers, represented by this *loved* maiden, live in the Spirit. They are as a dove in the singleness of their eye for Christ, completely separated unto Him. This *Bride* company has progressed and developed to fulness of love for the Lord Jesus.

The *Song of Songs* is the path of all those who have the *Bride* spirit, who desire to be fully and wholly identified with Him. God is ever ready to bestow much grace and accomplish much work within the life of any believer who will permit Him the liberty to carry on and complete His work in them. But those who allow that grace to work to its *full* end and complete accomplishment are few. *The choice is yours.*

The Spirit and the Bride say, "Come!"
And let him who is listening say, "Come!"
And let every one who is thirsty
(who is painfully conscious of his
need of those things by which the
soul is refreshed, supported, and
strengthened);
And whoever earnestly desires to do it,
Let him come and take and appropriate
(drink) the water of Life without
cost. —
Rev. 22:17

Lift up your heads O ye gates,
And be lifted up you ancient doors;
That the King of glory may come in.
Who is He then, this King of glory?
The Lord of Hosts, He is the King of
glory! —
Ps. 24:9-10

1. What is this song called? (Song 1:1)

    _____

2. Who sings this song? (Rev. 14:1-5)

    _____

3. Describe the character of the only ones that can learn this song. (Rev. 14:4-5)

    a. _____

    _____

    b. _____

    c. _____

    d. _____

    e. _____

Note: 144,000 is a symbolic number.

> 0 means *seed*

> 3 means the *fulness of God*

Therefore, 000 means a seed in the fulness and image of God.

> 12 means *divine government*

> 2 means *the matter is determined by God*

> 12 x 12 = 144 means divine government — the matter is determined by God

In conclusion, the 144,000 who were standing with the Lamb upon Mt. Zion, having the Father's name written on their foreheads (or having the renewed mind) are:

A seed in the fulness and image of God, under His divine government — the matter is determined by God!

4. This is a song of love of those who desire total transformation by the Lord. What contrast of the transformed life do we see in I Samuel 2:8? Answer is taken from the Amplified Bible, quoted below.

He raises the poor out of the dust
And lifts up the needy from the ash heap,
To make them sit with the noble,
And inherit the throne of glory.

5. What is the cry of the Bride spirit? (Song 1:2)

_____

This cry marks the starting point of real spiritual progress. It is an inward spiritual longing for the Lord Himself. If dissatisfaction with the ordinary and this pursuit for love's full end is not burning in the spirit of the believer, then it is utterly impossible to attain to *any* intimate relationship with the Lord. If there is not a hunger and thirst in the heart, then you will not understand what the Spirit of God means by this song.

6. What should you do if you do not have this intense desire? (Eph. 1:17-19)
    a. _____
    _____
    b. _____
    _____
    c. _____
    _____
    d. _____
    _____

7. What does the maiden say of God's love? (Song 1:2)

_____

The love of Jesus is better than the sweetest and most excellent product which this world can achieve. The things under the sun which men value most offer no comparison to His love.

8. What does she say about the character and name of her lover? (Song 1:3)
    a. _____
    b. _____

Therefore, the virgins love Him — because of who He is, the sweet oil of His graces, and because of His sweet name which is like purified oil that is emptied out. See marginal note.

9. That sweet ointment of His precious name has been poured out. What does Paul say of Him? (Phil. 2:6-11)
    a. (v. 7) _____
    b. (v. 8) _____
    c. (v. 9) _____
    _____
    d. (v. 10-11) _____
    _____

10. What prayer does the maiden utter? (Song 1:4)

_____

11. How does the Lord draw us to Himself? (Hosea 11:4)
    a. _____
    b. _____
    c. _____

It is the revelation of Jesus, given by the Spirit of His own beauty and magnificent glory, that draws us to Himself. Notice the one believer *drawn* to the Lord results in · *us* (many) running after Him (Song 1:4). Believers that are being drawn inspire others to press on to know Him.

12. How does the Lord answer her prayer? (Song 1:4)

_____

13. By what title does she recognize the Lord? (Song 1:4)

_____

Before we can know the Lord as the beloved Bridegroom of our souls, we must recognize Him as the reigning King. Complete dedication to His rule and authority always precedes a life of intimate love and devotion. This act of bringing the believer into His chamber, or secret place, marked the beginning of an intimate communion with her and a special revelation of Himself to her.

14. What has the beginning of knowing God in His inner chamber done for the believer? (Song 1:4)

_____

15. With what motives do these believers love the Lord? (Song 1:4)

_____

16. What is the goal of our instruction? (I Tim. 1:5)
    a. _____
    b. _____
    c. _____

May the Lord, by this sweet word of His Spirit, stir up many believers to become dissatisfied with anything else other than Bridal affection for the Lord of Glory. May He cause all of us who are His people to thirst and to reach out for those full and mature affections described in this song, which alone can satisfy His heart. It is the one who seeks after His heart with whom He will share His throne and His glory. Many are called and few are chosen. *Seek to be chosen.*

NOTES

STUDY 2

THE REVELATIONS IN THE
KING'S CHAMBERS

In the preceding study we noticed that as soon as the believer began to cry out to know God for Himself alone, that the King brought her into His chambers. Notice that this is not a banqueting house, but His chambers — a secret place — where she will be prepared for a fuller knowledge of the Lord.

1. What was the first revelation the maiden received in the King's chambers? (Song 1:5)

   _____

The Spirit of God will deal deeply with all those believers who make the confession of the maiden, *"We will run after Thee."* To those who utter this cry He will reveal all that is contrary to the mind of God in their hearts and lives.

The maiden's recognition of her *blackness* is not an acknowledgement of the former sins that have been put away; all that was knowingly wrong in her life has already been put away or she would never have been able to come to this place of intimate fellowship in the King's chambers.

The redeemed one's cry, "I am black," is a revelation of the blackness of the unrenewed mind — the mind that has been corrupted for so long by Satan. It is a revelation of soul-power, of everything that is a product of the soul-life. It is a revelation of the unsubmitted soul of man: mind, intellect, emotions and will, all of which must be brought into the control of the Spirit. Once the maiden only thought of the blackness as sin, but now she sees the blackness of her unrenewed soul.

2. What is the heart cry of the believer at this point in the revelation of God? (Job 42:5-6; Isa. 6:5)
   a. _____
   b. _____

Job cried out, "I abhor myself," while Isaiah cried out, "I am ruined." When this self-abhorrence is real and deep, the soul has no hesitation in acknowledging it. Many desire the *self-life* dealt with in secret, and are not willing to be as honest before others as they are before God. This pride must be broken before deliverance comes. Even our spiritually religious appearances must be surrendered so that we may be brought into a life of transparent reality both before God and man.

3. In realizing her blackness, what else does the believer realize? (Song 1:5)

   _____

4. What experience did Paul have along this line? (Phil. 3:8-9)
   a. _____
   b. _____

5. How and to what extent shall we be made righteous? (Rom. 5:18-19)
   a. _____
   b. _____
      _____

6. How does the maiden describe herself in symbolic terms? (Song 1:5)
   a. _____
   b. _____

Note: Kedar means dark *room* or *chamber*.

Therefore, the tents of Kedar point to her dark and unrenewed mind or soul. In like manner, the Church or believer is many times referred to in the symbolic language of the Bible as the *moon*. The moon is dark in itself, having no light of its own, but the light it gives off is a reflection of the light of the sun. The sun in scripture represents Jesus.

7. The *curtains of Solomon* were made of *fine linen*. What does fine linen in the scripture stand for? (Rev. 19:8)

_____

8. How are we made righteous? (Rom.4:3-5)

_____

Therefore, we see that the righteous acts of the saints are *faith* acts — believing God and acting on the truth of His Word. We see then that the maiden, though dark in her soul-life and in need of a renewed mind, believes God and it is accounted to her as righteousness.

9. In Isaiah what prophecy do we read concerning the Church? (Isa 30:26)

_____

The darkness of the moon (which symbolizes the unrenewed mind of the believer) has been totally transformed and filled with the light of the sun so that it too appears in the image of the sun itself.

Note: 7 means completion or spiritual perfection.
the light of 7 days — complete light flooding the church.

10. As a result of this revelation of *blackness*, what is the cry of the maiden to those around her? (Song 1:6)

_____

It is the discipline of the Lord that has withered the maiden's flesh and made the life of the flesh to be of no account to her. God is spoken of in scripture as being a sun, a consuming fire. He has scorched her with His terrible holiness and caused her to be black. Praise and esteem becomes most painful to the maiden because her soul is conscious of what she is within herself. She feels that she has been laid bare to every human as well as to the eye of God. Any desire within her to be admired or honored passes away. She only craves a deeper abasement so that her *Lord alone* may be seen.

11. What words of Jesus go along with this attitude of the heart? (Luke 14:26)

_____

12. What has she been caught up in and what has she neglected? (Song 1:6)
    a. _____
    b. _____

13. We can compare this to the story of Mary and Martha. What was Mary doing? What was Martha doing? (Luke 10:38-42)
    a. _____
    b. _____

14. What was Jesus' answer to Martha? (Luke 10:41-42)

_____

15. What exhortation did Jesus give of balance in the believer's life? (Matt. 23:23)

_____

16. What is meant in the Song by *my mother's sons*? (Gal. 4:26-29)

_____

17. Why were they persecuting her? (Gal 4:29)

_____

18. What cry does the maiden utter to the Lord? (Song 1:7)

_____

_____

Note: Noon symbolizes the perfect light of the day. It is the sun in full strength.

19. What is the pathway of the just likened to? (Prov. 4:18)

_____

_____

20. What does Job say about the path of the just and its result? (Job 11:13-19)

_____

The maiden asks the Lord for the pathway to spiritual maturity. She desires the path of rest with God in the fulness of His light and in divine union with His heart. She does not wish to be a part of companies of people who follow men of God (His companions) rather than the Lord Himself. This is symbolized by the flocks of his companions.

21. What were we called into? (I Cor. 1:9)

_____

22. What rebuke did the early Church receive? (I Cor. 1:12-13)

_____

23. In not wanting to be a veiled one, what did the maiden desire to do? (II Cor. 3:15-18)

_____

_____

Note: Wearing a veil was the custom of women during Bible times. Their faces could only be seen by their husbands. The maiden desires to have her face uncovered that she might look intently into the Bridegroom's face. (We as believers desire that our hearts might be opened to God so that we might receive the revelation of Himself.)

24. What instruction does the Bridegroom give? (Song 1:8)
    a. _____
    b. _____

25. What does this instruction refer to? (Heb. 6:12; Heb. 13:7; I Peter 2:21)
    a. _____
    b. _____
    _____
    c. _____

26. Who are the shepherds that the maiden is instructed to follow? (Eph. 4:11-13)

_____

27. What is meant by her *goats* or *kids*, and what is she supposed to do with them? (Song 1:8)
    a. _____
    b. _____

In the greatest pursuit of personal blessing, we must be careful not to neglect the younger *kids or goats*, the less mature ones, for whom we have the responsibility. Our attention here focuses on service and warns that in seeking for Christ in a fuller measure for ourselves our duty to younger and more immature ones must at the same time be carried out.

28. How does the King address her in this passage? (Song 1:8)

_____

Recognizing our own lack of self-worth and need for the Lord is the first requirement to becoming truly beautiful in the eyes of the King.

29. What kind of worshiper has she become? (John 4:23-24)

_____

30. What promise does she have from the Lord? (John 14:21)

_____

NOTES

STUDY 3

THE BANQUETING HOUSE

And the Master said, where is my guest
chamber, where I shall eat...
with my disciples? —
Mark 14:14

At His table the well-beloved opens His heart to His redeemed one. The Bridegroom has much to say to His own which cannot be said *at the beginning*. He must first say "follow Me" and must draw us away from other interests before He can tell us of a path that is *expedient* for us which will lead to a fuller knowledge of Himself.

1.   What does the Bridegroom compare His beloved to? (Song 1:9)

The Bridegroom compares the swiftness of the maiden running after Him to the choicest horse among Pharaoh's chariots.

2.   What words of Jesus describe this *swiftness* of seeking Him? (Matt. 11:12) Answer from the Amplified Version below.

And from the day of John the Baptist
until the present time,
The Kingdom of Heaven has endured
violent assault,
And violent men seize it by force (as
a precious prize) — a share in the
heavenly kingdom is sought for with
most ardent zeal and intense exertion.

3.   Describe the picture given in Job of this *horse* that is seeking for a share in the heavenly kingdom with most ardent zeal and intense exertion. (Job 39:19-25)
     a.   (v. 19-21) _____
     b.   (v. 22) _____
     c.   (v. 22) _____
     d.   (v. 24) _____
     e.   (v. 25) _____

This is intense pressing on to know the Lord and the consequential abandonment to the Holy Spirit for His work to be done at any cost. Once the will is wholly surrendered to God and the decision made to obey and follow at all costs, the Spirit is able to do His work. It is the delay and ceaseless controversy of the will against the Spirit that grieves and hinders the Lord. In addition, the child of God is unable to emerge from the region of strife into deepest rest.

4.   In this description of the maiden by the Bridegroom, what items point to the wealth and power that belong to the soul-life? (Song 1:9-10)

She is swift in movement and has a good measure of natural beauty, talent, and strength. The comparison is made to point out that in spite of the revelation of the inner chamber and a true quest for a spiritual life, one's natural endowments may come into much prominence in this pursuit. Many make no progress in spiritual life because of the intrusion of natural movements. Only what is wrought of God can be reckoned in terms of true values and carry us to our goal.

5. What promise of transformation does the Bridegroom give the maiden? (Song 1:11)

_____

Note: The word for *ornaments* in the original Hebrew means something like a *crown*—gold-braided wreath resembling a crown. *Gold* represents the *divine nature* while *silver* represents *redeemed* man. Therefore, the promise of the Bridegroom is that He will transform her through redemption and crown her with the divine life. The working of the gold into ornaments or a braided wreath requires *much fire* as gold is only workable when melted. This is the promise of the Bridegroom: to transform all that is of the natural life into the divine nature. The surrendered soul, pressing on for the prize of the high calling of God, is promised here that the work will be done. She *shall know* the divine life in union with the Glorified One; she *shall* sit down with Him in His throne and be a partaker of His glory. For those who have a longing heart, God has promised to fulfill *all* their desires. *Rest upon His Word!*

6. What words of assurance do we have from the mouth of the Lord? (Num. 23:19)

_____

7. Where is the maiden's attention directed now? (Song 1:12)

_____

8. What is the requirement in order to commune with the Lord at His banqueting table? (Rev. 3:20)

_____

9. Describe briefly the provision of the King's table. (I Kings 4:22-23)

_____

10. What type of maiden is this that is able to partake of the meat of the King's table? (Heb. 5:13-14)
    a. (v. 13) _____
    b. (v. 13) _____
    c. (v. 14) _____
    d. (v. 14) _____

11. As she partakes of this spiritual food, as she communes with the King, what happens? (Song 1:12)

_____

Note: Perfume in the original text is *nard* or *spikenard*.

12. What example do we see of this in John? (John 12:1-3)

_____

Mary anointed Jesus because of her love, her appreciation and her dedication to Him. As a result of this love-act, the fragrance of the spikenard filled the room.

13. As a result of feasting on the meat of the Word, what happens? (Jer. 15:16)

_____

The result of feasting upon the meat of the Word brings joy, resulting in true praise and a life of dedication and love toward the King. This type of life gives off a sweet smelling fragrance to God and to all those who come into its presence.

14. What picture do we see in Jeremiah of believers who are giving off this *type of fragrance*? (Jer. 31:12-14)
    a. (v. 12) _____
    b. (v. 12) _____
    c. (v. 12) _____
    d. (v. 13) _____
    e. (v. 14) _____

15. As a result of the revelations she has received at the banqueting table, in what new light has she seen the King, her Beloved? (Song 1:13)

_____

16. Below are the properties of myrrh. In studying them we will discover the new light in which the maiden has come to know the King through her spiritual banqueting with Him.

METAPHOR	PARALLEL
1. Myrrh is an embalming spice and was used in the embalming of Jesus.	1. Mark 10:38, 45; Phil. 3:10 _____
2. Myrrh has a preserving quality; it keeps things from corrupting, putrifying, and rotting.	2. II Peter 1:4-11 _____ _____
3. Myrrh has a beautifying quality. It is good to take away the wrinkles from the face and make the skin smooth and shining.	3. Eph. 5:25-27 _____ _____
4. Myrrh was the first and principle ingredient of the holy anointing oil that was appointed to be used for the anointing of Aaron and the tabernacle.	4. Isa. 10:27 (_Fatness_ means _anointing_) Isa. 61:1 _____ _____
5. Myrrh has a healing quality.	5. Prov. 4:20-22 _____
6. Myrrh has perfuming quality; it is used for perfuming garments and other things to make them cast a pleasant smell.	6. II Cor. 2:14-16 _____

Application:

In closest communion at the King's table, the soul now learns from the lips of the Lord that if she is to know Him fully, she must expect suffering and sacrifice. Up until now, she has only had glimpses of Christ in His glory. Now He asks her to follow Him, even though it may mean the cross. "Are you able to drink the cup that I drink, or to be baptized with the baptism that I am baptized with?" (Mark 10:38) Will she turn back? The decision must be made. It is only in partaking in the fellowship of His sufferings that we can partake of and know the power of His resurrection. Will she follow in the steps of Jesus, who for the joy set before Him, endured the cross, despising the shame, and sat down at the right hand of God? She reveals her _Bride Spirit_ by consenting to follow Him at all costs, clasps the myrrh to her breast and exclaims: "My beloved is unto me as a bundle of myrrh."

To her joy, by embracing the fellowship of His sufferings—total death to self—she finds that this precious myrrh that she holds so close to her heart begins to preserve her and keep her from corruption, thus allowing her to partake of the divine nature and making her calling and election sure. It has begun to beautify her with the water of the Word, taking away all blemishes, spots, and wrinkles. It has brought an anointing upon her life that has begun to break the yoke of the enemy over her and to set her free from bondage. This myrrh clasped to her breast has begun healing all her flesh. The perfuming quality of this myrrh has produced a fragrance upon her life that she has become a fragrance of Christ in every place. Men begin to marvel, not being able to cope with the wisdom and the Spirit with which she is speaking, and begin recognizing her as one who has been with Jesus.

> _O soul, what can you say to the King_
> _at His table?_
> _What can you say to Him with the pierced_
> _hands but "I will not leave thee,"_
> _"My heart is fixed O God, my heart is_
> _fixed."_

NOTES

STUDY 4

JESUS, LOVER OF MY SOUL

*The Lord loves the gates of Zion
More than all the other dwelling places
of Jacob.
Glorious things are spoken of you,
O city of God.
But of Zion it shall be said,
"This one and that one were born
in her;"
And the Most High Himself will establish
her.
The Lord shall count when He registers
the peoples,
This one was born there.
Then those who sing as well as those
who play the flutes shall say,
"All my springs of joy are in you."—
Psalm 87:2-3, 5-7*

1. What does the maiden compare the Bridegroom to? (Song 1:14)

_____

Henna flowers were used by Jewish maidens for adornment. Engedi was a place in the wilderness where David fled to hide. To find henna blossoms in the desolate place symbolizes the uniqueness of Jesus. She is adorned with Christ, so here is a visible manifestation of Jesus to the world.

2. What words of praise does the King speak to the maiden? (Song 1:15)

_____

The Bridegroom sees the holy dove, the spirit of the Father, shining through the eyes of the soul whose gaze is turned wholly toward Him in complete abandonment and trust. From the standpoint of function, the eyes of the dove can only see one thing at a time. This signifies singleness of purpose.

3. What does Jesus say about *clearness* or *singleness* of purpose? (Luke 11:34-36)
    a. _____
    b. _____
    c. _____

Therefore, we see that as we fix our eyes on Jesus, our life shall be completely illumined. We must be careful not to look at circumstances or the waves around us. In doing so we take our eyes off Jesus and begin to look at things that produce darkness in our minds and hearts.

4. As we keep our eyes fixed on Jesus what promise do we have? (John 8:12)

_____

5. What does the maiden reply in response to the King? (Song 1:16)

_____

6. What is said about their couch? (Song 1:16) Answer from the Amplified Version below.

_____

*Our arbor and couch are green and leafy.
(Green symbolizes freshness, vigor, prosperity
and that which is flourishing.)*

7. What is said about the righteous? (Prov. 11:28; Jer. 17:7-8)

a. _____

b. _____

8. What does the shepherd do for the sheep? (Ps. 23:2)

_____

Therefore, the maiden finds rest for her soul in their communion together, for from their fellowship springs all that is fresh, invigorating and flourishing in her life.

9. What does the maiden say about their house? (Song 1:17)

_____

10. Cedars are a type of the New Creation of God, of His saints. Let us study this type more closely.

1 . The cedar is a very noble and stately tree. It grows very high. It mounts high toward heaven.

1 . Isa. 33:15-17; Col. 3:1-2

_____

_____

2 . The cedar is a tree that takes deep root. As the tree grows high, it proportionately takes root downward. If it were weak at the roots, because of its tallness the wind would blow it down. Therefore, the root system must be equal to the height.

2 . Hosea 14:5; II Sam. 23:5

_____

_____

_____

3 . The cedar is a very strong tree.

3 . Ps. 84:7

_____

4 . The cedar is a tree full of sap. It also bears a sort of fruit. The shadow of this tree is very refreshing and all fowls of every wing dwell under it.

4 . Ps. 92:12-15; Ez. 17:23; Isa. 60:3-5

_____

_____

_____

5 . The cedar is a very profitable tree, and is excellent for building a house. Solomon made use of it in building the temple.

5 . Eph. 2:21-22

_____

_____

Inferences:

If the saints are likened unto cedars, excellent above others, well rooted, strong, durable, and useful to God and men, do we excel? Do we grow up high heavenward? Do we grow in humility? Are our hearts lowest, when our estates are highest? When we are most honored in the eyes of men, are we most humble in the eyes of God? Remember that the tree that takes deepest root spreads it branches farthest out and brings forth the most fruit. There are those who try to tear up the cedars of God by the roots to destroy them. They send many strong blasts and violent winds, yet the saints have stood, and will stand. *The Highest Himself will establish her.*

Finally, the cedar cast a shadow that enables birds of every wing to dwell under her. How happy is that the people or nation that sits under the shadow or protection of a righteous government, when righteousness and judgment shall be administered by the saints! All will seek shelter under them. This shall be accomplished in the latter days.

11. We have noticed in the Song that the maiden has said that their house was built of cedars and cypress. The cypress is also known as a funeral tree and is found commonly in the graveyard of Judea. The cypress signifies death. Thus, we see in these trees the life of the New Creation, and at the same time, death. What principle is the dwelling place of the believer and the Lord built upon? (Gal. 2:20)

_____

_____

Both the cedar and the cypress were used in the building of Solomon's temple. In other words, these were timbers that proved worthy for the construction of the habitation of God here on earth. Therefore we see that the basis for God's tabernacling among men lies on the death of the accursed old life and the resurrection of the new. Notice in the Song that the house is built not of *one* rafter but of *many*.

12. What does this symbolize? (Eph. 4:16)

_____

_____

Then it will come about in that day,
That nations will resort to the root of
Jesse who will stand as a signal for
the peoples;
And His resting place will be glorious.
And I shall glorify My glorious house.
The glory of Lebanon will come to you,
To beautify the place of My sanctuary;
And I shall make the place of My feet
glorious.
And the sons of those who afflicted you
will come bowing to you,
And all those who despised you will bow
themselves at the soles of your feet and
they will call you the city of the
Lord,
the Zion of the Holy One of Israel.
Then all your people will be righteous
and will possess the land forever,
The branch of My planting,
The work of My hands,
That I might be glorified. —
Portions of Isa. 11 and Isa. 60

NOTES

STUDY 5

THE OVERPOWERING LOVE OF GOD

As the hart pants for the water brooks,
So my soul pants for Thee O God.
How lovely are Thy dwelling places,
O Lord of hosts!
My soul longed and even yearned
for the courts of the Lord.
One thing I have asked from the Lord,
that I shall seek;
That I may dwell in the house of the Lord,
in His presence,
all the days of my life,
To behold and gaze upon the beauty
of the Lord,
And to meditate and inquire in His
temple.
For a day in Thy courts is better than a
thousand anywhere else.
I had rather be a doorkeeper and stand at
the threshold of the house of my God
Than to dwell at ease in the tents of
wickedness.
How blessed are those who dwell in Your
house;
They are ever praising Thee.
How blessed is the man whose strength is
in Thee;
In whose heart are the highways to Zion!
O Lord of hosts, blessed — happy, fortunate,
and to be envied — is the man who trusts
in You,
Leaning and believing on You,
Committing all and confidently looking to
You and that without fear or misgiving. —
Portions of Psalm 27; Psalm 84; Psalm 42

1. What opinion does the maiden have of herself? (Song 2:1)

_____

Sharon is a plain in Judea, and the rose mentioned here is a rambling rose or some ordinary flower that is common to the area. Thus she is saying, I am a very ordinary person, yet cared for and loved by God.

2. What does the King say of the maiden? (Song 2:2)

_____

3. What do thorns represent? (Gen. 3:18; Heb. 6:7-8)

_____

The work of man, apart from God, can only produce thorns and briers.

4. Let us study the type of the *lily* more closely.

SIMILE	PARALLEL
1. A lily is a very sweet flower, so fragrant that a man's senses will be easily turned with the strength of its fragrance.	1. II Cor. 2:14-15; Eph. 5:1-2 _____ _____
2. A lily is an exceedingly white flower, there is nothing more pure, nothing whiter.	2. Rev. 19:8; Dan. 12:10; Mal. 3:2-4 Note: fullers' soap is a whitening agent. _____
3. The lily is a very fruitful flower, often yielding fifty pods. Note: 50 is the number of *jubilee* - in the *year of jubilee* everything returns to its rightful owner!	3. Isa. 27:6; Num. 14:21; Hab. 2:14; Dan. 2:35, 44 _____ _____
4. The lily is a very tall flower—few others are taller.	4. Micah 4:1, 2 _____
5. The lily is a flower most gloriously adorned and lovely to look upon; Jesus said, "Solomon in all his glory was not arrayed like one of these." Its form is excellent. It has six white leaves, within are seven grains, and all within is the glory of gold. It hangs down its head. Much of the glory of the lily is inward.	5. Ps. 45:13 _____ _____

Six is the number of man.

White symbolizes purity and righteousness.

Therefore six white leaves symbolized man clothed with purity and righteousness.

Seven is the number of completion.

Gold symbolizes the divine nature.

Therefore, seven golden grains within stands for the completion of the divine nature within man.

Conclusion:

As a most fragrant lily, the Bride of Christ gives off the sweet fragrance of the knowledge of God in the midst of a cursed earth under the domain of darkness. As a lily among thorns, so the Bride of Christ stands forth in holiness and purity in the midst of a crooked and perverse generation. As a fruitful lily the Church will grow and multiply until it has become a great kingdom and has filled the whole earth with fruit. The year of jubilee will be ushered in, and everything will be returned to its rightful owner, for the kingdoms of this world shall become the kingdoms of our God and of His Christ. In the last days the Church will be exalted above every other kingdom and all nations will flow into it. The Bride of Christ as a beautiful lily will be completely transformed and the soul of each individual believer will be filled with the divine nature.

5. What has Jesus come to mean to the maiden? (Song 2:3)

_____

The maiden is now losing sight of all the *sons* or *trees* (Paul, Apollos), and has her sight fixed only upon Jesus. Dwelling under His shadow brings great rest and refreshing to the soul, and eating His fruit brings great sweetness to the spirit.

6.   The maiden said that under His shadow she found *great delight*. What will happen to those who *delight* in the Almighty? (Job 22:26-29)
   a. _____
   b. _____
   c. _____
   d. _____

7.   As the maiden partakes of these *apples*, what are they like? (Prov. 25:11)
   _____

We see then as we partake of the *fruit* of the tree of life, we eat of the divine nature (gold) and we receive from the Lord the perfect word that brings sweetness to our spirit.

8.   As we partake of these *apples*, what happens to our own tongue? (Isa. 50:4)
   _____

9.   What are the privileges of those who dwell under the shadow of the Almighty? (Ps. 121:5-8)
   a. _____
   b. _____
   c. _____
   d. _____

Note: The maiden *sat down* under the shade of this tree. This is a position of rest and trust and relaxing in the security of God. Notice that Jesus is *sitting* in heaven at the Father's right hand.

10.   As the Bridegroom brings the maiden into the banqueting house (literally the house of wine), what revelation of His nature is given to her? (Song 2:4)
   _____

This revelation of His love brings great joy to her. Wine in the scriptures symbolizes joy. Therefore, in this house of wine is found great joy at the revelation of His love.

11.   What does this banner signify? (Prov. 17:17; Prov. 18:24; John 15:13-15)
   _____

12.   At this deeper revelation of the love of God, what does the maiden cry out for? (Song 2:5)
   _____

Lovesick, according to Webster's Dictionary, means to be so much in love as to not be able to react in a normal way. Such was the experience of the saints of all ages when they came into a full realization of the Lord's special presence. Intense spiritual feeling such as this can produce physical exhaustion. The Lord has to enlarge the capacity of the soul to be able to enjoy and endure His glorious presence.

13.   What happened to the Apostle John when he saw Jesus in His glory? (Rev. 1:17)
   _____

14.   Although Jesus desires to reveal Himself to us in all His glory and beauty, why can't He? (John 16:12)
   _____

Therefore, we see that a process of strengthening and enlarging, a transformation from glory to glory, must take place. For Jesus to reveal the fulness of Himself to us when we first come to Him would be like a man who has lived in a dark cave for many years being suddenly brought out into the full strength of the noonday sun. This man must be taken through varying degrees of light before his eyes can bear the sun in full strength. So it is with us spiritually.

15. What is the maiden's desire? (Song 2:6)

_____

Note: *Hand* in the scripture symbolizes *the will in action*.

16. What does the left hand of God signify? (Matt. 25:41)

_____

_____

Therefore, the left hand signifies the action of God's will which is judgment against His enemies.

17. Jesus is the *Head* of the Church. What is under Him? (Eph. 1:20-23)

_____

Therefore, the maiden desires to see the Devil and his angels put under her Head, Jesus. As Paul says in Hebrews, "For in subjecting all things to Him, He left nothing that is not subject to Him. But now we do not yet see all things subjected to Him." The maiden desires to see God's will in action which is the believer rising up in the authority of Christ to tear down the strongholds of the enemy and put them under the Church.

18. What does the right hand of God signify? (Mark 16:19; Ps. 45:9; Rev. 3:21)

_____

_____

19. The psalmist David was a man after God's own heart. How did he express this desire to experience the love of God? (Ps. 27:4; Ps. 42:1-2, 7; Ps. 84)

_____

_____

20. After this great experience with the Lord, what position do we find the maiden in? (Song 2:7)

_____

Since the hour she said, "Draw me, we will run after Thee," the Lord has tested her surrender, and shown her more clearly the conditions of oneness with Him and His life. The Lord has tested her and found that she has *steadily purposed* to follow on to know the Lord. Her will is so fixed on this one purpose that the Lord will now be able to lead her through deeper testing without the delay of reasoning, or hesitation. The Lord now desires a time of spiritual rest for His beloved before He calls her to arise and follow on, so that she may be filled with all the fulness of God.

THE CALL TO ESCAPE FROM SELF
AND ENTER INTO THE
RESURRECTION POWER OF THE LAMB

Who is like the Lord our God,
Who is enthroned on high,
Who humbles Himself to behold
the things that are in heaven
and in the earth?
He raises the poor from the dust,
And lifts up the needy from the
ash heap,
To make them sit with princes
And inherit the throne of glory.
He makes the barren woman abide
in the house
As a joyful mother of children. —
Portions of Psalm 113; I Sam. 2:8

The maiden, resting in her Beloved, suddenly hears His voice calling her and recognizes it at once.

1. How does the king come to her? (Song 2:8-9)

_____

To regard the Lord as a gazelle or hart refers to the inspired title of Psalm 22, called *aijeleth hashshahar* or *hind of the morning*. Bible scholars agree that this Psalm points forward to the resurrection of Jesus. Morning is the beginning of the day and thus the resurrection of Christ is the beginning of new life. The hart is noted for its beauty and swiftness of escape from its enemies. The hart walks on the high places of the earth. We see Jesus then desiring for the maiden to follow Him in all the beauty, victory and swiftness of His resurrection life.

2. As a *resurrection* type, what is the King doing? (Song 2:8)

_____

Note: *Mountain* in the scripture symbolizes *kingdom*. In this passage we see Jesus in the power of His resurrection and in His victory over the kingdoms of darkness, and the kingdoms of this world. The Lord here manifests His triumph over every power, leaping and skipping over the power of the enemy with all things under His feet.

3. What message of revelation is the King bringing to the maiden? (Isa. 52:7)

_____

4. What does the King call the maiden to do? (Song 2:10)

_____

Up until now, the maiden has only known the sweetness of communion with the Lord, but little of the power for service or the fierce struggle of spiritual warfare.

5. What does the King desire to do in her life? (II Sam. 22:34-40)
    a. (v. 34) _____
    b. (v. 35) _____
    c. (v. 36) _____
    d. (v. 37) _____
    e. (v. 38-40)_____

6. When she learns these things, what will happen? (Isa. 35:5-10)

_____

_____

7. What stands between the maiden and the Lord? (Song 2:9)

_____

In the sweetness of her communion with the Lord, the maiden has built up a tabernacle or a wall in which she has enjoyed the Lord for herself. She has forgotten the multitude of men in the valley, men oppressed by sin and bound by demons. The Lord cannot be imprisoned behind her wall. He must move in the power of His resurrection in the hearts and lives of men. He must liberate the captives and set free those that are bound. He must heal the bruised and brokenhearted. He must proclaim unto Zion *Your God reigns!* For this He gave His life. For this He endured the cross. For this reason He was manifested, to destroy the works of the devil, to render him powerless, and to liberate the sons of men into the glorious liberty of the sons of God. He desires for her to follow Him into the ressurection power.

8. What cry of the ages has God heard? (Ps. 102:19-20)

_____

9. Job, which according to Bible scholars is the oldest book of the Bible, contains in it the hope of the ages. What is written there? (Job 19:25-27)

_____

_____

10. What part do the redeemed play in this? (Obadiah 21; Rom. 8:19-21)

_____

The risen Lord of Glory has come to answer this cry.

11. The Lord calls her to arise and come away, to come out from behind her wall. What attitude are we exhorted to have? (Phil. 2:4-7; Matt. 20:28)
   a. (v. 4) _____

   _____

   b. (v. 5,7) _____

   _____

   c. (v. 28) _____

   _____

12. How can the maiden break through this wall? (Ps. 18:29)

_____

13. The King is calling the maiden to follow him. What does he want to teach her and what should her response be? (Matt. 4:19-20)

_____

_____

In times past, the maiden has known the Lord's presence in connection with a certain place and a certain time in which she sought Him. Much of her realization of His presence was based on feelings. Any impact with the world or daily tasks seemed to trouble her and rob her of any real peace.

14. What does the Lord desire for her to learn? (Acts 17:27-28; Jer. 23:23-24; Ps. 139:1-18)

_____

We see then that the Lord desires for her to learn of His ever-abiding presence. He desires for her spirit to be released to touch His Spirit, to be able to fellowship with Him not only in times of quietness, but also in the times of heightened activity. He desires her to know a communion with Him that surpasses *feelings*, a communion of spirit. She must learn to recognize the King in all the circumstances of her life. The Lord is omni-present. The Lord's presence should be a reality, not only in her prayers, but a reality in the everyday affairs of this life.

15. What does the Lord liken her past period of rest to? (Song 2:11)

_____

During the winter season in nature, the sap goes downward to the roots and all outward manifestation of life appears stopped.

16. What has happened to the maiden during her winter period of rest when the rain of the Spirit fell upon her to prepare her for her new call? (Eph. 3:17-19)

_____

17. What time of the year has it become and how is this new life coming forth contrasted to the winter that has just past? (Song 2:12-13)

_____

We see in this graphic picture the abundance of the resurrection life. Paul said, "That I might know Him and the power of His resurrection." It is this resurrection life that we have been called to walk in. This is the sabbath rest of God. It is not a ceasing from much activity, as some believe, but rather a life in which every day is a day in which you do the Father's will. It is this life of fruitfulness to which the maiden is being called.

18. What is the sabbath rest of God? (Isa. 58:13-14)

_____

19. What should we avoid doing? (James 4:13-15)

_____

It is when our own plans are interrupted that aggravation and turmoil sets in. If our day is subject to the leading of the Spirit then we cannot be disappointed. It is only in seeking our own plans, no matter how spiritual, that we step out of God's rest.

20. Describe this type of follower of the Lord found in David's wilderness land. (I Chron. 12:8)
    a. _____
    b. _____
    c. _____
    d. _____

Note: Proverbs says "The righteous are as bold as a lion." Revelation says, "Behold, the Lion of the tribe of Judah, the Root of David has overcome."

21. In the life of the maiden, we have seen many phases or stages of progress and growth in her pursuit of the Lord. How does Ecclesiastes explain this variety? (Ecc. 3:1-11)

_____

NOTES

30.

STUDY 7

JESUS, THE ROCK OF MY SALVATION

In our previous study, the King has called the maiden to escape from self and to follow Him into the resurrection power of the Spirit. Together they will leap upon the mountains, putting the satanic kingdom under their feet. Together they will set the captives free and loose the men who are bound by the curse of sin.

1. In the calling of the maiden into this resurrection power, the King points out that the flowers have already appeared in the land. What do the *flowers* signify? (Job 14:1, 2)

   _____

2. What does He mean by the time for *pruning the vines*, and how does this relate to the life of the maiden? (John 15:2)

   _____

The *turtledove* was a bird used for sacrifices. It is therefore a type of the Spirit of God being poured out through the sacrifice of Jesus. This made the Baptism in the Holy Spirit possible. This passage relates to the maiden specifically, yet the passage is also prophetic for the end times. (Read Song 2:11-13)

The winter of the Church is over and gone. The time of restoration has come. The *fig tree* represents *Israel*. The *vine* represents the *Church*. The Holy Spirit is poured out in the earth, Israel begins to become ripe to receive the Gospel (as well as being nationally restored), and the Church begins to produce fruit. It is at this time that God wants us to go forth and minister in resurrection power.

3. What is written in the New Testament concerning the fig tree and the Restoration? (Matt. 24:32-33; Acts 3:20-21)
   a. _____
   b. _____

4. Will Israel or the Church go back into darkness or defeat again, after God returns and begins to restore them? (Isa. 54:5-10)

   _____

5. What does the King call the maiden? (Song 2:14)

   _____

Before the Lord has spoken of her eye being as a dove's eye; here He addresses her as her whole being manifesting the full life of the Spirit. This is a future position to which she has not yet attained.

6. Why, then, is the King calling her by this name? (Rom. 4:17; Rom. 8:29)

   _____

Therefore, as God sees us through the eyes of faith, we too must see others through the eyes of faith, believing and praying for them that God will accomplish His work in their lives when they appear to fall short.

7. In what position is the maiden found? (Song 2:14)

   _____

8. Who is the *Rock*? (II Sam. 23:3; I Cor. 10:4)

   _____

9. What then does the *cleft Rock* signify? (Compare John 19:33-34; Ex. 17:6)

   _____

10. Being placed in the cleft of the rock refers to what specific position of the believer? (Phil. 3:10 compared with Ex. 33:21-22)

_____

We see an exhortation from the King that only as the maiden takes her place in the death of the Messiah, allowing all that is earthly and soulish in her life to die, can she walk in pure resurrection life. Only resurrection life makes it through the cross, the complete death to a life ruled by the soulish nature.

11. Let us look further into the metaphor of the *Rock* to discover more information about the maiden's position in the Messiah. (Now a metaphor is a figure of speech containing an implied comparison in which a word or phrase ordinarily and primarily used for one thing is applied to another.)

METAPHOR	PARALLEL
1. A rock is a firm and immovable thing, good for a foundation.	1. Luke 6:47-48
2. Rocks in ancient times were used for habitations; people dwelt in them, they hewed out houses in the rocks.	2. Ps. 90:1; I John 4:16
3. A rock is a high place. Though they have their root low and deep, yet their high and soaring tops are lifted far above the surface of the earth.	3. Col. 3:1-4; Rev. 14:1; Eph. 2:6
4. Rocks, being high, are useful for seeing things far off.	4. Heb. 11:13; John 8:56
5. Rocks are strong, and were used for defense. They are impregnable.	5. Ps. 94:22
6. Rocks are durable, permanent, and lasting. There is NO removing a rock. They continue the same from generation to generation.	6. Ps. 90:2; Heb. 13:8
7. Rocks yield honey.	7. Ps. 19:10
8. Precious stones and jewels are the *sweat* of rocks. All rich mines of gold and silver are in and among rocks.	8. Col. 2:3; Job. 28:1-21 Note: This passage in Job is an allegory on wisdom and knowledge.
9. Rocks yield oil.	9. Job 29:6; Deut. 32:12-13 Note: Oil symbolizes the *anointing oil* — the Holy Spirit.
10. Rocks yield the purest water, and most pleasant springs proceed from them. No water is so clear as that which comes through rocks.	10. Rev. 22:1; Ezk. 47:1-12

11.	Rocks are dangerous to stumble over or to fall on, especially from the top of one. When a man gets up almost to the top of a high and mighty rock, and suddenly, out of carelessness, falls, he is broken in pieces and may perish.

11.	Rom. 9:33; I Cor. 10:12; Matt. 21:44

_____
_____
_____
_____
_____

Application:

    As this maiden takes her place in the cleft Rock, all that is fleshly and soulish will be broken to pieces. In her position in the Rock, she will receive heavenly vision and spiritual eyesight to see those things afar off. As she makes the Rock her dwelling place, she finds herself dwelling in love, dwelling *in* God. The Rock becomes her stronghold, her fortress, and as she dwells there she lives *above* the circumstances of the earthly life. As she takes her place in the clefts of the Rock, she sees that the promises of God are like honey and they are sure, steadfast and everlasting. In the *Rock* she digs deep and finds all the treasure of wisdom and knowledge. These treasures are hidden from birds and from men who dwell on the earth, but to her they are revealed. She digs deep shafts down in the Rock and searches out the riches that are found there. She is able to bring these hidden truths and precious stones to the light where they reflect the brilliance of the Son. As she dwells in the Rock, it pours out oil upon her head. From it she drinks water as pure as crystal which washes her from every spot and wrinkle. Consider the Rock in which she dwells, for such is God.

NOTES

NOTES

STUDY 8

THE CALL TO INTIMATE FELLOWSHIP

In the last study, we found that the Lord has called the maiden to escape from self into His resurrection life. He has asked her to take her place in the cleft rock, the crucified life, so that all that is of the soulish power might die. He desires for her life to be controlled by His resurrection power. He cannot be imprisoned behind her wall, but He must go forth and deliver the creation. He wants her to move out of her circumstances and into Him. He desires for her to abide constantly in Him wherever He may lead. In these circumstances there are no bounds of time and place. He desires for her to be one with Him in His interests and service. He wants to bring her out of incomplete union and incomplete fellowship into a life of complete fellowship with the King. The King is seeking one with whom He can share His heart, His purpose, and His plans. He is not merely looking for someone who is concerned only with their own life and blessing. It is this fellowship that He desires from her and it is His desire to lead her into it.

1. How does the Lord portray her union in His resurrection? (Song 2:14)

_____

Notice that the *steep pathway* in other translations is called the *secret places of the stairs* or *the secret of the steep places*. This is a *call to ascend with the risen Christ*. Positionally we are seated with Christ in heavenly places with all enemies under our feet, yet there must be an experiential working out of these things. There must be a taking of our inheritance and a rising above of the earthly ways. We must ascend upward into a fuller knowledge of Him and be transformed from glory to glory.

2. Where is the Bride of Christ found in Revelation? (Rev. 21:9-10)

_____

We find the Bride on top of a very high mountain. She got there through the secret places of the stairs, through the steep pathway into His glory and inheritance. We see a picture of these stairs of ascension in the Word.

3. What picture do we see in Genesis? (Gen. 28:12-17)

_____

We see the Lord standing at top of the ladder with the promise of inheritance. Between the time that Jacob received this promise and the time that the Israelites took their inheritance, there were many stairs to be climbed and many trials to be endured.

4. What picture do we see in Ezekiel? (Ezk. 40:2, 6) Note: *East* represents *the mind of Christ* or *an openness toward God*. *Gate* represents *the mind of man*. *One* is the number of *God*.

_____

Here is a picture of the mind of a man facing the mind of Christ. There must be an *ascending* of the stairs before the mind (gate) can be measured by the measurement of God and be found in His image.

5. How is the way of the *secret places of the stairs* found? Note: *Secret* also means *counsel* or *intimacy*. (Ps. 25:14; Job 11:6; Matt. 13:35; Dan. 2:22)

    a. _____
    b. _____
    c. _____
    d. _____

6. What is the next matter brought to the maiden's attention? (Song 2:15)

_____

Little foxes hide themselves behind the vines. If unnoticed they can easily destroy the fruit of the vine. The vines with tender grapes represent the *beginning* of resurrection and ascension life. The fruit of life is full of promise. If unwatched or unguarded now, the little things can ruin it all. Therefore it is very important for the vine to have a caretaker so that the little foxes can be caught and taken care of.

7. What are the little foxes? (Eccl. 10:1; Prov. 16:18, 28, 32; Prov. 18:9, 13)

_____

These are just some of the little foxes that spoil the vines. Remember that these little foxes hide. These are not necessarily grave sins. We must therefore be wise and discerning and also have a caretaker who is able to help us watch.

8. In light of this, what should we do? (Prov. 19:20; Prov. 20:30; Prov. 27:5, 6)

_____

9. How does she regard her relationship with the Lord? (Song 2:16)

_____

We find that she realizes God's love for her, yet she sees herself as the center of attention and not the Lord. Notice how she says, "My beloved is *mine.*" Later in the song, we see her perspective change as she says "I am my beloved's."

10. Where does He pasture His flock? (Song 2:16)

_____

Note: The lilies here are those people with dedicated and pure hearts toward God. Among such a company, the Lord really feeds His flock.

We remember that at the first of this chapter, the Lord has called her to rise up from behind her wall and follow Him in this resurrection life.

11. What is her response? (Song 2:17)

_____

Bether means *separation.* What she is actually saying is that she wants the Lord to turn back and be enclosed in *her* circumstances. She desires to be separated from the world until her life is more perfected (until the shadows flee away). She has preferred to have Him in hiding behind her own wall. She has deliberately chosen to shut herself out from any environment in the world, and this at the expense of having the Lord labor there alone without her help. The result is an incomplete union with the Lord both in His interests and service. Therefore, the Lord employs a new method of teaching.

12. What method does the Lord employ? (Hosea 5:15)

_____

He withdraws the sense of His presence from her that He might draw her out of herself into a quest for Him. This is the maiden's first awakening to actually going out to the Beloved in *His* circumstances.

13. What do we find the maiden doing now? (Song 3:1)

_____

The maiden has begun to seek the Lord. The bed here represents a place of spiritual rest. She seeks the Lord in her old retreat but seems to not find Him. She seeks to recover her past feelings and experiences. The shadows have deepened instead of fleeing away.

14. What must she learn about service? (Isa. 58:10-11)
   a. _____
   b. _____
   c. _____

15. What experience is she having that is similar to Job's? (Job 23:8-10)

_____

    1. Her first step of Christian experience was to forsake all to follow Him and to know His cross.

    2. Her second step was to know Jesus as an indwelling reality which involved feasting at His banqueting table and enjoying deep communion with Him.

    3. The third step, which she has not taken as yet, is abiding constantly in Jesus wherever He may lead. In these circumstances there are no bounds of time or place.

16. What do we see her stirred to do? (Song 3:2)

_____

The Lord has succeeded in His purpose. He has called her to *arise* but she did not obey. By hiding His face, He aroused her. By His silence, He has drawn her to seek Him diligently. He has broken down the wall of reserve and drawn her out of herself.

17. Who found her? (Song 3:3)

_____

We observe now in the maiden a new humility and honesty about her need for help. She has let down all her walls of pride and self-sufficiency and sees her need for others in the Body of Christ.

18. What is the watchman's duty? (Ezk. 33:2-7)

_____

19. What must she do? (Heb. 13:7, 17)

_____

She must remember that the watchmen can point out the way for her and show her the path, but they cannot seek the Lord for her. This she must do for herself.

20. As she follows their instruction, what happens? (Song 3:4)

_____

21. What has actually happened to the maiden during this experience? (Heb. 12:7-10; James 1:2-4)

_____

The Lord did not test her more than she was able to endure. He allowed her to find Him and allowed Himself to even be led by her. The *mother's house* represents *the system of grace*, the *chamber of conception* indicates the *love of God*. God used the principle of grace and love to bring her forth. But because she cannot yet completely discern what is of the Spirit and of the soul, the Lord meets her at that level. She soulishly clings to Him. She must learn to rely upon the Word of God alone out of a heart of complete trust. As she goes on to know Him, the maiden will make an important discovery: He will not veil His presence from her when she loses all thought of herself. In order to dwell in Him and live by Him, as He lived by the Father, she must yield up her own life.

22. What promise does she have as she endures testing? (James 1:12)

_____

Notice that this crown of life is given not to those who endure until death, but those who endure through trials, for

> *Blessed, happy, to be envied is the man*
> *who is patient under trial and stands*
> *up under temptation,*

For when he has stood the test and been
approved,
He will receive the victor's crown of
life which God has promised to those
who love Him. —
James 1:12 Amplified Version

NOTES

STUDY 9

TRANSFIGURATION, A LIFE OF INTIMATE UNION

And all of us, as with unveiled face,
Because we continued to behold in the
Word of God as in a mirror the glory
of the Lord,
And constantly being transfigured into
His very own image in ever increasing
splendor
And from one degree of glory to another;
For this comes from the Lord which is
the Spirit. —
II Cor. 3:18 Amplified Version

The maiden in the previous study has gone through many dark nights of trial because of disobedience to follow the Lord's call. Therefore, the Lord had to employ other methods to draw her out of herself. Sins are relative. To the soul that walks in close union with the Lord, even the very smallest act of unfaithfulness becomes great. A sin which a stranger would regard as trivial would appear a serious crime to the trusted servant. Others may be content with being kept from what is considered gross sin, but an obedient heart that seeks to walk in unbroken communion with Him, cannot excuse even the smallest act of disobedience or insensitivity to God's will.

1. What has the valley of trouble become to her? (Hosea 2:14,15) Note: The Hebrew meaning of *achor* is *trouble*.

    _____

2. What different type of relationship has the Lord brought the maiden into through this wilderness experience? (Hosea 2:16, 19) Note: The Hebrew meaning of *Baali* is *my Master*. *Ishi* means *my Husband*.

    _____

After the period of rest commanded by the Lord in Song 3:5, the daughters see the *betrothed* one emerging from the wilderness. She who had been desolate, broken and weeping is now appearing with the glory of God upon her.

3. Where is she coming from? (Song 3:6)

    _____

4. What happened to Jesus after He came out of the wilderness of testing? (Luke 4:13-14)

    _____

It is important to remember that the Israelites wandered for 40 years because of unbelief, murmuring and complaining. It took Jesus 40 days. It was never God's will for the Israelites to wander in the wilderness. It was His plan to lead them straight through it into the promised land. He became so aggravated with them because of their constant complaining that He destroyed that generation and raised up another one to take the inheritance. Likewise, we can take ten years to learn one year's lesson, or we can take one year to learn ten year's lessons. This all depends on our attitude during testing. We can either walk forward through the valley of trouble in faith and confidence with a glad heart, or we can be dragged through with *heel marks* all the way. If we choose the latter course, it is doubtful that we will ever walk in the fulness of what God intends for us. We also risk the chance of grieving the Holy Spirit of God and being *set aside*.

5. What happened to the murmurers in the wilderness? (Num. 14:20-45)

    _____

6. Were they the only ones who suffered for their unfaithfulness? (Num. 14:33)

_____

In the maiden of this study, we see one who is *faithful*. She passes through the *nights* of trial and comes up out of the wilderness with a glad heart.

7. As she comes up out of the wilderness, what is she likened to? (Song 3:6)

_____

8. What other two references do we see in the scriptures to this column or pillar of smoke? (Ex. 13:21-22; Joel 2:28-30)
   a. _____
   b. _____

We find this expression used when Joel was describing God's wonders in the days when He will pour out of His Spirit in Pentecostal fulness on His servants. We also see that it was in the pillar of cloud that God manifested His presence to Israel in the wilderness. From these references we see the maiden emerging from the wilderness of testing in the power of the Holy Spirit, just as Jesus did.

9. What is she perfumed with? What fragrance is she giving off? (Song 3:6)
   a. _____
   b. _____
   c. _____

Note: *Myrrh* is used to symbolize three things in particular:

1. It is an embalming spice. This denotes the maiden's union with Jesus in His death. "I am crucified with Christ. It is no longer I that live, but Christ lives in me."

2. It is a beautifying ointment which takes away wrinkles. She is being washed in the water of the Word so that she might be without spot or wrinkle.

3. It is the principle ingredient in the holy anointing oil of Aaron. She has been anointed by the Holy Spirit to be a *priest* unto God.

10. *Frankincense* is a fragrant spice, used in making the priestly incense that was to be burned before the Lord. What does this refer to? (Rev. 8:3-4)

_____

11. What do the *powders of the merchant* refer to? (Matt. 13:45-46)

_____

Notice that there is a price involved. The maiden, in seeking the Kingdom of God, has had to pay the price which is total surrender of her life. Jesus said, "If anyone will come after Me he must deny himself, take up his cross and follow Me."

12. What is this *betrothed* one said to be? (Song 3:7)

_____

This couch is the resting place of the King of Peace. (Solomon means peace.)

13. What parable does Jesus give in Matthew 8:20?

_____

Here is a life that has become a *resting place* for the King, a place where He can lay His head. Here is a life which has come under His Lordship, His Headship. This life is the life of one who is in divine and intimate union with the King.

14. How many men are around this resting place of divine union? (Song 3:7)

_____

These men are also symbolic. Sixty men, or threescore men, would be 3 x 20. The number twenty is the number of expectancy:

- Twenty years Jacob waited to get possession ot his wives.
- Twenty years Israel waited for a deliverer from Jabin's oppression.
- Twenty years the Ark of the Covenant waited for Kirjaithjearim.
- Twenty years Solomon was waiting for the completion of two houses.

Three is the number of fulness or divine completion:

- God's attributes—omniscience, omnipresence, omnipotence
- Time—past, present, future
- Human capability—thought, word, deed
- Kingdoms—animal, vegetable, mineral

Sixty men would be waiting in expectancy for God to complete His divine plan. This symbolizes the expectancy and hope of those who are called into the Bride of Christ.

15. How else does this passage describe those 60 men who symbolize those who have the Bride calling? (Song 3:7-8)
    a. _____
    b. _____
    c. _____

In the wilderness the Lord has trained the maiden to be a warrior. We no longer see a sheep lying down in green pastures, but a mighty man of war.

16. Give a description of the King's chair or throne. (Song 3:9-10)
    a. _____
    b. _____
    c. _____
    d. _____
    e. _____

Here is the symbolism:
Timber or cedar of Lebanon—Saints
Silver—Redemption
Gold—Divine nature
Purple—Kingly authority

The King's throne itself represents the life where Jesus dwells inwardly as Lord and King. The King's chair then represents those saints, who having been redeemed through the blood of Jesus, are being supported and filled with the divine nature. It represents those who are under the Lordship of Jesus, and because of this His Kingly authority is being exercised through their lives.

17. What does the phrase "the interior lovingly fitted out by the daughters of Jerusalem" mean? (Eph. 4:15-16)

_____

18. What is this procession coming up out of the wilderness proclaimed to be? (Song 3:11)

_____

The daughters of Zion represent those who have already been brought into union with the Lord. They are overcomers, members of the Bride who rejoice to see the *Bride Spirit* in other souls, and are glad for the gladness of His heart.

19. What does the crown symbolize? (Isa. 62:3-5)

Here is the entrance of the maiden into divine union with the King. She has become betrothed to Him in faithfulness, in lovingkindness and compassion, in righteousness and justice; betrothed to Him forever. Here is the place where the one who goes on to know the Lord experiences what is meant by the scripture, "the man who is joined to the Lord is 'one spirit' with Him." The maiden, as she seeks Him, begins to enter into a union with Him that can only be known by those who are "married to Him who made the heavens and the earth." Just as earthly marriage is the beginning of two lives being blended together into one, the beginning of two people discovering and learning to know one another, so it is with those who are married to the Lord. In this relationship Jesus begins to share with His Bride His love, His thoughts, His plans and purposes in the earth. He provides for her every need. This is the beginning of intimate union with Jesus in the life of the believer and the beginning of deep knowledge of Him.

This Bridal union is a spiritual relationship with Jesus that we are not waiting to receive someday when He comes, but it is a place in the Spirit that we can enter now. We see Jesus demonstrating this relationship with the Father when He came up from the wilderness in the power of the Spirit. Jesus' prayer for those who believed in Him was that they might be part of His Bride, in intimate union.

That they may all be one; even as
Thou, Father, art in Me and I in Thee...
I have made Thy name known to them,
And will make it known;
That the love wherewith Thou didst love me
may be in them, and I in them. —
John 17:21a, 26

And you shall call me "Ishi," that is
"my husband,"
For your husband is your maker, whose
name is the Lord of Hosts.
You will be called, "My delight is in her,"
and your land, "married."
And as the bridegroom rejoices over the
bride,
So your God will rejoice over you. —
Portions of Hosea and Isaiah

It is this intimate union that God desires to bring you into now, that you may be filled with all the fulness of God.

The Spirit and the Bride say, "come."
And let the one who is thirsty come
And drink the water of life without cost. —
Portions of Revelation

NOTES

STUDY 10

THE BEAUTY OF THE NEW CREATION

In our previous study we have seen that the believer has become to the Lord a *crown of beauty*. His Bride has become a royal diadem upon His head. There follows a praise to the Bride from the lips of the King, describing the beauty of the *New Creation*. There are seven attributes described here which point to the spiritual perfection of the New Creation. As Jesus spoke in parables, telling a story in which people, things and happenings have a hidden or symbolic meaning, so it is here. The beauty of the Bride is spoken of in natural terms, yet as we look into the parable, we receive spiritual insight and understanding of the attributes of the New Creation of God and of the individual believer who is going on in maturity to know the Lord.

> *But blessed are your eyes, because they*
> *see;*
> *And your ears, because they hear.*
> *For truly I say to you,*
> *That many prophets and righteous men*
> *desired to see what you see,*
> *And did not see it;*
> *And to hear what you hear,*
> *And did not hear. —*
> *Matt. 13:16-18*

I. THE EYES

1. What is the first feature of the Bride that is mentioned and how does the King describe it? (Song 4:1)

   _____

The King, beholding the presence of the Holy Spirit, represented by the *dove* in the eyes of the Bride, sees her as the temple of the Holy Spirit. The *eyes like doves* point to spiritual insight. The ability to perceive things in the Spirit is one of the most prominent features in those going on to maturity. Doves' eyes, too, can only focus on one thing at a time. The maiden, likewise, has single vision: eyes only focused on Jesus and His will.

2. What prayer does Paul pray concerning spiritual insight? (Eph. 1:17-19)
   a. _____ _____
   b. _____ _____

3. What has the god of this world done? (II Cor. 4:4)

   _____

In contrast, the maiden is described as one whose eyes have been opened to see the light of the gospel of the glory of God.

4. What is said about Leah? (Gen. 29:17)

   _____

Leah represents those believers of *weak* spiritual insight.

5. What is said about Rachel? (Gen. 29:17-18, 30)

   _____

Jacob, who represents a type of Jesus, fulfilled his lawful duty to Leah. Yet, because of Leah's weakness in spiritual things, he loved Rachel more. Rachel represents those who are strong in spiritual things and those who walk in holiness before the Lord. *Beauty* in the scriptures represents *holiness*.

6. How has this spiritual insight, *dove's eyes*, been developed in her life? (Heb. 5:13-14)

_____

In Ephesians 4:13 we are told that we are all being built up until we become a *mature man* and reach the *measure of the stature which belongs to the fulness of Christ*.

7. In Amos we see the Lord *measuring* His people. What is He measuring them with? (Amos 7:7-8)

_____

A *plumb line*, according to Webster's Dictionary, is a weight on the end of a line used especially by builders to show vertical direction.

8. We find out more about this *plumb line* in Zechariah. Describe this *plumb line*. (Zech. 4:9-10; Zech. 3:9) See Marginal Notes.

_____

The significance of the *plumb line* is this: Jesus is measuring His people by the plumb line of complete spiritual insight. (The number seven means *completion*, or *spiritual perfection*.) In Isaiah we find out what this measurement is.

9. What are the *seven eyes*, or the *seven spirits* of God which Jesus desires His Church to measure up to? (Isa 11:2-3)

1. _____   5. _____
2. _____   6. _____
3. _____   7. _____
4. _____

Note: For those with NAS Bibles, verse 3 reads in the King James Version, "and shall make him of quick understanding in the fear of the Lord."

10. In Ezekiel we find a symbolic description of the overcomers. What is written about their spiritual insight? (Ezek. 1:18)

_____

Finally, these eyes are behind the Bride's veil. The people of this world cannot see or understand what a believer with spiritual insight sees. Spiritual perceptions must be hidden from the world. Some believers flippantly, and without discrimination, express the things that they have received from the Spirit of God. In contrast, we see that the eyes of the Bride are veiled, lest she *cast her pearls before swine* or cast what is *holy to the dogs*.

II. THE HAIR

1. Describe the hair of the Bride. (Song 4:1)

_____

2. What does hair signify in scripture? (Num. 6:1-5)

_____

3. Samson's separation unto God was the secret of his strength. When his hair was cut, or his separation unto God was broken, what happened? (Judges 16:17)

_____

So it is in the life of the Bride. The strength of God is manifested only as she remains separated unto His will and for His pleasure.

4. The hair of the Bride is described as a *flock of goats that have descended from Mount Gilead*. Mt. Gilead was the mountain on which the sheep and goats grazed, awaiting sacrifice in the temple.

What were two of the offerings in which goats were given for sacrifices? (Lev. 1:10; Lev. 3:6)

a. _____

b. _____

The *burnt offerings* and the *peace offerings* were *fellowship offerings*. They were *free-will* offerings to the Lord. The *burnt offering* symbolized the *entire surrender* to God of the individual. As a man gave the offering voluntarily, he was offering up his own body as a living sacrifice to live a life pleasing to God. The *peace offering* was a sacrifice offered in communion with God, given on behalf of those who desired a *closer fellowship* with God. Consequently, the reference to the maiden's hair (her separation unto God) being like a flock of goats points to a consecreted and dedicated offering of ourselves to the Lord. In such a dedication lies the strength and obedience of the believer.

5. What promise do those have who have wholly given themselves unto God and desire most earnestly His fellowship? (IIChron. 16:9)

_____

6. What was goat hair used for in the construction of the tabernacle? (Ex. 26:7)

_____

The tabernacle in the wilderness was where God met with Israel. The curtains of *goat hair* or skin covered the place where God met with man, and designated the *meeting place* of those set apart by God. The reference to the maiden's hair being as a *flock of goats* designates that her life is a place where God is *tabernacling*, and that she is being built together with other members of the Body as a dwelling of God in the Spirit.

7. What is one of the first things said about the Bride of Christ in Revelation? (Rev. 21:2-3)

_____

III. THE TEETH

1. What are the teeth of the Bride compared to? (Song 4:2)

_____

_____

The teeth indicate the ability to appropriate food. This reference then denotes the ability to receive and appropriate the provision of the Lord and to partake of the *strong meat* of the Word.

2. Who are those who can eat the *strong meat* of the Word? (Heb. 5:13-14)

_____

_____

According to the *Song*, the teeth are seen as a flock of shorn ewes which have come up from their *washing*.

3. What *washing* has the Bride received? (Eph. 5:26)

_____

As we receive the Word and meditate on it our mind is washed and renewed. Therefore, taking the *teeth* to signify the *mind*, we discover that these *ewes coming up from their washing* signify that the mind of the Bride has been washed in the water of the Word and been transformed, sanctified and cleansed.

4. What type of *ewes* or sheep are these? (Song 4:2)

_____

5. What does *wool* typify in the scriptures? (Ezek. 44:17-18; Gen. 3:17-19)

_____

The priests who ministered to the Lord within the veil were not allowed to enter with woolen garments upon them or with anything that caused sweat. *Wool* suggests the *earthly life that the Lord has cursed.* The ewes shorn of their wool, which caused them to be deceptive in size and weight, describes the *renewed mind* which has been *shorn of the wisdom of this world, freed from the curses of this earth* and *renewed in the wisdom and knowledge of God.*

6. *As we interpret the teeth* to signify the renewed *mind* what does the writer mean by "all of which bear twins?" (Job 11:5-6; Ecc. 7:18)

   _____

7. We have learned earlier that the Bride has been feasting at King Solomon's table and eating the strong meat found there. As a result of feasting on this strong meat found in I Kings 4:22-23 at Solomon's table, what has happened to the *mind* of the Bride? (I Kings 4:29-30)

   _____
   _____

This is a beautiful picture of the renewed mind, full of the balance of wisdom and discernment.

IV. THE LIPS

1. Describe the lips and mouth of the Bride. (Song 4:3)

   _____

2. Where else do we find the scarlet thread mentioned in scripture and what does it signify? (Josh. 2:18-19)

   _____
   _____

The scarlet thread brought redemption to Rahab and her household. In comparison, the lips of the Bride bring redemption and deliverance to men.

3. What are the lips of the Bride speaking? (Rom 10:14-15; Isaiah 52:7-10)
   a. (v. 14)_____
   b. (v. 7) _____
   c. (v. 7) _____
   d. (v. 8) _____

The lips of the Bride are not only speaking of redemption to others, but her lips themselves have been redeemed and brought under the Lordship and cleansing of Jesus.

4. Describe the constrast of the lips of the heathen who reject His authority. (Psalm 12:3-4)

   _____
   _____

5. Describe the words which the Bride speaks from lips that are subject to the Lordship of Jesus. (Ps. 12:6)

   _____
   _____

6. What was found in the mouth of the overcomers, and what are they considered to be? (Rev. 14:4-5)

   _____

7. This goes along with what teaching in James? (James 3:2)

   _____
   _____

V. THE TEMPLES

1. Describe the *temples* of the Bride. (Song 4:3)

    _____

    The *temples* represent the *seat of man's thoughts*. In describing the temples as a *sliced* pomegranate, we see that the thoughts of the Bride are *opened* and *exposed before God*. Notice that the temples are veiled from the outward world, but open and laid bare before God.

2. How does the psalmist describe the openness of thought toward God? (Ps. 19:14; Ps. 139:23-24)

    _____

    _____

    So it is with one whose thoughts are open toward God.

    The seeds of the pomegranate are crystal seeds tinged with red. Likewise, the thoughts of the Bride have been cleansed and purified. Her thoughts are as pure and clear as crystal, allowing the light of God and the wisdom of God to shine through them. Her thoughts have been redeemed (signified by the red).

3. What was found carved on the pillars of Solomon's temple? (I Kings 7:20)

    _____

4. What are the overcomers likened to? (Rev. 3:12)

    _____

    The Bride has laid her thoughts bare before the most high God to be tried and tested. As a result, her thoughts have been purified and refined that the light of God might shine through. She has qualified as an overcomer.

5. What are the weapons of her warfare and what are they able to do? (II Cor. 10:3-5)

    a. _____
    b. _____
    c. _____

VI. THE NECK

1. Describe the neck of the Bride. (Song 4:4)

    _____

    _____

2. Contrast the description of the neck of those who are disobedient to God. (Isa. 48:4)

    _____

    The *neck* in scripture signifies the *will*. The neck of the Bride represents a will in submission to the will of the Lord.

3. What does describing the Bride's *neck* or *will* as a tower suggest? (Ps. 61:3)

    _____

4. This tower is called the tower of David. The will of the Bride is said to be a stronghold of strength against the enemy as was David. What was the secret of David's strength? (Acts 13:22)

    _____

    _____

In having a submissive will toward God, we see the Bride's *will* as *a tower of strength* fixed on one purpose—to do all of God's will.

5. What promise do those have whose will is as *a tower of strength* fixed to do God's will? (Micah 4:8)

    _____

    _____

This tower, which the will of the Bride is compared to, was a tower built as an armory, a storehouse for weapons.

6. What type of weapons were they? (Song 4:4)

    _____

7. In the weapons of our warfare, what is our shield and what is its purpose? (Eph. 6:16)

    _____

    _____

8. Describe these *mighty men* to whom the shields belonged. (I Chron. 12:8)
    a. _____
    b. _____
    c. _____
    d. _____
    e. _____

The Bride's will and desire to do the will of God has been strengthened through the example and *faith* (shields) of these mighty men of valor. We note from the above passage that these men were skilled in tearing down the strongholds of Satan. They were said to have *faces like lions*. The lion in scripture symbolizes Kingly *authority*, Jesus Himself being the Lion of Judah. These men had the authority of the King upon their lives. When the enemy looked into their faces, it was the same as looking into the face of Jesus. They were said to be *as swift as the gazelles on the mountains*. In our earlier studies, we noted that this refers to Jesus in His resurrection life and power. These were men that were led by the Spirit of God and followed the Lamb in His resurrection power.

9. How are the mighty men of God described by Paul? (Heb. 11:32-40)
    a. _____   g. _____
    b. _____   h. _____
    c. _____   i. _____
    d. _____   j. _____
    e. _____   k. _____
    f. _____

10. What are we exhorted to do? (Heb. 6:12)

    _____

    _____

Therefore, through these examples of faith, the Bride has been strengthened to do the will of God.

VII. THE BREASTS

In this parable of the Bride, we come to the *seventh* feature, which *completes* the picture of the individual believer who is pressing on in God. This parable is a corporate description of the Bride of Christ as well.

1. Describe the seventh feature that is mentioned here. (Song 4:5)

    _____

    _____

2. In our spiritual armor, what is our *breastplate*? (I Thes. 5:8)

_____

3. What other two spiritual qualities are our *breastplate*? (Eph. 6:14; Ex. 28:15)

_____

The breastplate of judgment was worn by the high priest who went in within the veil to minister to the Lord. Through the blood of Jesus, the way has been opened into the holiest for us, that we too may enter in. In studying this portion of the high priest's clothing, we can discover some truth about the priesthood of the believer.

The two breasts signify the inward qualities of faith and love. The faith within produces righteousness (right standing with God) for it is written that Abraham believed God and it was accounted to him as righteousness. The result of love is the ability to judge with righteous judgment. Also, it is the love of God that causes judgment to come on the Church and the world. As it is written in Hebrews, "If we are without correction, we are bastards and not sons."

The two breasts of the breastplate of the Bride could be written:

```
FAITH ───────── produces ─────────→ LOVE
  │                                    │
produces                            produces
  ↓                                    ↓
RIGHTEOUSNESS ───── produces ───────→ JUDGMENT
```

Notice the progression in the development of the breasts as well as the balance.

Therefore, it is written in the Song that they are as *twins*. They *balance* one another. Let us study this further.

4. In constructing the breastpiece of judgment, what type of workman must one be? (Ex. 28:15)

_____

5. Applying this spiritually, to be able to judge with righteous judgments which the breastplate signifies, what type of skill must we be exercised in? (Heb. 5:13-14)

_____

_____

The *breasts* of the Bride signify that the Bride has been developed in faith and in love. Through studying the Word diligently, she has become skilled in the Word of righteousness. By reason of use, her senses have been exercised to discern or judge between good and evil.

6. What was carried inside the breastplate of judgment and for what were they used? (Ex. 28:30; Num. 27:21)

_____

_____

Urim means *lights*. *Urim* represents the *supernatural revelation of the Word of God*. It is by this revelation that God makes known His counsel and His will.

7. What was Paul's prayer for the believer? (Eph. 1:17-18)
   a. _____

   _____

   b. _____

8. Paul desired for them to receive revelation of what three-fold vision? (Eph. 1:18-19)
   a. _____
   b. _____
   c. _____

Revelation knowledge is deeper than *faith* knowledge. However, we must first have faith before we can receive revelation from the Word.

9. How does God give revelation, teach knowledge and interpret a message from the Word? (Isa. 28:9-10)

_____

_____

Faith knowledge is like understanding the basic mathematic equation, multiplication, subtraction and addition. *Revelation* knowledge is like understanding *geometry*. Unless there has been a line upon line understanding of basic math, geometry can never be understood. So it is with the Word of God. Notice the progression of development in the breasts or breastplate of the Bride.

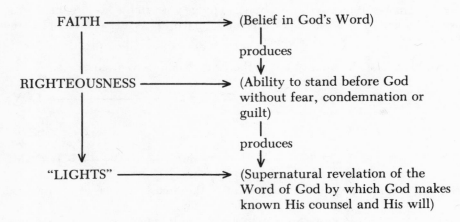

Let us look at the *twin* of the Urim as the Song compared the breasts to twins. *Thummim* means *perfections*. The *Thummim* represents the *perfect measurement* by *which the believer is being judged* and *also judging others*.

10. What is the measurement by which we are being judged? (Eph. 4:13)

_____

_____

11. The *lights* is closely related to the *perfections* in what way? (Eph. 5:26-27; Heb. 4:12-13)

_____

_____

We must also note that as we submit to the love of God, He judges our lives.

12. What does the scripture say concerning this judgment and what was the result? (Ps. 66:10-12; Mal. 3:2-3)

a. _____

_____

b. _____

_____

Notice the development:

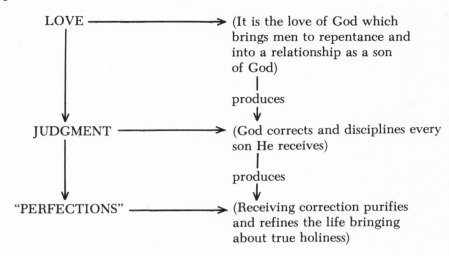

LOVE ⟶ (It is the love of God which brings men to repentance and into a relationship as a son of God)

produces

JUDGMENT ⟶ (God corrects and disciplines every son He receives)

produces

"PERFECTIONS" ⟶ (Receiving correction purifies and refines the life bringing about true holiness)

13. When the individual believer as well as the corporate Bride of Christ has been judged by God and been perfected, what commandment of Jesus will they fulfill? (Matt. 5:48)

_____

Notice the development, balance and progression of the breasts or breastplate of the believer:

FAITH	LOVE
RIGHTEOUSNESS	JUDGMENT
"LIGHTS"	"PERFECTIONS"

The breasts of the Bride are compared to a fawn, which is a young deer. A fawn is very *sensitive* as are these qualities of the Spirit. These fawns are said to be twins of a gazelle. A *gazelle* represents the *victory of the resurrection life.* Therefore, these qualities of the Spirit developed in the believer are a product of that victorious resurrection life.

14. Where are these fawns feeding? (Song 4:5)

_____

We discovered in an earlier study that the *lilies* signified those *saints with dedicated and pure hearts toward God.*

15. Where are these fawns feeding, that they might become fully developed? (Eph. 4:11-13, 16)

_____

All those who have progressed this far in their spiritual walk have, according to Paul, been

renewed in the spirit of their mind,
And have put on the new self,
Which in the likeness of God has been
created in righteousness and true
holiness.
Therefore, if any man is in Christ he is
a new creation.
The old things passed away;
Behold, new things have come. —
Eph. 4:23-24; II Cor. 5:17

NOTES

STUDY 11

THE DESIRE OF THE KING

Listen, O daughter, give attention and
incline your ear;
Forget your people and your father's
house;
Then the King will desire your beauty;
Because He is your Lord, bow down to
Him. —
Ps. 45:10-11

Throughout the Song, the Lord always shows Himself at the place to which He desires to draw the soul. He is the *magnet* of the story.

1. Where does the Lord desire to draw the maiden? (Song 4:6)

    _____

The *hill of frankincense* historically is *Calvary.* We studied earlier that myrrh has many uses. Among those, we noted that it was used for an embalming spice; it was used to take away wrinkles; and was used in the anointing oil of Aaron. Through these symbols, the Lord is calling the maiden into a deeper union with His death that all wrinkles might be taken away in order that she might come forth with a greater anointing, even the anointing of the High Priest Himself.

2. What must continually happen in her life and why? (II Cor. 4:10)

    _____

    _____

Therefore, the more we die to self, the more His life can come forth.

3. What does Paul say will bring about a deeper knowledge of Him? (Phil. 3:10)
    a. _____
    b. _____
    c. _____

The desire of this maiden from the beginning was to be drawn into intimate fellowship with the King. The path is one of total death to self. Through this death, there will spring up within a transcendent overcoming power, a greater degree of spiritual perception, a closer relationship between the soul and God and a more complete deliverance from this wilderness world. The Lord sends forth a call to come up higher to victory.

4. What question does the Lord continue to ask the maiden? (Mark 10:37-38)

    _____

    _____

5. Not only does the Lord call her into a deeper identification with His death, but what else does He call her to share in? (Song 4:8)

    _____

We learned earlier that the *leaping* upon or *journeying* upon *the mountain speaks of* the *resurrection power of the Lamb* in His exaltation above the kingdoms of this world. The risen Lord desires for her to look with Him from the top.
Amana means *integrity and truth.*
Senir means *a coat of mail.*
Hermon means *destruction.*

In integrity and through the revelation of the truth, covered with the whole armor of God, and hidden in Him who was manifested to destroy the works of the devil, the maiden is exhorted to look and see that she is seated far above every principality and power because of the triumphant victory at Calvary.

6. What else will she encounter there in the heavenlies? (Song 4:8)

_____

Not only has a call been given to the maiden to enter into a deeper identification with the Lord's death and resurrection, but a call has also been given to enter into spiritual warfare as indicated by the *den of lions* and the *mountains of leopards* which inhabit the very regions of the heavenlies.

7. Where is our battle and who is it with? (Eph. 6:12)

_____
_____
_____

That which we are confronted with before experiencing the spiritual elevation into the realm of the heavenlies is no more than the enemy's work upon the earth. Experience in the heavenly realm brings us to the enemy's *hide-out*, that we may come to grips with him face to face, in order to break his power.

8. The psalmist gives a prophetic word concerning this same experience. Analyze. (Ps. 18:33-42)
Position: _____
Preparation:
    a. _____
    b. _____
    c. _____
    d. _____
    e. _____
Source of strength: _____
Purpose and result:
    a. _____
    b. _____
    c. _____

This is a beautiful picture of a warrior of God, of the overcomer. God's desire for the maiden is to enter into spiritual warfare in the heavenlies and to totally subdue the enemy under her feet as she learns to overcome through the blood of the Lamb.

9. For the first time, how does the Lord address the maiden? (Song 4:8)

_____

Notice that in this passage instead of asking her to "come away" as previously, He now is able to say "come *with* me" because of her union with Him.

10. What does the Word say about the man who is joined to the Lord? (I Cor. 6:17)

_____

God's spirit becomes so mingled with the spirit of man that you cannot separate them. They are no longer two but one.

In calling the maiden His *Bride*, the King is expressing that His desire for her is as her desire for Him. The King looks upon her as one in whom He could confide and with whom He could now share everything. Her affections for Him have gone beyond the ordinary, and being mature and pure, she is capable of entering into deep intimacy with God. Both Jesus and Paul speak of this entering into deep intimacy with the Lord in which He reveals the deep things of His heart.

11. What did Jesus and Paul say about this? (John 16:12; I Cor. 3:1-3)

a. _____

_____

b. _____

_____

The believer in this *Song* has come to a place of maturity that she could share in the sufferings of Christ. The believer has entered into such an intimate relationship with the Lord that He could share His plans and desires with her, as well as receive love and affection from her. With such a believer, the Lord will share the intimate and deep things of His heart. The believer has entered into such a union with Him that her spirit responds as His Spirit, being quenched when His Spirit is quenched, rejoicing when He rejoices, weeping when He weeps.

12. What else does the King call His Bride? (Song 4:9)

_____

13. Why does He call His Bride His sister? (Heb. 2:11)

_____

_____

Jesus recognizes their kindred nature. Abraham's wife, Sarah, was his half-sister. Issac and Jacob both married close relatives, in contrast with Esau who took a heathen wife. So it is with Jesus, who gives Himself and His love to that one company of people, who being born of the Father in heaven, possess the same eternal life as Himself.

14. What has the Bride done to the King's heart? (Song 4:9)

_____

Jesus has found satisfaction with the believer's love. She has caused His heart to rejoice over her. The King finds satisfaction in being close to her. Up until now, much has been said of the maiden's love and affection for the King. Yet, this is the first time the King expresses the satisfaction and joy that He is now able to receive from the maiden.

15. What two things have ravished the heart of the King? (Song 4:9)

a. _____

b. _____

The message of the eye can be very eloquent.

16. What did one glance of the Lord's eye do to Peter? (Luke 22:61-62)

_____

The glance of the eye between lovers can communicate the deep affections of the soul. A stranger cannot interpret a lover's eye, but the loved one can interpret it most clearly. Notice also that the Bride's eye was *single*. The Lord was moved with love because of the singleness of her dedication and separation unto Him.

17. What did Jesus say about those who have a *single* or clear eye? (Luke 11:34-36)

_____

The *eye* also signifies *insight* and *perception*.

18. How did that spiritual insight develop? (Ps. 119:98-100)

_____

As a result of this meditation, God has been able to communicate the deep things of His heart. Her affection and meditation upon Him have captured His love.

19. What is meant by a *single strand of your necklace*? (Prov. 1:8-9)

_____

The maiden has heard the Word of God and held it fast. She has been a doer of the Word and not a hearer only, therefore, the King's heart is filled with love for her.

20. What does the King say about His Bride's love? (Song 4:10)

_____

We remember that from the first chapter of this Song that the maiden extolled the King's love more than wine. Yet this is the first time that the maiden has given back to the King as much love in return. Now the King extols her love as also better than wine. Wine in the scripture signifies joy. (Ps. 104:15) The King is saying that the Bride's love is greater than joy to Him, that it is itself the delight of His heart.

21. The psalmist David prophesied concerning this great love between the believer and her God in Psalm 45, a Psalm celebrating the King's marriage. There are many noble ladies present, yet who stands at the King's right hand? (Ps. 45:6-9)

_____

Note that the queen is clothed in *gold*, symbolizing the *divine nature*.

22. What has caused the King to desire her beauty? (Ps. 45:10-11)
    a. _____
    b. _____

23. What does the Lord say about her fragrance? (Song 4:10)

_____

Oil in the scripture signifies the *Holy Spirit*. The reference to *her oils* is a reference to the *release of the Spirit* in the life of the believer. This great fragrance has come forth from the brokenness in her life. Her soul powers have been subdued by the Spirit of God through the trials and testing of her faith.

24. What has the Bride begun to do? (I Cor. 2:14-16)

_____

25. The Lord's rejoicing over that believer who is a member of His Bride is recorded by the prophet Isaiah. Describe that rejoicing and the way the Lord looks upon this believer. (Isa. 62:3-5)
    a. _____
    b. _____
    c. _____
    d. _____

26. What does the Lord say about the lips and tongue of this believer? (Song 4:11)

_____

27. What does the *honey* signify? (Prov. 24:13-14)

_____

From the lips of the believer comes wisdom which she has learned from the King. He sees in her the very beauty He has put there. The milk she gives forth is the milk of the Word for sustaining the young in the Lord. (1Peter 2:2)

28. What qualities did the maiden display in her life that caused the King to impart His wisdom to her? (Ps. 81:11-16)

_____

29. What does the King say about her garments? (Song 4:11)

_____

Garments in scripture speak of *all that has to do with outward attitudes, behavior* — all that has to do with *external appearance*.

30. What has happened in the life of the believer? (Ezek. 17:22-23; Ps. 92:12-15)

_____

What about you, dear brother and sister in the Lord? Have you ever had the experience of sensing a certain spiritual quality about a believer from whom there seemed to ooze forth a special spiritual influence over you that you could not find words to describe? That is *fragrance*. It is the fruit of a life obedient to the Holy Spirit.

NOTES

NOTES

STUDY 12

THE GARDEN OF THE LORD

The Lord will comfort Zion;
He will comfort all her waste places.
And her wilderness He will make like Eden,
And her desert like the garden of the Lord. —
Isaiah 51:3

1. What figurative language does the King use to describe the Bride? (Song 4:12)

    _____

One of God's original thoughts at the beginning of creation was a garden. A garden is not ground for mere agricultural purposes, rather it is for the production of something for beauty and pleasure. Although there may be trees and fruit, it is not for commercial use. Its one objective is to produce flowers and blossoms which are to be gathered as something beautiful and exotic. So it is with the Bride who exists for the pleasure and satisfaction of her Bridegroom the King.

2. What has the Lord done in the life of the maiden? (Isa. 51:3)

    _____

The *garden* represents the *soul* of the believer. It includes all that involves her *personality*, her *mind*, *emotions*, and *will*. We read in the Song that this is not a public garden, but a garden locked up.

3. What does the scripture tell us about an open vessel? (Num. 19:15)

    _____

The maiden is *set apart*, separated unto God for His use only.

4. What has the maiden kept herself from and what is the Lord's attitude toward her? (James 4:4-5)

    _____

This garden was not only a garden locked up, it was also a *rock* garden. In the marginal notes we find that *rock* literally means *stone heap*.

5. What does the reference to a *stone heap* signify? (Deut. 27:5-7)

    _____

6. What was offered to the Lord on this altar? (Deut. 27:6-7)

    _____

From our previous lesson, we learned that burnt offerings and peace offerings were free-will offerings for those who desired a closer union and *fellowship* with the Lord. The believer's soul has become the altar of sacrifice through which God can fellowship with His Bride.

7. What do we find the Lord God doing in the garden in the beginning? (Gen. 3:8-9)

    _____

This was God's original thought in creating His man and the garden in which they fellowshipped. The soul of the believer has become a place where the Lord God can walk and fellowship intimately with the desire of His heart. The Father's desire for fellowship has been fulfilled in her.

8. What grows in the garden or soul of the maiden? (Song 4:13-14)
    a. _____
    b. _____
    c. _____

d. _____
e. _____
f. _____
g. _____
h. _____

As we study the symbolism of these spices and fruits, we will learn what the Bride's garden, her transformed soul-life, was like.

The first thing we discover in the *garden* or *soul* of the Bride is an *orchard of pomegranates*. We have previously learned that *pomegranates* signify *pure and godly thoughts*. The literal translation for the word *orchard* is *paradise*. The Bride's mind has become a *paradise of godly thoughts*.

9. How has this orchard or paradise of godly thoughts been cultivated and grown? (Phil. 4:8; Ps. 119:44-48; Ps. 119:97-105) Briefly summarize.

_____
_____
_____

10. As a result of this orchard of pomegranates having been grown in the maiden's garden (or this paradise of godly thoughts filling the believer's mind), what ability does the believer have? (Ps. 119:98-100)
a. _____
b. _____
c. _____

So is the life of one whose mind is fixed upon God's Word—to seek fellowship with Him.

11. Secondly, her garden contains *choice fruits*. What is this a reference to? (Gal. 5:22-23; Col. 1:9-11)

_____
_____

Through the renewing of the mind, the fruit of the Spirit springs forth in the life of the believer. Through the knowledge of His will in all wisdom and spiritual understanding, she is bringing forth fruit for every good work.

12. *Henna and nard* plants were also found in the garden. Previously, what did the maiden use henna blossoms to describe? (Song 1:14)

_____

The maiden has compared the Lord to *henna blossoms*. In pointing out that, these same blossoms were found in the maiden's garden, the King signifies that he recognizes *His image* being reproduced in the life of the believer. These blossoms were also used for outward adornment. The Lord recognizes that *His image is her outward adornment before the world*.

13. What is actually happening in her soul? (II Cor. 3:18)

_____

14. The next plant brought to our attention is the *nard* or *spikenard* plant. Previously, when did the maiden's *nard* (perfume) give forth its fragrance? (Song 1:12) See marginal reference.

_____

We found earlier that the table was where the maiden fed upon the strong meat of God's Word. It was from this intimate communion that this fragrance of spikenard came forth from the maiden. *Nard is the fragrance of her love* and *appreciation for Him*.

15. What did Mary do to express her deep devotion to the Lord? (John 12:3)

_____

Note that as a result of her expression of love toward the Lord that the whole house was filled with the fragrance of the ointment and everyone in her presence was blessed. Likewise, the lives of those believers who go on to know the Lord are filled with this fragrance of appreciation and love for their King.

16. Among other fragrances found in the garden were *cinnamon and the finest spices*. What other reference do we find in regard to this fragrance? (Ex. 30:23-25)

_____

17. What was the holy anointing oil used for? (Ex. 30:26-30)

_____

Smelling of *cinnamon* and *all the finest spices*, the maiden has been *anointed* as a *holy place* where God can meet with her. As one who has the privilege of ministering to God, she has been *anointed* as *holy unto the Lord, set apart as a meeting place for Him alone.*

18. In the garden of the maiden was also found *all the trees of frankincense*. What was one thing that frankincense was used for? (Ex. 30:34-37)

_____

19. This *incense* was offered morning and evening. With what was this *incense* offered? (Rev. 5:8; Rev. 8:3-4)

_____

20. What portion of this prayer life does the frankincense symbolize? (Isa. 60:6; Ps. 100:4)

_____

21. On what sacrificial offering do we find frankincense being placed? (Lev. 2:1)

_____

The *grain offering* could be brought only with burnt or peace offering. It could never be offered with the sin offering. This offering relates only to the offerings of those who desire fellowship with the Lord and desire to consecrate their lives to God. *Grain*, according to Matthew 13 refers to the *sons of the Kingdom*.

22. What does the frankincense poured out on the grain represent? (Ps. 149:1-6; Ps. 84:4)

_____

The fragrance of all the *trees of frankincense* coming up from the garden of the maiden is a reference to the *soothing aroma of a life filled with praise* unto God, and that with much *variety*.

23. List some of the varieties of praise given in Ps. 149:1-6.
    a. (v. 1) _____
    b. (v. 2) _____
    c. (v. 3) _____
    d. (v. 3) _____
    e. (v. 5) _____
    f. (v. 6) _____

24. Finally, found in the garden of the believer are *myrrh and aloes*. In Psalm 45, a song celebrating the King's marriage, what is mentioned as having this fragrance? (Ps. 45:8)

_____

Garments have to do with all *outward attitudes, behavior, and external appearances.*

25. With what was Jesus anointed at His death? (John 19:38-40)

_____

26. What was Jesus' death an external manifestation of? (Rom. 5:8)

_____

Myrrh and aloes signify *suffering love*. Jesus demonstrates His *suffering love* for us. The maiden's garden smells of this *suffering love*.

27.   How is she demonstrating this suffering love? (I Peter 4:12-19)

_____

28.   How did the apostles demonstrate this suffering love? (Acts 5:40-42; I Cor. 4:9-13)

_____

29.   This *suffering love*, this fragrance that flows forth from the maiden's garden, is described in its extent in the end of the Song. What is the extent of this suffering love? (Song 8:6-7)

_____

From studying the symbolism of these spices and fruits, we have discovered the following about the soul-life of the believer:

1.   Her mind is a paradise of godly thoughts. (orchard of pomegranates)
2.   She is manifesting the fruit of the Spirit in her life and bringing forth fruit unto God. (choice fruits)
3.   She is being transformed into the image of the Lord from glory to glory. His image can be seen in her. (henna and nard)
4.   She is filled with the fragrance of love and appreciation for the King. (nard and saffron)
5.   She has been appointed as a holy place set apart as a meeting place for Him alone. (calamus and cinnamon)
6.   She gives forth the fragrance of a life filled with praise unto God. (frankincense)
7.   She brings forth the quality of *suffering love* giving her life as a ransom for many. (myrrh and aloes)

30.   What has brought forth this beautiful foliage in her garden or this transformation of her soul-life? (Song 4:15)

_____

31.   What has happened in the life of the believer? (John 4:14; John 7:38)

_____

The *well* and its water *in the midst of the garden* is a beautiful parable of the *renewed spirit* of the believer in the *midst of her soul*.

32.   What request does the maiden make of the Lord? (Song 4:16)
      a. _____
      b. _____

33.   What does *wind* in the scriptures represent? (John 3:8; Acts 2:2, 4)

_____

In the natural, the north wind is very cold and penetrating. In contrast, the south wind is very pleasant, gentle and mild.

34.   What are the north and south winds representative of? (Phil 4:11-12)

_____

We see, then, the *north* and *south winds represent the different circumstances appointed by God to develop the fragrance of the garden*, and cause its fragrance to *flow out* to the world.

35.   What does Paul say happens through this north and south wind experience? (Phil. 1:20)

_____

The Amplified Version say it this way:

> *... but that with the utmost freedom of speech*
> *and unfailing courage, now as always,*
> *Christ, the Messiah, will be magnified and get*
> *glory and praise in this body of mine*
> *And be boldly exalted in my person, whether*
> *through life or through death. —*
> *Phil. 1:20*

The maiden has reached a place in her relationship with the Lord that external circumstances are not her delight, but rather the joy of the Lord, Himself, and her delight in Him is her strength.

36. We see a picture of this north wind experience in the breaking of the alabaster vial. What happened when the vial was broken? (Mark 14:3; John 12:3)

_____

As we are broken by the Spirit of God through north wind experiences, the fragrant perfume of the Spirit will flow out of us and minister to others who are around us. We must also point out in this passage that the ministry of this fragrance to others was merely a by-product.

37. For whom was the spikenard which flowed out of the alabaster vial intended? (Mark 14:3)

_____

Those around the woman scolded her for wasting this costly ointment on Jesus when it could have been given to the poor.

38. Yet, what did Jesus himself say of the woman's offering of ointment? (Mark 14:6-7)

_____

This breaking of the soul of man, represented by the alabaster vial, caused the precious ointment to flow out and fill the whole house with its fragrance. But Jesus emphasized in this passage that, more than ministering to others, the sweet smell ministered to Him, doing a good deed unto Him. Likewise, the whole garden of the maiden's inner life was for her Beloved and so were its fruits. They are for the sole purpose of the Lord and for the sole glory of God to do with as He will.

39. We see another picture of the north wind experience in the story of Gideon's army. What was inside the pitchers? (Judges 7:16)

_____

40. As they surrounded the camp of the enemy what did they do? (Judges 7:20)

_____

When they smashed the pitchers the torches could be seen burning brightly. So also as our earthen vessels are broken and brought into subjection through the Spirit of God, the torches of our spirit will be seen burning brightly in the darkness of this world. We will truly be a sword for the Lord.

41. A contrasting picture of the south and north wind experience is found in the prophecy of Ezekiel over the dry bones. When Ezekiel prophesied to the four winds to come and breathe upon the slain, what happened? (Ezk. 37:9-10)

_____

The Spirit of God breathing upon our lives has a quickening effect. It will quicken all that is dead within us, bringing it to life.

42. As the Spirit of God breathes upon our garden, what will happen? (Rom. 8:11)

_____

This is a south wind experience.

In conclusion, we find that the maiden has entreated the Lord for two things:

One, to bring about any circumstance in her life that He sees fit, to cause the fragrance in her garden to flow out.

Two, she invites the Lord to come into the garden Himself and partake of the fruit. Thus, we too should be able to entreat the Lord to come to us and find the relationship and fruit He desires to satisfy the need of His heart.

43.   What is the essense of her prayer here in asking the Lord to come to her and partake of the fruit in her life? (Ps. 19:14; I Peter 2:5; Rom. 12:1; Eph. 5:10; II Cor. 5:9)

_____

44.   How does the Lord respond to her invitation to come into her garden? (Song 5:1)

_____

Every dedication to the Lord is accepted by Him. Each time this maiden cried out to the Lord for a deeper union with Him, the Lord responded. This made up her spiritual history. Let us remember that our first dedication to the Lord made us truly His, yet only a deep and earnest desire as well as an *invitation* on our part will cause the Lord to come to His garden in this manner.

45.   How does Paul explain this desire? What does he press on to attain? (Phil. 3:12)

_____

46.   What condition does the Lord give those who desire to have Him answer them? (Jer. 33:3)

_____

The God of this universe *never* imposes His presence or His will upon men without their personal invitation. It is His *desire* to bring all of His born again ones into intimate union with Himself. Yet, he will never do this *against* our will. There must be an *intense desire* to know Him and be close to Him on behalf of those who call upon Him.

Of the multitudes that followed Jesus, He had twelve disciples and a few women that were closest to Him. Of those disciples He had three, Peter, James and John, to whom He revealed Himself on the Mount of Transfiguration in all His glory. Of the three He had one, John the beloved. John calls himself the disciple whom Jesus loved. When Jesus was crucified there were four people who stood at the foot of the cross—Mary (the mother of Jesus), Mary (His mother's sister), Mary Magdelane, and John. The other disciples stood at a distance with the multitudes. To so identify with Jesus' crucifixion meant certain death. Yet, John and these three women did not count their life dear in order that they might be near Him. Jesus said, "greater love has no man than this, that he would lay down his life for his friend." (John 15:13) These four showed by their actions this greater love.

John was the only disciple who did not die a martyr's death—for he had already in a sense given his life. It is the gospel of John that gives us the deepest revelation of who Jesus really was—the very God of the universe Himself. It was to Mary Magdalene that Jesus *first* revealed Himself after His resurrection. Mary had stayed at the tomb seeking Him with all her heart. For Jesus said, "He who loves me...I will love him and will disclose myself to Him." (John 14:21)

Did Jesus have favorites? *No*, each disciple, each woman *chose* for themselves the degree of relationship they desired with the Master.

47.   In order to have God listen to us, what must we do? (Jer. 29:12)

_____

48.   What must we do before God will let us find Him? (Jer. 29:13)

_____

There must be a *wholeheartedness* about our desire and entreating of the Lord. This is perhaps the kind of prayer which most easily gains an answer. This advanced dedication is different than earlier ones. The former and earlier dedication of ourselves to Him is to allow Him to plant and cultivate His garden and to have His way with us. This present committal, however, results from His full work within us. It is offering to Him a life full of His own work and labor of love. It is to give him the opportunity to enjoy all that has grown up with us.

49. As the Lord sees the *toilsome labor* of His soul when He enters into His garden, what happens? (Isa. 53:11; Song 5:1)

_____

50. Who does the Lord bring with Him into the garden? (Song 5:1)

_____

51. Who are the Lord's friends and lovers? (John 15:14-15; John 14:21)

_____

The Lord shares the fruit of the maiden's life with those who truly love Him with all their heart, soul, mind and strength. To these, He gives the intimate fruit of the maiden's life, with which to be satisfied and with which to feed their soul.

52. The maiden is a source of life and strength to God's flock. What is she doing? (Luke 12:42)

_____

53. Is this garden a public garden? (Song 4:12)

_____

54. What kind of spring is the maiden compared to? (Song 4:12)

_____

Notice that the maiden is a spring sealed up. These fountains are not for public usage nor are they to run at random into every outside place. This is a private garden belonging to the Lord of glory. The spring of waters within it are owned by Him. It is the Lord Himself that *invites* His friends and lovers to partake of the fruit He has grown there, as well as to drink the living water He has placed there. It is not the maiden's prerogative or choice to give these things out to those who pass by.

We find a beautiful picture of this in a story about Jacob. (Read Genesis 29:1-10). In this parable, *Jacob* represents *Jesus*. The *sons of the east* represent *those who have a heart that is opened to God*.

55. What does this *well* have in common with the *well* or *spring* that the maiden in the Song is compared to? (Gen. 29:2; Song 4:12)

_____

56. There were other flocks of sheep waiting to be watered. But what did Jacob (representing Jesus) do when he saw Rachel coming with the sheep of Laban, his mother's brother? (Gen. 29:9-10)

_____

57. Who do the sheep of Laban, his mother's brother, represent? (Mark 3:33-35)

_____

In interpreting this parable we see that Jacob himself rolled the stone from the mouth of the well and watered those who desired God's will. *The well did not water the sheep on its own; it could not, for it was sealed. Someone* had to roll away the stone or unseal the well *so that the water could flow out.* Likewise, within us is that everlasting water and that precious fruit that He has grown. We need not fret and worry about giving out this precious life — for it is not ours to give. Only Jesus can *unlock* the garden or *unseal* the spring. Only He can give permission for others to enter.

No matter how much we might long to witness to someone or desire to share with others, unless the Lord Himself removes the seal from the well, or unlocks the garden, all our striving is in vain. On the other hand, we may find ourselves in situations where the idea of actually ministering to the person with whom we are speaking is the farthest thing from our mind. Suddenly, we may become aware that the Spirit of God is ministering to that person through us, watering and feeding that soul. What has happened? The Lord has brought His friends and lovers into *His* garden. The Lord knows those who are His and those who are thirsty; He is well able to quench their thirst and give them the water of life without cost.

As we have allowed the Lord to cultivate the garden of our soul, He will take what He has grown there and with it He will feed His sheep.

58. When the souls of the priests are filled, saturated with abundance and fatness, what will happen to God's people? (Jer. 31:14)

_____

59. What does the Lord desire to do for His sheep? (Ezk. 34:14-15)

_____

Jesus, as any good shepherd would do, goes ahead of His sheep, searching for rich grazing areas and fertile ground. In this ground He plants and cultivates rich feed. He takes out any poisonous weeds that would cause harm to His sheep, checking for any holes that would cause His sheep to stumble and be cast down. Then He goes and gathers His sheep, leading them to the pasture which He has prepared.

The *maiden* in the Song has become that *pasture land*, that *grazing ground*. She has become a place where the Lord of Glory can bring His friends and lovers and feed them upon her soul.

Jesus desires to cultivate us into rich pasture lands, not for our own enjoyment alone, but that He may bring His sheep there and cause them to drink and imbibe deeply.

60. If we love the Lord, what will we desire to do? (John 21:15-17)

_____

NOTES

STUDY 13

GETHSEMANE – THE FELLOWSHIP
OF HIS SUFFERINGS

We are...fellow heirs with Christ –
Sharing His inheritance with Him;
Only we must share His sufferings if we
are to share His glory.
But what of that?
For I consider that the sufferings of
this present time are not worth being
compared with the glory that is about
to be revealed in us.
For even the whole creation, all nature,
Waits expectantly and longs earnestly,
for God's sons to be made known. –
Rom. 8:17-19 Amplified Version

Thus far in our study, there have been three distinct revelations of the Lord Jesus to the Bridal soul:

1. As *King*, taking possession of the throne of the heart.
2. As the *Risen One*, bringing her through crucifixion of self, (dying to the world and self interests) into resurrection glory and union with the Lord of Life.
3. As the *Lover* of the soul, the Lord rejoicing over the fruit of the New Creation life.

We come now to Jesus' revelation of Himself as "the man of sorrows and acquainted with grief." The Lord desires to bring His loved one into a deeper sense of the fellowship of His sufferings, in order that she may know His heart and might partake of His glory.

1. What does the Bridal soul say about herself? (Song 5:2a)

_____

2. This is the same testimony that Paul the apostle gives. What does he say about himself? (Gal. 2:20)

_____

She was asleep. Her fleshly activity had ceased. Through the workings of God in her life she had entered into the *Vine-Branch* relationship; as she abides in Him, she brings forth fruit. The cross had truly been worked into her life. She is asleep to her own separate activities, but ever more *awake* unto Him. The outward life abides in the rest and calm of the Lord. The inward life is alive and active, her inner self being like a "watered garden and like a spring of water whose water fail not." As we have seen in Song 5:1 she has become a *place* where the Lord can bring His friends and lovers and let them feast upon the luscious fruit within.

3. As she rests in the Lord she hears a voice. Whose voice does she say it was? (Song 5:2)

_____

4. What three things does Jesus say characterize His sheep? (John 10:27)
   a. _____
   b. _____
   c. _____

As a young lamb we saw that she failed in the beginning to understand the intent of His calling. But through the knowledge of the Lord and the intimate knowing that He has had of her, she has come to recognize and understand His voice immediately.

5. As Jesus stands knocking at the door of her heart, what does He ask her to do? (Song 5:2)

_____

Jesus calls for her to open her heart further to Him. He does not push His way in. He does not force her to follow. She must always follow Him by her own voluntary consent.

6. By what four titles did Jesus address her and what does each title signify? (Song 5:2) Note: *My darling* is used by David in the Psalms to represent his own *soul* or his *life*. (Use this meaning to interpret part b. of this question.) Jesus is saying the Bride is as His own soul and is as an extension of His life in the earth.

TITLE   SIGNIFICANCE

a. _____   Matt. 12:50 _____

b. _____   II Cor. 3:3 _____

 _____

c. _____   Matt. 3:16 _____

d. _____   Heb. 6:12; James 1:12 _____

 _____

 _____

Note here that He does not call her *His Bride*. Does the omission signify that her answer to His new call will determine whether or not she will apprehend that for which Jesus apprehended her? Let us see what this new call is all about.

7. What figurative language does the Lord use to represent this new call and revelation of Himself to His Bride? (Song 5:2) Note: the word for *damp* is literally *drops* (see the marginal reference).

 _____

 _____

Historically, these words refer to the agony of Jesus in Gethsemane.

8. As Jesus was struggling there in prayer, what happened? (Luke 22:44)

 _____

 _____

9. Jesus was totally man and totally God. In His humanity, with what was He struggling? (Matt. 26:39, 42)

 _____

10. Although Jesus in His humanity was shrinking back from this cup of suffering, humiliation and death, what was the intent of His will? (Matt. 26:39, 42)

 _____

There is a moment when, through the revelation of the Spirit, the meaning of conformity to Christ stands revealed. All preconceived ideas vanish and the believer finds that she has overlooked His reminder that the servant is not greater than his Lord. The crucified Christ must have crucified followers. She had only thought of His power and His glory.

11. Thinking of His power and His glory, two disciples asked Jesus for a place of honor in His Kingdom. What was Jesus' question to them? (Mark 10:35-38)

 _____

 _____

12. What was their response to that question as well as the other disciples' response to Him when He spoke about His death? (Mark 10:39; Mark 14:31)

 _____

13. Although Jesus had spoken to them of His cross and the death He must suffer, how did they react when the reality of what was going to happen came upon them? (Mark 14:48-51)

 _____

Having seen that this new call involves entering into the fellowship of the Lord's suffering and His agony in Gethsemane, let us turn back to our picture lesson in the history of the Bridal soul. This call is completely unexpected to many, for they have thus far experienced many aspects of the cross in their life. They have seen the effect of the cross in the forgiveness of their sins, in the world and the corruption of self.

In our lesson, the maiden has been aware that there is a peculiar suffering attached to the cross, but up until now she has not become aware of its real depth and breadth. She has known in the past the application of the cross to her inward life, but she has not realized the extent of how the cross would mold and shape her whole being.

There is yet another deep phase of the cross in its application to the believer, for in the measure that we would know His resurrection power, we must in the same proportion enter into the fellowship of His sufferings.

14. How does Paul explain this? (II Cor. 4:10-11)

_____

_____

It is into the depth and breadth of this death that Jesus now desires to take His Bride.

15. How does the maiden respond to the Master's call? (Song 5:3)
    a. _____
    b. _____

16. In speaking of the *putting off* of her dress, what is the maiden referring to? What things has the cross already dealt with in her life? (Col. 3:9-10; Eph. 4:22-24)

_____

In failing to comprehend the depth of this call of God upon her life, the maiden is saying that she has already experienced the cross in her outward life. She has already seen the effect of the cross in delivering her from the appeal of the world and the corruption of self. "Is it not enough," she reasons, "to have had such a deep experience with the cross that my old nature and way of life has been completely put off?"

Here she is looking only at the negative side of the cross, failing to comprehend what Paul speaks of as "always carrying about the liability and exposure to the same putting to death that the Lord Jesus suffered, so that the *resurrection life* of Jesus also may be *shown forth* by and in our bodies." (II Cor. 4:10 Amplified Version)

17. In saying "I have washed my feet" in what other aspects has she already experienced the cross in her life? (John 13:6-10)

_____

Not only had she put off the old self and her former manner of life, but her inner life had been fully cleansed and purified from sins. Here again we see that to her, the intent and purpose of the cross was to keep one in a clean state, which is the *negative only*. The maiden had washed her feet, putting off her shoes. Bare feet signifies in the scripture *a slave in the presence of his master*. Being *barefoot*, she had submitted to His Lordship in her life. "Is is not enough," she reasoned, "that my life has been totally dedicated to Him, that my feet have been washed and I have been fully cleansed inwardly? Is it not enough that the cross has been applied to all those little foxes that spoil the vine?"

Yet, Jesus was asking her to walk in her bare feet, to follow His call. The meaning of this she failed to comprehend.

18. When Jesus humbled Himself unto the death of the cross what did He receive? (Phil. 2:7-11)

_____

This is the *positive* application of the cross — *dominion*, the possession of your inheritance. Yet, this cannot be experienced without the cross.

19. What did the Lord tell Joshua about his bare feet? (Josh. 1:3)

_____

_____

Notice that the Lord told Joshua that every place he put the *sole* of his foot would be his. He did not say the *sole* of his shoes, for without shoes, feet become more sensitive. Stepping upon sharp things causes pain. Every pebble, every thorn, every rock can be felt. This call that Jesus is calling the maiden to now is a path in which she must walk *barefooted*. Things before that she did not feel, or was not sensitive to because she had walked with her shoes on, now she will feel. It is a path in which she shares in the sufferings of her Lord. It is a path in which her spirit responds to sin in the same way God's Spirit responds. It is a path in which she will feel God's heartbreak over the rebellion of man and His hurt in being rejected by His creation whom He loves. She will feel the depths of His love that caused Him to lay down His life. His heart will become her heart. The reproaches that fell upon Christ will fall upon her. The Spirit of Christ will flow through her so fully that the world will attack, not her, but the Spirit of Christ within her. She will know what Jesus meant when He said, "Zeal for Thy house has eaten me up." She will be jealous on behalf of her God to see His holiness go forth in the earth.

However, through fear — fear of consequences, fear of losing present blessing, fear of the unknown, fear of being deprived of familiar comforts, and an undefinable fear of the reality of suffering — the maiden shrinks back from the Lord's call.

It is here that many Christians fail to go on and apprehend that for which Christ apprehended them — total conformity to His death, that His resurrection life might be manifested in our mortal bodies.

20. As Peter tells us in I Peter 2:21, Jesus left us an example that we might follow in His steps. What did Jesus say that is an example to us? (John 12:27-28)
    a. _____
    b. _____

21. As Jesus put His *nail scarred hand* through the door of her heart, and made His appeal to her to enter into this deeper fellowship with Him, what was her response? (Song 5:4-5)

_____

22. When Thomas saw those same nail pierced hands, what was His response? (John 20:24-28)

_____

She had shrunk back from His call in her humanity for a moment, but not in the purpose of her will. One look at the *nail scarred hand* and she could not ignore her love for Him, which surpassed her concern for herself. If her actions had been a deliberate rejection of Him on the part of her will, the Lord could have done no more until she had yielded. He sees, however, that it is a surface shrinking and that she must be able to ignore it and act by her will alone.

23. We see a picture of this in the life of Peter as he, too, was shrinking back in his humanity, because of fear, when Jesus was arrested to be crucified. With that one look, Jesus touched that spring in Peter's heart. What did Peter do? (Luke 22;59-62)

_____

24. As the maiden opened the door, what dropped from her hands and fingers? (Song 5:5)

_____

One use for *myrrh*, which we discovered from an earlier study was its use as an *embalming spice*. The use of *myrrh* in this passage denotes Jesus in His *death*. *Hands* in the scripture signify *the will in action*. Her *hands and fingers dripping with this liquid myrrh* denotes that *through her action she has shown that the inner most depths* of her *will* are *steadfastly purposed to follow Him to the death*. She made her choice. She lays aside her fears and arises to unlock the bolt which she herself has put upon the door of her heart and bids the man of sorrows to enter in.

25. When she opened the door to her beloved, what did she discover? (Song 5:6)

_____

As she agrees to enter into that suffering she opens the door. As she does that, she enters into a deeper working of that cross. Now the soul begins to taste of that cup which she has decided to drink. To see what this darkness is all about, let us look at Jesus as He arises from His struggle in the garden of Gethsemane, having submitted His will unto the will of the Father. Jesus was met by the chief priests and officers of the temple and elders, along with a cohort of Roman soldiers.

26. When Jesus saw what faced Him, what did He say? (John 18:11)

_____

27. What did Jesus say about what He was about to face? (Luke 22:53; John 19:10-11)

_____
_____

28. When Jesus stood before the chief priests and the religious leaders, what did they do to Him? (Matt. 26:67)

_____

29. What happened to the maiden as she, too, was found by the _watchman_, which here signifies _the worldly religious leaders_? (Song 5:7)

_____

This could have been a spiritual wounding. As Jesus said of His own situation, these would have had no power over her unless it had been permitted by God.

30. When David, who was a man after God's own heart, had to leave Jerusalem to flee from his son, Absalom, there was a man standing beside the road cursing him and throwing stones at him. Abishai, like Peter, wanted to cut off the man's head. What was David's response? (II Sam. 16:9-13)

_____
_____

31. Who did Jesus name as the inspiration behind these religious leaders? (Luke 22:53)

_____

32. What did Jesus tell Peter about the trial that he would face? (Luke 22:31)

_____

33. What assurances did Jesus give in this trial? (Luke 22:32)

_____

34. What promise did Jesus give to His disciples who stood by Him in His trials? (Luke 22:28-30)

_____
_____

35. We see this sifting of darkness coming upon righteous Job. What was God's testimony concerning Job? (Job 1:8)

_____
_____

36. What accusation did Satan make? (Job 1:10-11)

_____
_____

37. What did God permit Satan to do? (Job 1:12)

_____
_____

38. This testing, known as the *dark night* of the soul, is described very well by Job. Read Job 30:16-31. In going through this experience, we may have some or all of the trials that Job describes. Briefly summarize the description given in this passage. (Job 30:16-31)

(v. 16) _____

(v. 18) _____
_____

(v. 20) _____

(v. 21) _____

(v. 24) _____

(v. 26) _____
_____

(v. 27) _____

(v. 28) _____

(v. 29) _____
_____

(v. 31) _____

This darkness is:

1. A complete withdrawal of the *sense* or feeling of God's presence.
2. No emotions of joy.
3. Little ability to worship and commune with the Father.
4. Difficulty in accomplishing very much, (the feeling of your hands being tied).
5. Very little spiritual edification of the soul
6. God is silent—no amount of calling or pleading can cause Him to respond or answer.
7. There is a sense of being in a dry place.

39. What did David say about this darkness? (Ps. 139:7-12)

_____

Whether we sense God's presence or not, we can have the same assurance that David had. There is no way to escape God's presence, for He is everywhere at one time, filling every particle of the atmosphere with His energy. As Paul said, the God whom we seek is not far from each one of us for "in Him we live and move and exist." (Acts 17:27-28)

40. What did Job say about his *sense* of God's presence during this dark hour of testing? (Job 23:8-10)

_____

41. Jesus, too, *felt* that utter aloneness. At the culmination of that dark hour—which every soul who is going on with the Lord must taste of—what did Jesus cry out? (Matt. 27:46)

_____

42. What did David say about this sifting and testing that had come upon him? (II Sam. 16:12)

_____

As we turn back to the story of the maiden, we see powers of darkness aiming their attack upon this soul as she follows her Lord through the valley of the shadow of death. They aim at beating her back from her position in Him. They press upon her to admit the thought that God has laid upon her more than is right, and that she must retreat into an easier path. They shout to her "curse God and die." They taunt her with the silence of her Lord and tell her that if He delighted in her, if she were right with Him, He would have spared her from all this sorrow. They present to her some compromise which appears to be a *way of escape*. Her flesh and her heart fail her.

43. What was David's testimony during this hour of trial? (Ps. 73:25-26)

_____

44. What was Job's testimony? (Job 1:21-22)

a. _____

_____

b. _____

45. What was Jesus' testimony in this? (I Peter 2:22-23)

_____

46. What are we to do with the example that Jesus left us? (I Peter 2:21)

_____

The maiden lays her hand of faith afresh upon the Head of the sacrifice on Calvary's cross and waits for God to explain.

47. Turning back to our Song, what did the guardsmen do to the Maiden? (Song 5:7) Note: *Shawl* is more literally translated *veil*.

_____

48. What did the Roman soldiers do to Jesus? (Matt. 27:27-29)

_____

49. When the guardsmen took away her veil, it seemed as though she had been exposed to the world, yet what was actually happening? (I Peter 4:12-14)

_____

50. Paul tells us that Moses had to cover his face with a veil so that the children of Israel could not see the glory of the Lord. Yet, under the new covenant what kind of face are we to have? (II Cor. 3:12-13, 18)

_____

Consequently, we see that in the maiden's life the persecution immediately *removed the veil* so that God's glory could be seen in her. This is what Paul speaks of as always bearing about in the body the dying of the Lord Jesus, so that the life of the Lord Jesus could be manifested in our bodies.

51. As Stephen was speaking to those religious leaders who were persecuting him, how did his countenance appear? (Acts 6:10-15)

_____

52. What are the fiery ordeals that come upon us designed to prove? (I Peter 1:6-7)

_____

53. What are we to greatly rejoice in? (I Peter 1:3-6a)

_____

54. In all this, what are we protected by? (I Peter 1:5)

_____

55. Turning back to our Song, what was the maiden's tesimony to the daughters of Jerusalem as she was in the midst of this dark trial? (Song 5:8)

_____

Will they tell Him who made heaven and earth that the hardness of His love is as sweet to her as all His favors? The fact that she can use such words now, even when He has appeared to withdraw Himself from her, shows the depth of His work in her and her union with her Lord. She has stood the test and proved that she loves Him for Himself alone. Satan has been defeated once again.

Many waters cannot quench love,
Nor will rivers overflow it;
For love is as strong as death; ...
Love bears all things,
Believes all things,
Hopes all things,
Endures all things.
Love never fails. —
Portions of Song 8 and I Cor. 13

The Word of God tells us that David was cursed by his people and rejected. Likewise, Job became a curse and a byword to his wife, his friends, and even his children despised him. Satan had devised a plan to show God that two of the men who were the most dedicated to Him did not truly love Him—but his plan failed. For Job boldly proclaimed "though He slays me yet will I trust Him," and David cried out, "Besides Thee I desire nothing on earth." The maiden now joins that chorus: "Tell Him whom my soul loveth that I am sick with love."

After that struggle in Gethsemane, Satan had devised to totally crush the living God and wipe Him from the universe forever—but this plan also failed. What Satan sent Job, David, the maiden and even Jesus, was for their destruction. But what was meant for the bad became Satan's own mousetrap, for following the *crucifixion* inevitably came the *resurrection*!

NOTES

STUDY 14

THE KING OF GLORY

Lift up your heads, O gates,
And lift them up, O ancient doors,
That the King of glory may come in!
Who is He, then, this King of glory?
The Lord of hosts, He is the King of glory. —
Ps. 24:9-10 Amplified Version

The question now asked by the daughters of Jerusalem, "What is your beloved more than another?"; stirs the maiden's being. How can she describe Him who is the *radiance* of God's glory, the One who is the *image* of the invisible God? Under the inspiration of the Holy Spirit, she blurts out a vivid word-picture of Him who made heaven and earth. This is a fresh vision of the Lord that has come to this one because she has followed on to know Him, being made conformable to His death.

1. How does the Bridal soul describe His appearance? (Song 5:10) Note: *dazzling* here means *dazzling white* as when wholly illumined by the sun.
    a. _____
    b. _____
    c. _____

2. In the latter days of Jesus' ministry, He took three of His disciples, Peter, James and John — those who were the closest to Him at this time — up on a high mountain and revealed to them His glory. How did they describe His appearance? (Matt. 17:2; Luke 9:29) Note marginal reference.
    a. _____
    b. _____

The Amplified Version says it this way:

And as He was praying, the appearance of
His countenance became altered (different) and
His raiment became dazzling white — flashing
with the brilliance of lightning. —
Luke 9:29

This revelation of the dazzling white light of His glory is now being revealed to the maiden.

3. What is the Lord our God? (Ps. 84:11)

    _____

4. What is the Lord's radiance like? (Hab. 3:4)

    _____

5. We find that John was given an even greater revelation of this dazzling Savior when he was exiled on the Isle of Patmos. How did the Lord's countenance appear? (Rev. 1:12-18)

    _____

6. Who does the Lord of Glory identify Himself as? (Rev. 1:13-18)

    _____

7. We find this same revelation given to the prophet Daniel. Compare Daniel 7:9-10 to Rev. 1:12-18. Who does Daniel identify Him as? (Dan. 7:9)

    _____

8. In Isaiah's prophecy of the coming of the Messiah, what titles does Isaiah give Him? (Isa. 9:6)

   a. _____

   b. _____

   c. _____

   d. _____

   e. _____

9. To whom does the Lord reveal His identity? (John 14:21; Prov. 8:17)

   a. _____

   b. _____

10. When Moses saw the burning bush and God called to him from its midst, telling him to go lead Israel out of Egypt, who did God identify Himself as? (Ex. 3:13-14)

   _____

11. When Jesus was being questioned by the Jews, they said to Him, "You are not yet fifty years old, and you have seen Abraham?" How did Jesus respond to them? (John 8:56-58)

   _____

   Thus Jesus identified Himself as the great "I AM" who spoke to Moses in the burning bush.

12. How did the Lord speak to Moses? (Ex. 33:11)

   _____

13. What type of man was Moses that caused the Lord of glory to reveal Himself to him in such an intimate way? (Num. 12:6-8)

   _____

We, under the new covenant, stand not as servants of God but as sons. Therefore, we have the opportunity of receiving an even deeper revelation of the Lord of Glory to our hearts as well as the opportunity of having an even deeper relationship with Him than His servant Moses did.

We find the maiden of the Song describing Him for the first time in the glory of that white dazzling light — which is the terrible crystal which surrounds the throne of God. We find the maiden understanding more of the Lord's true identity. Yet, at the same time that the Lord appears to her in that dazzling white light, He also has a *ruddy* appearance. What could this mean? Let us search the scriptures.

14. How does John describe the appearance of the Lord of Glory as He sits upon His throne? (Rev. 4:2-3)

   a. _____

   b. _____

To discover what these stones represent and to interpret their meaning accordingly, we may find one clue by looking at their numerical value as designated by their position in the breastplate of the High Priest (Ex. 28) and also by looking at their position in the foundation of the Holy City (Rev. 21).

The *sardius* stone is the *first* stone in the breastplate of the High Priest and the *sixth* stone of the Holy City.

The number *one* represents *God*.

The number *six* represents *man*.

This reveals to us that the *One* who sits in the midst of the throne is *both God and man*.

The *jasper* stone is the *twelfth* stone in the breastplate of the High Priest and the *first* stone of the Holy City.

The number *twelve* represents *divine government*.

The number *one* represents *God*.

This reveals to us that He who sits on the throne is the God of divine government or the God who is the supreme ruler of the universe.

15. The *first* stone in the breastplate of the High Priest is the *sardius* and the last stone in the breastplate is the *jasper*. What does this reveal to us? (Rev. 1:8, 17-18)

    _____

    _____

16. Describe the *One* who is the "Alpha and the Omega" from verse 8. (Rev. 1:8)

    a. _____

    b. _____

    c. _____

    d. _____

17. Describe the *One* who is called the "first and the last" from verse 18. (Rev. 1:17-18)

    a. _____

    b. _____

    c. _____

    d. _____

The book of Revelation, according to John, is called the Revelation of Jesus Christ. The one who is, who was, and who is to come is Jesus Christ. The one who was dead and is now alive forever more is the same Jesus. And according to His own testimony, He identifies Himself as the *Almighty*. Therefore we can conclude that the One who sits upon the throne is *God Almighty Himself, Jesus Christ, the Lord of Glory*.

Both the sardius and the jasper stone have a *red glowing* appearance. From the center of the throne, in the midst of the dazzling white light of God's glory, emanates a *red* glowing which equals the brilliance of shining jewels. This *red* brilliance is the very mark of His passion, for He has redeemed us unto Himself by His own blood.

Hear now His testimony:

> *For I am the Lord your God,*
> *The Holy one of Israel, your Savior.*
> *Before Me there was no God formed,*
> *And there will be none after Me.*
> *There is no savior besides Me,*
> *So you are My witnesses,*
> *Declares the Lord that I am God.*
> *Even from eternity I am He.*
> *Thus says the Lord, your Redeemer,*
> *The Holy One of Israel, I am the Lord.*
> *Your Holy One, the Creator of Israel,*
> *your King.*
> *I am the First and the Last and there*
> *is no God besides Me.*
> *Is there any God besides Me or is there*
> *any other Rock? I know of none.*
> *Thus says the Lord your Redeemer,*
> *The One who formed you from the womb,*
> *I the Lord, am the Maker of all things,*
> *Stretching out the heavens by Myself*
> *And spreading out the earth, all alone.*
> *There is no other God and a Savior.*

Turn to Me and be saved all the ends
of the earth,
For I am God and there is no other.
I have sworn by Myself, the Word has
gone forth from My mouth in
righteousness and will not turn
back.
That to Me every knee will bow and
every tongue will swear allegiance. —
Portions of Isaiah 43, 44 and 45

NOTES

STUDY 15

THE KING OF GLORY:
THE HEAD OF GOLD

And I saw heaven opened;
And behold a white horse and He who sat
upon it is called faithful and true;
And in righteousness He judges and wages war.
And His eyes are a flame of fire and upon
His head are many diadems
And He has a name written upon Him which no
one knows except Himself.
And He is clothed with a robe dipped in
blood;
And His name is called the Word of God.
And the armies which are in heaven clothed
in fine linen, white and clean,
Were following Him on white horses,
And from His mouth comes a sharp sword,
So that with it He may smite the nations;
And He will rule them with a rod of iron;
And He treads the wine press of the fierce
wrath of God, the Almighty.
And on His robe, and on His thigh He has a
name written
KING OF KINGS, AND LORD OF LORDS. —
Rev. 19:11-15

1. What other words does the maiden use to describe her Lord in verse 10? (Song 5:10)

_____

The word *outstanding* is literally translated *a lifted up banner*. See the marginal reference.

2. How did Jesus describe the manner in which He would be lifted up as a banner? (John 3:14-15)

_____
_____

3. Why did Moses lift up the serpent in the wilderness? (Num. 21:6-9)

_____
_____
_____

Bronze in the scriptures signifies judgment. In the cross of Jesus Christ we see the serpent judged, his dominion and curse broken over mankind that whoever looks upon Jesus and believes shall truly live. The Beloved of the maiden is truly a Banner lifted up among ten thousand. He is her Champion, her Deliverer. He is the Desired of all ages and the One of whom Job spoke when he said,

And as for me,
I know that my Redeemer lives
And at last He will take His stand
on the earth. —
Job 19:25

4. What did Enoch prophesy? (Jude 14)

_____

The literal translation is "the Lord came with His holy ten thousand." See marginal note.

5. Looking in Revelation at this coming of the Lord, which John as well as Enoch prophesied, give a description of Him who comes with ten thousand of His holy ones. (Rev. 19:11-16)
   a. (v. 12) _____
   b. (v. 12) _____
   c. (v. 13) _____
   d. (v. 15) _____
   e. (v. 16) _____

6. In Psalms we find a reference again unto the Lord and His ten thousands. What are the ten thousands called here? (Ps. 68:17) Note: the marginal reference's literal translation is *twice ten thousand*.
   _____

As earthly kingdoms are dependent on warlike preparations for their defense, a single prophet (like Elijah for example) can do more for the preservation and prosperity of the Church than all natural means of defense. In the proper context, *chariots* indicate this in scripture. The *chariots of God* here signify those who move in the *prophetic* anointing; this is the restored Church where each member is a prophet, a priest, and a king.

It might also be noted here that the number 10,000 literally means *a seed in the image of God, through the fulness of testing.*

   0 = seed

   3 zeros = the number three meaning the perfection, fulness or image of God

   10 = the fulness of testing

7. How does the Lord appear among those sons in His image? (Ps. 68:17)
   a. _____
   b. _____

8. Describe how the Lord appeared at Sinai to the Israelite nation, to those people who did not know Him intimately as Moses did. (Ex. 19:16-21)
   a. _____   d. _____
   b. _____   e. _____
   c. _____   f. _____

9. Why was Moses able to go up and speak with the Lord face to face and the Israelite nation was not? (Isa 33:14-17)
   a. (v. 14) _____
   b. (v. 15) _____
   c. (v. 15) _____
   d. (v. 15) _____
   e. (v. 15) _____
   f. (v. 15) _____
   g. (v. 15) _____

10. As a result of this holiness in his life, what was his privilege? (Isa. 33:16-17)
   a. (v. 16) _____
   b. (v. 16) _____
   c. (v. 16) _____
   d. (v. 16) _____
   e. (v. 17) _____
   f. (v. 17) _____

This promise extends to all those who walk in holiness before Him. From these scriptures we see that the revelation of the Lord which the soul of the maiden is now receiving is a face to face relationship as a man would speak to his friend. She has become one who has the privilege of seeing the King in His beauty. It is this revelation that is now unfolding before her. She has become one who is able to behold a far-distant land, one with prophetic vision. She is one of whom it could be said, "Surely the Lord God does nothing unless He reveals His secret counsel to His servants the prophets." (Amos 3:17)

11. As we continue in the revelation of the beloved Bridegroom to the heart of His Bride, how does the maiden describe His head? (Song 5:11)

_____

Gold in the scripture signifies the *divine nature*.

The maiden is receiving a revelation of Jesus not as some lesser member of the Godhead but as the Creator of the universe and the *Head* of *all* things.

12. For who is Jesus? (II Cor. 4:4)

_____

13. For what dwells in Jesus? (Col. 2:9)

_____

14. What is Jesus the *Head* over? (Col. 2:10)

_____

15. What was Jesus' testimony of Himself? (John 14:8-9)

_____

16. In the Revelation of Jesus, when He appears with 10,000 of His holy ones, what is found upon His head? (Rev. 19:12)

_____

A *diadem* with over 2 or 3 fillets signified *dominion* over 2 or 3 countries, hence the *many diadems* here is a reference to *the dominion* of the Messiah as the *supreme ruler of the earth* which is also signified by His name, KING OF KINGS AND LORD OF LORDS.

17. What has the Lord become to the maiden? (Isa. 28:5-6)
    a. _____
    b. _____
    c. _____

There are three types of crowns primarily mentioned in the scriptures:

1. The royal crown.
2. The priestly crown.
3. The victor's crown.

Her beloved has become to her all three.

THE ROYAL CROWN

18. The *diadem* is the symbol of the power to rule. What have we — as those who have received of God's abundant grace and gift of righteouness — been promised? (Rom. 5:17)

_____

As the Amplified Version says it, "...We are to reign as kings in life through the One, Jesus the Messiah..."

19. Seeing Jesus with the *head of gold*, with the head crowned with *many diadems* and identifying herself with Him, what is she able to exercise? (Luke 10:19)

_____

_____

20. Being born of God, what has she come to realize? (I John 5:18) Answer this question from the Amplified Version quoted below:

> We know (absolutely) that anyone born of
> God does not (deliberately and know-
> ingly) practice committing sin,
> But the One who was begotten of God
> carefully watches over and protects
> him —
> Christ's divine presence within him
> preserves him against evil —
> And the wicked one does not lay
> hold (get a grip) on him or touch him.

    a. _____

    b. _____

21. What is her inheritance? (Dan. 7:27)

_____

_____

22. How has this maiden come into an experiential knowledge of reigning in this life with Jesus and exercising dominion over the power of darkness? (II Tim. 2:12; Luke 22:28-30)

_____

In partaking of the sufferings of Christ, she has begun to reign experientially.

23. As she follows on to know the Lord, in what measure will she find herself reigning in this life? (Rom. 5:21)

_____

_____

THE PRIESTLY CROWN

In addition to the Lord becoming to her a diadem, a royal crown, we found that He also has become to her "a spirit of justice for him who sits in judgment." This represents the *crown of the priest*.

24. How has she learned to judge or make a decision? (Isa. 11:3-4)

    a. _____

    b. _____

    c. _____

    d. _____

25. In being able to stand with the Lord in judgment, what three qualities must be developed in your life? (Deut. 1:13)

    a. _____

    b. _____

    c. _____

26. In judgment, what two things must you be careful to do and what one thing must you know? (Deut. 1:17)

    a. _____

    b. _____

    c. _____

27. How has the Bride come to experience the Lord as this *priestly crown* of judgment in her life? (Ps. 119:97-104)
    a. _____
    b. _____
    c. _____
    d. _____
    e. _____

28. How have her senses been trained to discern good and evil? (Heb. 5:14)
    _____

29. Because these qualities have been developed in the life of the Bride, what is she able to say along with Jesus, her Bridegroom? (John 12:48-50)
    _____
    _____
    _____

THE VICTOR'S CROWN

30. Finally, the Lord has become to her a "strength for repelling the onslaught at the gate." This represents the *crown of the victor*. For who has given us the victory? (I Cor. 15:57)
    _____

31. What has she learned to trust in? (II Chron. 32:7-8)
    a. _____
    b. _____

32. The maiden testifies along with the psalmist, "Whom shall I fear, whom shall I dread?" For what has the Lord become to her? (Ps. 27:1)
    a. _____
    b. _____
    c. _____

33. Though a host encamp about her, or a war rise up against her, what was her testimony? (Ps. 27:3)
    a. _____
    b. _____

34. Who is able to overcome the world? (I John 5:4)
    _____

Those who are born of God have the potential, the ability, and the power to overcome the world.

35. Yet, what is the *victory* that overcomes the world? (I John 5:4)
    _____

36. Speaking of this *faith* and this *victory* what did Jesus teach? (Mark 11:22-24)
    _____
    _____
    _____

This truly is the essence of faith that is the crown of the victor and will repel the *onslaught at the gate*, as well as make aggressive advances against the enemy.

In the all glorious *head of gold*, the maiden sees Jesus as the Head of all things to His Bride, the Church. She sees Him as the ultimate Crown and Head of all authority and power whom every power in heaven and earth must obey, the fulness of Diety dwelling in Him in bodily form. She sees Him as the great Judge, as the *Discerner of the thoughts and intents of the heart*, and as the Living Word. Through Him, she has come to judge righteously in every situation. Finally, in the great *head of gold*, she sees the crown of the victor, and through Him the power to conquer all the enemies in her own life as well as in the Church. She has come to realize that "He who is born of God overcomes the world. Christ's divine presence within him preserves him against evil — and the wicked one does not lay hold, get a grip on, or touch him!" (I John 5:18, Amp. Version)

"Crown Him with many crowns,
The Lamb upon His throne;
Hark: how the heavenly anthem drowns
All music but its own.
Awake, my soul, and sing
Of Him who died for thee,
And hail Him as thy matchless King
Through all eternity."

"Crown Him the Lord of Life,
Who triumphed o'er the grave,
And rose victorious in the strife
For those He came to save;
His glories now we sing
Who died, and rose on high,
Who died — eternal life to bring
And lives, that death may die."

"Crown Him the Lord of peace,
Whose power a scepter sways
From pole to pole, that wars may cease,
And all be prayer and praise:
His reign shall know no end,
And round His pierced feet
Fair flowers of paradise extend
Their fragrance ever sweet."

"Crown Him the Lord of love.
Behold His hands and side,
Those wounds, yet visable above,
In beauty glorified:
All hail, Redeemer, hail!
For Thou hast died for me:
Thy praise and glory shall not fail
Throughout eternity."
"Crown Him with Many Crowns"
by Matthew Bridges, 1800-1894

NOTES

STUDY 16

THE KING OF GLORY:
HIS HIDING PLACE, THE WATER OF LIFE,
HIS HUMILITY AND OBEDIENCE

One thing I have asked from the Lord,
that I shall seek;
That I may dwell in the house of the
Lord all the days of my life,
To behold the beauty of the Lord,
And to meditate in His temple. —
Ps. 27:4

1. How does the maiden describe her Lord's hair? (Song 5:11)

   _____

2. What do the locks of hair represent in the Word? (Num. 6:5)

   _____

Long hair, then signifies *separation unto God*.

3. In what way was Jesus separate from man? (Heb. 7:26)
   a. _____
   b. _____
   c. _____
   d. _____
   e. _____

4. Because of God's holiness, what does He do? (Isa. 45:15)

   _____

5. We discovered in our last lesson that because of God's holiness and purity in contrast to the sinfulness of the people, He had to hide Himself from Israel when he appeared on Mount Sinai. Why? (Ex. 19:20-21)

   _____

6. What has the Lord made His hiding place? (Ps. 18:9-12)

   _____

The *blackness of His locks* thus signify God's *hiding place* where he hides Himself in His terrible holiness from the eyes of men.

7. For *without holiness* or *sanctification*, what does the scripture teach concerning man? (Heb. 12:14)

   _____

8. We have seen that the maiden has gone through periods of discipline and dealing from the Lord. Prior to this description of the Lord that she is now giving, she went through a very great period of darkness and testing, a dark night of the soul. What was the purpose of this discipline? (Heb. 12:10)

   _____

9. Although discipline does not seem joyful but sorrowful, what does it yield to those who have been trained by it? (Heb. 12:11)

   _____

In like manner, the reference to the Lord's hair (His separation) being as *clusters of dates* refers to that peaceful fruit of righteousness that has been developed in the believer's life through the darkness of testing.

This testing has come upon the believer that he might be a partåker of God's holiness and might receive a greater revelation of the Lord.

10. Give four characteristics of God's dwelling place. (Isa. 57:15)

    a. _____

    b. _____

    c. _____

    d. _____

11. What does the Lord love and who shall behold His face? (Ps. 11:7)

    a. _____

    b. _____

12. What promises has the Lord given to those who believe and trust in Him? (John 12:46; Isa. 45:3)

    a. _____

    b. _____

Through the discipline of the Holy Spirit the maiden has received a deeper capacity to behold the glory of the Lord and to partake of His holiness. Therefore, the treasures of God's darkness and the hidden wealth of His secret places have been revealed to her. Consequently, there follows in the maiden's Song a deeper revelation of the glory of God in the face of Jesus Christ.

13. How does the maiden describe His eyes? (Song 5:12)

_____

14. Who are the eyes of the Lord toward? (Ps. 34:15)

_____

The *eyes* are the *seat of the expression*. The expression in the eyes is for, and can be read by, those who are very close. Words and letters are for those at a distance or in a far-off country. Here we learn how close to Him this maiden has come when she could describe such expression.

As the dove returned to Noah with an olive branch in his mouth, signifying that the waters of the flood had subsided and that the time of trial was over, so the maiden reads in the dove eyes of the Lord that her period of testing and trial has come to an end. As the dove fixes his eye only on his mate, so the maiden sees that the eyes of the Lord are fixed on her.

15. In comparing her Lord's eyes to doves *beside streams of water*, what has the Lord become to her? (Isa. 33:21)

_____

16. We see a picture of this same thing written by Ezekiel. In Ezekiel's vision, what were the stages of the water that was flowing from the *house of God*, whose house we are? (Ezk. 47:1-5)

    a. _____

    b. _____

    c. _____

    d. _____

    e. _____

17. This is a fulfillment of what promise? (John 7:38; John 4:14)

_____

This spring becomes a fountain that will grow and increase from a well to rivers of living water. This deep pool, produced by an everlasting spring within the believer, will *leap up* to grasp, comprehend and apprehend *infinity*, which is an immortal, deathless, imperishable existence and endless vitality.

18. For those who take refuge in the shadow of God's wings, of what do they drink? (Ps. 36:8-9)

    a. _____

    b. _____

The river of God is given to those in whom God delights.

19. From where does that river flow? (Rev. 22:1)

    _____

Consequently, the believer who is under the Lordship of Jesus Christ — His throne being established in their heart — will have the privilege of drinking from the river of the water of life.

20. What will happen to those who drink from this river? (Ps. 46:4)

    _____

The maiden in this Song has come into a relationship with the Lord where the Spirit of the Lord, represented by the *dove's eyes*, has become to her a place of rivers, waters enough to swim in.

21. What has become evident in her life? (Ps. 46:4-5)

    _____

The maiden has become a *holy dwelling place* of the most High, her God is in the midst of her, and she shall not be moved.

22. In the trials and darkness that went before this deeper revelation of the Lord, what has it seemed like to the maiden? (Ps. 42:7)

    _____

As the water torrent reaches the sea, and can evermore plunge deeper into the fathomless ocean, so now is the maiden lifted out of herself to find a limitless capacity in God. It is out of a broken life that *deep calls unto deep*.

23. How does the maiden describe the Lord's cheeks? (Song 5:13)

    _____

24. When Jesus was upon earth, what did He give His cheeks to and what did He not hide from? (Isa. 50:6)

    _____

25. As He set His face like flint, enduring this type of treatment, what did He know? (Isa. 50:7)

    _____

26. Paul exhorts us to have this same attitude which Jesus had. Summarize this attitude. (Phil. 2:5-8)

    _____

27. Since Jesus has suffered in the flesh, what are we exhorted to do? (I Peter 4:1)

    _____

28. What has he who has suffered in the flesh ceased from and what does he live for? (I Peter 4:1-2)

    a. _____

    b. _____

29. What example did Jesus leave for us to follow? (I Peter 2:21-28)

    a. _____

    b. _____

    c. _____

    d. _____

    e. _____

In the Lord's cheek's, His Bride sees that example of humility and obedience to the point of death that Jesus has set before us, and like the Holy One who called her, she is reminded to be holy in all her behavior.

The Hebrew word which the maiden uses to refer to the cheeks of her Lord as herbs or spices is *bosem* which means *creating desire*. It is the remembrance of Him with the marks of His passion that has caused the redeemed of all ages to cry out, "Draw me after you and let us run together." (Song 1:4)

NOTES

STUDY 17

THE KING OF GLORY:
THE LIPS OF THE KING

My heart overflows with a good theme;
I address my verses to the King;
My tongue is the pen of the ready writer.
Thou art fairer than the sons of men;
Grace is poured upon thy lips;
Therefore God has blessed thee forever. —
Ps. 45 A Song Celebrating the King's Marriage

1.   How does the maiden describe her Lord's lips? (Song 5:13)

   _____

Lips are used in scripture to signify *the speech* or *the words that proceed from the mouth*. In a previous study we discovered that one of the properties of *myrrh* was that is was a *most fragrant perfume*, casting an intoxicating odor. We also learned previously that one of the characteristics of the *lily* was its *sweet smell*. In fact, it is so fragrant that a man's senses will be easily turned with the strength of its aroma. It is to this *overpowering sweetness of aroma* that the maiden compares the *lips* of her Lord and the *words* which dropped from them.

2.   What has God prepared for those who love Him? (I Cor. 2:9)
   a. _____
   b. _____
   c. _____

Notice that the things which God has prepared for those who love Him are things not perceived by the natural senses, things not perceived by the eye or words not *heard* by the ear.

3.   How then can we know these things, and perceive these words of the Lord that are like lilies and sweet smelling myrrh? (I Cor. 2:10-12)

   _____

4.   The scripture goes on to say that these things are not found in words taught by human wisdom, but taught by the Spirit of God. In what manner does the Spirit of God teach these things to us? (I Cor. 2:13)

   _____

It is these spiritual thoughts and spiritual words imparted to the spirit of man that the maiden is referring to in this passage.

5.   Elijah had an experience with that precious voice of the Spirit of God. Describe the three things that the Lord's voice was not in. Then describe the way the voice of the Lord came to Elijah. (I Kings 19:11-13)
   a. _____
   _____
   b. _____
   c. _____
   d. _____

The Amplified Version records it this way:

A sound of gentle stillness and a still small voice.

It is that still small voice, not audible by the *natural* ear, but heard only by the *spiritual* ear, that can impart things to the spirit of man in a split second of time, the truth of which continues to minister fragrance and sweetness for a lifetime.

6. What did Jeremiah say about the words of the Lord? (Jer. 15:16)

   _____

   _____

7. Speaking of this spiritual ear, what did the prophet Isaiah write? (Isa. 50:4-5)

   _____

8. What was his attitude toward what he heard with his spiritual ear? (Isa. 50:5)

   _____

Likewise, this maiden's ear has been awakened by the Lord of glory to listen as a disciple. She was not disobedient, nor did she harden her heart to the things which the Spirit was saying to her.

9. The psalmist also had an ear awakened to that still small voice. What did he say about the Lord's words to him? (Ps. 119:161-162)
   a. _____
   b. _____

10. As one who had become tuned in to the voice of His God, David heard with spiritual ears. In what way was the Lord able to commune with David's spirit? (Ps. 23:1-3)
    a. _____
    b. _____
    c. _____
    d. _____

Oh, the tranquility of that voice, the calmness of that voice, the peacefulness of that voice — like a cold drink of water on a hot sweltering day: it restores and renews our souls. It guides us down the right path. It stills and quiets our every troubling thought and fear.

11. That voice which is so still and so peaceful can at the same time lay bare the heart. Describe other qualities of that voice. (Ps. 29:4-9) Note: *cedars of Lebanon* in the scripture represents the *righteous man* — Ps. 92:12)
    a. (v. 4) _____
    b. (v. 4) _____
    c. (v. 5) _____
    d. (v. 6) _____
    e. (v. 7) _____
    f. (v. 8) _____
    g. (v. 9) _____
    h. (v. 9) _____

That precious voice that is so gentle and so peaceful is at the same time packed with power and majesty. That voice, while so kind and loving, is at the same time able to break through our hardness and soulishness and bring about true repentance and brokenness. That voice can cause our hearts to leap up with joy and make our feet to dance before Him. That voice can be as the prophet Jeremiah said, "as a burning fire shut up in our bones," as the Lord is with us like a "dread companion." That voice to our heart can be like a purifying fire, shaking everything that can be shaken from our lives so that only that which is from His Spirit will remain. That voice can cause His people to reproduce spiritually through guidance and instruction, revealing how to speak the Word of God to the one who is weary and lost. That voice can strip the forest bare, as it is written in Hebrews 4:12-13:

For the Word of God is living and active
And sharper than any two-edged sword,
And piercing as far as the division of
soul and spirit,
Of both joints and marrow and able to
judge the thoughts and intentions of
the heart.
And there is no creature hidden from His
sight,
But all things are open and laid bare to
the eyes of Him with whom we have to do.

12. What was the attitude of Job and the prophet Habakkuk toward the words of their Master, the King of Glory? (Job 23:12; Hab. 2:1)
    a. (Job)_____
    b. (Job) _____
    c. (Hab.) _____

13. As a result of this careful listening and diligent watching, what did the Lord speak to Habakkuk's heart? (Hab. 2:2-3)
    _____

14. The maiden spoke of her Bridegroom's lips being as lilies dripping liquid myrrh. In Solomon's temple, what do we find adorned with lily work? (I Kings 7:19, 22)
    _____

We find that the top of the pillars were crowned and adorned with lily design. The lily design was four cubits in depth. The number *four* speaks of the *completion of the New Creation*. Therefore we learn from this parable that the maturity or completion of the new creation man, which is the crowning glory of God's handiwork, will be adorned with the words of the Lord. Worked into their spirits will be the familiarity of that still small voice, penetrating and gracing their spirits.

15. What does Jesus say that the pillars in the temple of God represent? (Rev. 3:12)
    _____

16. What was the height of the capitals that were on top of the pillars and what were they made of? (I Kings 7:16)
    a. _____
    b. _____

Bronze represents *judgment*.

Five represents *God's grace*.

Consequently, this parable implies that by His grace, He has judged the sin in the soul of the maiden through the still small voice of His Spirit. He has caused His voice to be wrought within and without the spirit of His beloved Bride.

17. In the symbolic description of the sons of God — the overcomers — given by Ezekiel, what is written about the leadership of the voice of the Spirit of God in their life? (Ezk. 1:12)
    _____

18. Who are the sons of God? (Rom. 8:14)
    _____

19. What furniture in Solomon's temple was adorned with lily work? (I Kings 7:23-26)
    _____

This cast metal sea had the same function as the brazen laver in the tabernacle of Moses. It was used for the priests to wash their hands in before entering the Holy Place.

20. Give the dimensions of the cast metal sea. (I Kings 7:23)
    a. Diameter (from brim to brim)_____
    b. Height_____
    c. Circumference _____

The measurements speak to us of a spiritual truth.

10 = fulness of testing

5 = number of grace

30 = number of consecration for priestly ministry, maturity

The daily washing of the priests in the cast metal sea represents the washing in the water of the Word in order that we as a kingdom of priests might enter into a deeper fellowship and revelation of the Lord.

The meaning of the sea's measurements speaks to us of the same thing. By the grace of God and through the fulness of testing we shall grow up into maturity and be truly consecrated for priestly ministry.

21. Describe the stand on which the cast metal sea rested. (I Kings 7:25)
_____

22. What do the *oxen* in scripture represent? (I Tim. 5:18)
_____

The *ox* is a broken domesticated animal and represents *the one who labors* and *gives service to the Lord*, his will being subjected to the will of the Lord.

23. What do the oxen facing north, south, east, and west represent? (Matt. 28:19-20)
_____

The lesson we find hidden here is this — the instruction given to the maiden by the still small voice of His Spirit is not meant for herself alone, but is to be passed on to the whole world, "teaching them to observe all" that the Lord has commanded her.

The number of oxen and their grouping also reveals to us a spiritual truth.

12 = divine government

3 = the fulness of God

We can conclude that these ministers of the gospel go forth into the world under God's divine government, in His fulness and image.

24. What does Jesus say about the man God sends? (John 3:34)
_____

25. Jesus taught His disciples to observe the lilies. What did He say about them? (Matt. 6:28-29)
_____

26. What was Solomon's glory? (I Kings 4:29-34)
_____

We under the new covenant have the opportunity of having an even *greater wisdom* than Solomon had, because we have Jesus — the *source* of all wisdom and knowledge — dwelling within our hearts. When

Jesus said, "Even Solomon in all his glory was not arrayed like one of these," He was speaking of those who have had the *inner ear* of the Spirit developed within. Truly their hearts have been wrought with lily work—and their wisdom, discernment and breadth of mind is greater than that of Solomon's.

27. Actually, what do we under the new covenant possess within our vessels and what potential do we have? (Col. 2:2-3)

    a. _____

    b. _____

I come to the garden alone
While the dew is still on the roses;
And the voice I hear,
Falling on my ear
The Son of God discloses.

And He walks with me,
And He talks with me,
And He tells me I am His own;
And the joy we share, as we tarry
there,
None other has ever known.

He speaks and the sound of His
voice,
Is so sweet, the birds hush their
singing,
And the melody, that He gave to me,
Within my heart is ringing.

And He walks with me,
And He talks with me,
And He tells me I am His own,
And the joy we share, as we tarry
there,
None other has ever known.
C. Austin Miles

NOTES

THE KING OF GLORY:
HIS HANDS

And He is the head over all things
to the church, which is His body,
The fulness of Him who fills all in all. —
Eph. 1:22-23

Thou dost open Thy hand
And dost satisfy the desire of every
living thing. —
Ps. 145:16

Thus far, the maiden has described the Lord of Glory as the all Glorious Head. Each aspect of His character has been related to His position as the *Head* of all things to the Church, thus describing His head of gold, His hair, His eyes, His cheeks and His lips. The remainder of this revelation speaks of His body, the Church. It speaks of that *many-membered man, the sons of God,* who have grown up unto the measure of the stature of the fulness of Christ. As John the revelator, on the isle of Patmos, received that glorious vision of Jesus and His many-membered man that spoke with the voice of many waters, so also the maiden is receiving a deeper revelation of Jesus and those sons of God in His image. Jesus cannot be separated from His body which is the fulness of Him who fills all in all. Consequently, we will examine the rest of this revelation in light of the *body* of Christ — *His many-membered man* of which the maiden is a part.

1. What vision or goal does Jesus desire for His body to attain? (Eph. 4:12-13)
   a. _____
   b. _____
   c. _____
   d. _____

2. What is His body the Church? (Eph. 1:22-23)
   _____

Let us examine His hands in the light of the body of Christ.

3. How does the maiden describe her Beloved's hands? (Song 5:14)
   _____

From our previous studies we have learned that:

the *hands* represent *the will in action*

rod represents *authority to rule*

and *gold* represents *the divine nature*

We can conclude that God's will in action is to take His divine authority and rule.

4. Exactly how does God desire to rule here on earth? (Ps. 110:2)
   _____

5. Who does Zion represent? (Ps. 125:1)
   _____

God's will in action, then, is to rule by His great power through the lives of those who trust Him — and

He desires to do this *right now* in the *midst* of His enemies. He desires to rule through the divine nature that He has wrought in the hearts of those who are completely His.

Let us look at the *hands* more specifically and see what truth they reveal about this many-membered man, the sons of God in His image. Remember that *hands* signify in this passage *God's will in action*.

6.   What attitude do the members of this manchild company have which is represented by these hands that are as rods of gold? (John 4:34)

_____

7.   What do they seek? (John 5:30)

_____

8.   What can the Lord say about them that He also said about David? (Acts 13:22)

_____

We discover that those who make up this many-membered body are *doers* of the Word and *not hearers only*. They are literally *God's will in action* being expressed on earth.

9.   What does the prophet Habakkuk prophesy concerning this *hand* ministry, speaking of those who are doers of the Word and who act out God's will? (Hab. 3:4)
    a. _____
    b. _____

God's power is hidden in His sons who desire to perform all His will.

10.   What do they speak and what has God given to them? (John 3:34)
    a. _____
    b. _____

11.   More specifically, what do these rays that were flashing from His hand represent? (Job 36:32-33a)

_____

Lightning in the scripture represents the *anointed Word* going forth. We could translate the passage in Habakkuk and Job in this way:

> *The anointed word flashes forth from*
> *His sons;*
> *He covers His sons with the anointed*
> *word and commands them to strike*
> *the mark.*

12.   Jeremiah spoke of this anointed word. How did he describe it? (Jer. 23:29)

_____

13.   In a symbolic description of the sons of God given by Ezekiel, what did Ezekiel say was in the midst of them? (Ezk. 1:13)

_____

This anointed word, that is like a fire and like a hammer that shatters the rock, is found deep within the spirit of the sons of God.

14.   Not only did Ezekiel see this anointed Word abiding in the vessel of the overcomer, but how did he describe their actions? (Ezk. 1:14)

_____

They did not hold that word in, but they let it flash forth. They let the anointed word go forth from their mouths like a hammer, burning like fire and striking the mark, shattering the hardness in people's lives. By their very actions, they brought forth God's anointed Word. They are His will in action, going forth where the Spirit sends them and speaking the words which God has put in their hearts.

15. What does David say prophetically concerning this *hand* ministry? (Ps. 145:16)

16. Paul himself refers to this same event. How does he describe it? (Rom. 8:19-21)

Through this *hand* ministry, the Lord of Glory will satisfy the desire of every living thing. When the Lord sends forth this hand ministry, creation itself will be delivered from satanic bondage and will enter into the liberty of the sons of God.

17. With what were her Beloved's hands set? (Song 5:14)

In searching for what *beryl* represents in the Word, we find that its numerical value appeared in both the breastplate of the High Priest and in the foundation stones of the Holy City. We find that the beryl stone is:

in the *fourth* row of the breastplate (Ex. 28:20).
it is the *tenth* stone of the breastplate (Ex. 28:20).
and it is the *eighth* stone in the Holy City (Rev. 21:20).

The numbers signify the following:

4 = the completion of the New Creation

10 = the fulness of testing

8 = resurrection

The beryl stone signifies that through the fulness of testing the New Creation will be completed and will go forth in the power of the resurrection. It is a *green* color which also signifies *eternal* or *never ending resurrection life.*

18. The fact that resurrection power was a goal to run toward and attain is evident in the teachings of Paul, for what did Paul say was his desire? (Phil. 3:1)
    a. _____
    b. _____
    c. _____
    d. _____

19. If we have been united with Him in the likeness of His death, accomplished by the dealings of God through the Spirit, what also can we expect? (Rom. 6:5)

20. Again, in the symbolic description of the overcomers given by Ezekiel, what was the appearance of their wheels? (Ezk. 1:16)

21. What does the *wheel* represent? (Ezk. 1:20)

The spirit of these overcomers was charged with resurrection life.

22. To discover a little more of what the beryl stone signifies, we will look again at the breastplate of the high priest. What was engraved on each stone in the breastplate? (Ex. 28:21)

These names were engraved on the stones according to the order of their birth. The meaning of the names of the twelve tribes of Israel represent twelve *natures* that God is working into His people. These attributes will bring His people under His divine government represented by the number twelve.

On the tenth stone of the breastplate of the High Priest was engraved the name *Zebulun*. Zebulun was the tenth son of Jacob although the sixth son of Leah.

23. What does the name *Zebulun* mean, and why did Leah give him this name? (Gen. 30:20)

_____

The name *Zebulun* engraved upon the beryl represents the desire of His bride to dwell in the immediate presence of her Lord. We have said that those hands of gold set with beryl represent those who are God's will in action, partaking of His resurrection life and power. The name Zebulun reveals to us the *secret* of these sons. This we will look into further.

24. What are the four groups of believers listed in our Song? (Song 6:8-9)
    a. _____
    b. _____
    c. _____
    d. _____

The queens and concubines represent those believers who have varying degrees of relationship and intimate communion with the Lord.

60 queens = 30 x 2

30 = the matter of consecration and maturity for ministry. (David was 30 when he became King, Jesus was 30 when he began His ministry.)

2 = the matter is determined by God; He will establish it; He will confirm it and He will bring it to pass.

The sixty queens represent those believers who have matured for ministry through their relationship and fellowship with the Lord. They go forth and preach the Word as the Lord confirms and establishes the Word with signs following.

80 concubines = 40 x 2

40 = the number of testing and probation which ends either in victory or judgment (Israel was 40 years in the wilderness. Jesus was 40 days in the wilderness. During Noah's flood it rained 40 days and 40 nights).

2 = the matter is determined by God; He will establish it; He will confirm it and He will bring it to pass.

The *eighty concubines* represent those believers who have stood through many testings and tryings of God. Through the many testings and tryings of God and through this relationship with Him, they have come forth in victory, being established by God Himself.

The *virgins*, or *maidens* without number represent those children of grace who have been born again, but have developed no intimate fellowship with the Lord.

But, *my dove, my undefiled one*, the Shulamite maiden of our Song, represents those believers who have sought the Lord of Glory for Himself alone, not for His mighty acts, or the conquering of the enemy in their own lives. They have sought Him out of an appreciation and love for Him as a person and a desire to be close to His heart. This company of believers are as a dove in the singleness of their eye for Jesus, being completely separated unto Him. This *Bride* company has progressed and developed unto fulness of love for the Lord. It is this company that the *beryl stone*, engraved with the name *Zebulun*, represents. It is those people who have desired to *dwell* with the Lord in most intimate communion, longing to be those closest to His heart.

25. The psalmist David captures the intense desire of this *Zebulun company*. Describe their desire to dwell in the Lord's presence. (Ps. 84:1-2, 10)
    a. (v. 1) _____
    b. (v. 2) _____
    c. (v. 10) _____
    d. (v. 10) _____

26. What one thing has this *Zebulun company* asked and sought of the Lord? (Ps. 27:4)
    _____

Their whole life is consumed with this burning desire and passion. This is the secret of the power and anointing of this great *hand* company. Their life, their ministry, and their anointing is the outflowing of the deep relationship and intimate communion they share with the Lord of life.

27. What is the Lord's attitude toward this company of believers? (Ps. 68:16; Ps. 87:1-3) Note: *Zion* represents *those who trust wholly in the Lord. Mountain* represents *kingdom.*
    a. (v. 16) _____
    b. (v. 16) _____
    c. (v. 1-3)_____

28. What promises are given to those people with whom God has chosen to dwell in intimate communion? (Ps. 132:13-18) Note: the *horn of David* represents the *increase of power and glory of the Messianic Kingdom.*
    a. (v. 15) _____
    b. (v. 15) _____
    c. (v. 16) _____
    d. (v. 16) _____
    e. (v. 17) _____
    f. (v. 17) _____
    g. (v. 18) _____

29. What type of ministry will this *Zebulun company* have? (Isa. 58:12; Hosea 14:5-7) Note: the *cedar* of Lebanon represents the *righteous man*. The *roots* of the cedars of Lebanon are as deep as the trees are high.
    a. (v. 12) _____
    b. (v. 12) _____
    c. (v. 12) _____
    d. (v. 12) _____
    e. (Hosea v. 7)_____

This is a beautiful picture of the restoration that this *Zebulun company* will bring forth in the earth.

Although this *hand* ministry is a corporate company of people, the calling can only be attained to as each individual believer earnestly desires the Lord with his whole heart, sets his eye on the prize of the High calling of God in Christ Jesus, and presses on toward that goal by the grace of God.

> *Do you not know that in a race all the*
> *runners compete,*
> *But only one receives the prize?*
> *So run your race that you may lay hold*
> *of the prize and make it yours.*
> *Therefore, I do not run uncertainly —*
> *without definite aim.*
> *I do not box as one beating the air and*

striking without an adversary.
For my determined purpose is that I
may know Him —
That I may progressively become more
deeply and intimately acquainted
with Him,
Perceiving and recognizing and under-
standing the wonders of His person
more strongly and clearly.
And that I may in that same way come
to know the power outflowing
from His resurrection which it
exerts over believers.
Not that I have now attained this ideal
or am already made perfect,
But I press on to lay hold of, grasp,
and make my own
That for which Jesus has laid hold of me
and made me His own.
I do not consider, brethren,
That I have captured and made it my own
yet;
But one thing I do — it is my aspiration;
Forgetting what lies behind and straining
forward to what lies ahead,
I press on toward the goal to win the
supreme and heavenly prize
To which God in Christ Jesus is calling
us upward.
So let those of us who are spiritually
mature and full-grown have this in
mind and hold these convictions. —
Portions of I Cor. 9:24-27; and
Phil. 3:10-15 Amplified Version

NOTES

STUDY 19

THE KING OF GLORY:
HIS THRONE, HIS LORDSHIP

I kept looking until thrones were set up
And the Ancient of Days took His seat;
His vesture was like white snow
And the hair of His head like pure wool.
His throne was ablaze with flames.
Its wheels were a burning fire.
A river of fire was flowing
And coming out from before Him. —
Daniel 7:9-10a

We come now to the abdomen or belly of our Glorious Savior.

1. How is His abdomen described? (Song 5:14)

   _____

2. During the reign of Solomon, what did he construct of ivory? (I Kings 10:18)

   _____

   The *belly of ivory* represents the *King's throne.*

3. What did Jesus say would flow from the belly or innermost being of the believer? (John 7:38)

   _____

   The scripture goes on to say that "This He spoke of the Spirit whom those who believed in Him were to receive." (John 7:39)

   The belly of the Body of Christ then, represents the spirit of the believer where Jesus, by His precious Holy Spirit, reigns as King on His glorious throne.

   Let us look at the throne of Solomon to discover more about the spirit of the man in which God sets up His reign as King.

4. Describe the throne of ivory. (I Kings 10:18-20)

   _____
   _____
   _____
   _____

   Now this throne is a type and a shadow of the spirit of the believer where Jesus is enthroned as King. As we examine the throne we will discover truths about the spirit of the man who is submitted to His Lordship.

5. One thing that is immediately apparent is that this throne is surrounded by *lions*. These lions are metaphoric. Remember that a metaphor is a figure of speech containing an implied comparison in which a word or phrase ordinarily and primarily used of one thing is applied to another. Let us examine the metaphor of the *lion* to glean truths that are hidden there.

METAPHOR	PARALLEL
a. The lion is a very courageous creature. He does not run or flee from fear of either man or beast.	a. Prov. 28:1; Ps. 27:1-3; Acts 4:29-31 _____ _____

b. Lions are great conquerors. Although other beasts may be much bigger, they are not able to stand before lions.

b. Rom. 8:37

_____
_____
_____

c. A lion is a creature that other beasts are afraid of.

c. Saints are men that the wicked often fear. They dread the effects of their prayers. It was said that Mary Queen of Scotts was more afraid of the prayers of John Knox than an army of 20,000 men. (Mark 6:20)

_____
_____

d. A lion is a very strong creature.

d. Give reasons for this great strength. (Eph. 6:10)
   1. Prov. 14:26-27
   _____
   2. Prov. 18:10
   _____
   3. Prov. 24:5-6
   _____
   _____
   4. Dan. 11:32
   _____
   5. Heb. 11:34; Ps. 105:24
   _____
   6. Ps. 61:3-4
   _____
   _____

e. The lion treds down and makes a prey of his enemies.

e. Micah 5:8; Rev. 12:9-11

_____
_____
_____

Conclusion:

The maiden of our song is a believer who has enthroned Jesus as King of her life. As a result, she has a spirit that, as our metaphor tells us, is full of lions. She is a believer who is as bold as a lion, fearless in the face of her enemy. She does not run or flee from fear. She is more than a conqueror. She is a believer who is righteous and holy; therefore, the wicked fear her. She is a believer who is strong in the Lord and the strength of His might. He that prevails against her, whether men or devils, must prevail against and overcome the mighty God; and who is a match for Him? She has and uses His precious name. She knows her God, is strong, and does exploits. As the mighty lion tramples down all other beasts, so shall she trample down her enemy and there will be none to rescue.

Therefore, let the saints show themselves bold and courageous in the cause and interest of their God. A fearful and timid spirit does not become a Christian, as it denies the *very* work that Jesus has done for them. For He Himself has filled their spirits with great and mighty lions.

Let us look again at King Solomon's throne (the King of Peace, as his name indicates) to see what other truths are found there.

6. How many lions were found there and in what order? (I Kings 10:18-20)

_____
_____

The number of these lions speaks to us of another spiritual truth.

There were twelve lions on the six steps, six on one side and six on the other.

12 = divine government

6 = man

This represents man under God's authority, and divine government.

The stairs that lead up to the throne also have meaning. As we discovered earlier in our Song, *stairs* represent the *call to ascend with the risen Christ*. Positionally we are seated with Christ in heavenly places with all enemies under our feet, yet there must be an experiential working out of these things. There must be a taking of our inheritance and a rising above the earthly ways. This will *not* be done by those who sit complacently. This will be done by those who are bold as a lion and who are aggressive against the enemy.

7. What do the two remaining lions on either side of the throne represent? (Zech. 4:2-6)

_____

These two lions standing on either side of the throne represent the *Spirit* and the *Word*. It is the Word of God, enlightened and anointed by the Spirit, and the empowering of the Holy Ghost that will allow the believers to go forth as mighty lions. They aggressively pull down the strongholds of the enemy, boldly and fearlessly proclaiming the way of salvation.

8. What other descriptive terms does the maiden use to describe the belly of her beloved? (Song 5:14)

_____

9. In what instances does the Bible mention the sapphire? (Ex. 24:10; Ezk. 1:26-28) Note: *lapis lazuli* used in NAS is, in Hebrew, *the sapphire stone* — see marginal references.
    a. _____
    b. _____

Again we find the *belly inlaid with sapphires* is the very *throne* of the Lord God of Hosts.

10. What numerical position does the sapphire stone hold in the breastplate of the high priest and the foundation stones of the New Jerusalem? (Ex. 28:17-18; Rev. 21:19)

_____

5 = grace

2 = the matter is determined by God; He will establish it and bring it to pass

It is God Himself who establishes His residence in our lives and brings to pass His work in us. It is the grace of God that causes Him who made heaven and earth to choose to take up His abode in our hearts.

The color of the sapphire speaks to us of still another spiritual truth. The sapphire is a very deep ultramarine blue. Blue in the scripture signifies the *presence of the revealed God*. To the Hebrews it was the Jehovah color. It also signifies *the anointing*.

It is the Lordship of Jesus in the life of the believer that brings forth the *anointing* of the Spirit.

11. Describe the throne of the Lord of Glory. (Dan. 7:9-10)

_____

12. What is the Lord our God? (Heb. 12:29)

_____

13. Who can live under the Lordship of Jesus? (Isa. 33:14-15)

a. _____

b. _____

c. _____

d. _____

e. _____

The fire of His presence, in the life of those who are His, consumes and burns away all impurities.

14. What else does this fire signify? (Jer. 20:8-9; Jer. 23:29)

_____

This word which Jeremiah the prophet speaks, which he describes as a burning fire that he cannot refrain from speaking, is the *prophetic* word. When the *prophetic* word goes forth from the mouth of the believer, it will truly be like fire and like a hammer that shatters the rock. It will accomplish the purpose for which the Lord sent it. Note: We are not speaking here of the gift of prophecy in a meeting, of which Paul says, "all may prophesy."

In the latter days, God will have a seed that will come to maturity. He will have a people that have become so pure from the fire of the abiding presence of His throne in their hearts that they will *all* be prophetic. As Moses said, "Would that all God's people were prophets." From this seed the Word will go forth like fire. Just as Jesus was ruthless against those who had defiled His Father's house and drove them out of the temple, so that seed will be ruthless against sin and anything that would defile the Church of the living God. As it was written about Jesus, so it will be said about them: "Zeal for Thy house has consumed me."

...He said, take these things away —
out of here!
...And His disciples remembered that
it is written in the Holy Scriptures,
"The zeal — the fervor of love — for Your
house will eat me up. —
I will be consumed with jealousy for the
honor of Your house." —
John 2:16-17 Amplified Version

NOTES

STUDY 20

THE KING OF GLORY:
THE REVEALED WORD

*The secret things belong to the Lord
our God,
But the things revealed, belong to us
and to our sons forever. —
Deut. 29:29*

1. Describe the legs of the body of the beloved Bridegroom. (Song 5:15)

   _____

   It is on the *legs* that the whole body stands. Likewise, it is the legs of Jesus on which the body of Christ stands.

2. What do the legs of Jesus represent? (Ps. 33:9; Ps. 33:11; Isa. 14:24; Isa. 40:8)
   a. _____
   b. _____
   c. _____

3. What does John tell us about Jesus' legs when giving the account of the crucifixion? (John 19:33)

   _____

4. What does the Lord say concerning His covenant and about the utterance of His lips? (Ps. 89:34)

   _____

   It is the Word of God, His plans, His counsel, and in short, His covenant, on which the Body of Christ stands. All are sure and steadfast, unalterable, and cannot be broken.

   As we examine the legs of the Bridegroom further, we find a deeper truth concerning God's Word and covenant to His people.

5. As we discovered above, the legs on which we stand as believers represent more than just the written Word of God. They represent His plans, His counsel, and His Words as they are *revealed* to the heart of the believer. With whom does the Lord reveal His plans and the counsels of His heart? Gen. 18:17; James 2:23; John 15:14-15; Amos 3:7)
   a. _____
   b. _____

6. How does a believer become a friend of the Lord? (John 15:14)

   _____

7. As we continue with the description given to us of these legs, we find that they appeared as pillars. In the Old Testament, what did the pillar of stone or pillar of cloud indicate? (Gen. 28:12-18, 22; Gen. 35:9-15; Ex. 33:9-11) Summarize.

   _____

   _____

   We can conclude that the *pillar* of stone or cloud *marked the place where God spoke with man* face to face as with a friend revealing His plans, His counsel and His purposes.

8. In each instance where God appeared and spoke with Jacob, what did Jacob pour on top of the pillar? (Gen. 28:18; Gen. 35:14)

These legs according to our maiden were pillars made of *alabaster*. The only other mention of alabaster in the scripture are the accounts in the gospels of the women possessing alabaster vials full of precious ointment.

9.   A woman who was a sinner came to Jesus at the house of a Pharisee. In this account given by Luke, what did the woman do? (Luke 7:37-38)

_____

_____

10.   What was the Pharisee's response? (Luke 7:39)

_____

_____

11.   What was Jesus' reply? (Luke 7:40-47) Summarize.

_____

_____

12.   After Lazarus was raised from the dead, Jesus was again anointed with oil from the alabaster vial, this time by Mary the sister of Lazarus. In this account given in Matthew, what did Mary do? (Matt. 26:7)

_____

13.   What was the disciples' response? (Matt. 26:8-9)

_____

_____

14.   What was Jesus' response? (Matt. 26:10-12)

_____

_____

Both the disciples of Jesus and the Pharisee missed the significance of these women's acts of love unto the Lord. The woman, who was a sinner, had knelt at Jesus' feet, anointing them with oil, worshipped Him and wept in repentance. Jesus received her worship and forgave her sins. Israelites were to worship only the true God, for only God alone could forgive sins. The woman, through her worship, her repentance and her offering of oil poured out upon Jesus, was acknowledging Him as the Redeemer and the Holy One of Israel. The Pharisee failed to recognize the One who was seated at his table. He was a man who was forgiven little. This was because he had repented of only a little. The Redeemer of Jacob was seated beside him, yet he did not realize it nor did he call upon Him.

Mary, the sister of Lazarus, poured oil upon Jesus' head from a heart of devotion and adoration toward Him. In doing so, Mary was acknowledging Him as the God of Israel, her Messiah. As Jacob had anointed the pillar of stone as the place where he had met with God face to face, so she anointed Jesus. Flesh and blood had not revealed to her who He was. The disciples, too, were short-sighted; in their efforts to be religious they missed the meaning of a true act of worship.

But to all believers who, from a true heart of worship and adoration, seek Him, He will receive their worship and reveal unto them His plans, His purposes and His counsel through His Holy Word. He will also make known to them His covenant. As a result, those who seek Him in truth will have strong legs on which to stand, like pillars of alabaster.

Having loins girded with truth, they will be able to stand against the world, the flesh and the devil. They will be able to run through a troop, leap over a wall, and be able to pull down the strongholds of the enemy.

15.   Finally, upon what did the legs rest? (Song 5:15)

_____

16. What do the pedestals of pure gold represent? Remember *gold* represents *the divine nature*. (Jer. 1:12; Ps. 57:2)

_____

_____

17. What two things do we have as a surety of the unchangeableness of God's promises and purposes? (Heb. 6:13, 17)

a. _____

b. _____

Since God could swear by none greater, He swore by Himself and confirmed His promises with an oath. It is God that stands behind His Word. He Himself was the surety for His covenant, sealing it in His own blood. He ever lives to make intercession for the saints, to make good His promises unto them, and to fulfill everything that has been written concerning His body, which is the Church of Jesus Christ and the House of the Living God.

18. Who are those that are the blessed of God? (Luke 1:45)

_____

_____

19. What description does the maiden give her Lord's overall appearance? (Song 5:15)

_____

20. Who do the cedars of Lebanon represent? (Ps. 92:12)

_____

The Bridegroom is described as the *choice* cedars of Lebanon. This passage definitely points to the *humanity* of our Savior.

21. In which way was Jesus the choice cedar of Lebanon? (Rom. 8:29; I Cor. 15:45, 47)

a. _____

b. _____

Jesus, the last Adam, who is the first-born of a new race of people, is the choice cedar of Lebanon. He, in His humanity, fulfilled all things that the first Adam failed to do. He came as the first Adam came, begotten of God. Yet, He in His flesh overcame the world, the flesh, and the devil that He might bring forth a new race of people—the race that Adam failed to bring forth—who are the Godmen.

22. Contrast the first Adam and the last Adam, the Man Christ Jesus. (Rom. 5:14-21)

FIRST ADAM	THE MAN CHRIST JESUS— THE CHOICE CEDAR OF LEBANON
1. Through him sin and death entered the world and spread to all men.	1. Rom. 5:21 _____ _____
2. Judgment arose from his transgression resulting in condemnation.	2. Rom. 5:16 _____ _____
3. By his transgression death reigned.	3. Rom. 5:17 _____ _____
4. Through his transgression there resulted condemnation to all men.	4. Rom. 5:18 _____ _____

5. Through his disobedience the many were made sinners.

5. Rom. 5:19

_____

_____

23. As we have borne the image of the earthy, what must we also bear? (I Cor. 15:49; Rom. 8:29)

_____

_____

The first-born of the New Creation of God, the Man Jesus who is the last Adam, is truly the choice cedar of Labanon. It is His image that His body and His Bride is destined to bear before the world. As the world has borne to the fullest measure the image of the first Adam, so the New Creation of God, the blood-bought believer of the new covenant, must bear before the world the full image of the last Adam.

Just as Jesus went forth into the world, in like manner are His sons predestined to go forth into the world. His glorious body of sons will come to maturity. As they go forth, Jesus Himself will send out through them the sacred and imperishable news of eternal salvation.

NOTES

STUDY 21

THE KING OF GLORY:
HE IS THE DESIRE OF ALL NATIONS

Whom have I in heaven but Thee?
And besides Thee,
I desire nothing on earth. —
Ps. 73:25

1. How does the maiden describe the mouth of her Bridegroom? (Song 5:16)

   _____

   The mouth is the organ of speech through which one man communicates with another. Consequently, the mouth of the Bridegroom represents the means by which He communicates with His Bride. It is a fellowship that is sweet.

2. What did the psalmist David say about this sweet fellowship? (Ps. 119:103)

   _____

3. Within a riddle of Samson lies a type and shadow of Jesus. Give the type and shadow and explain what it means. (Judges 14:8, 14)

   _____

   _____

   _____

   _____

   The death of Jesus (who is the Lion of Judah) made it possible for man to experience the sweetness of fellowship and communion with the living God.

4. What does Proverbs identify this *sweetness of honey* as? (Prov. 24:13-14)

   _____

   We are exhorted in Proverbs to eat the honey, the sweetness of His Words, from which comes this heavenly wisdom. In the process of eating, the food is broken up, swallowed, digested, and distributed to all parts of the body, becoming part of the body itself. Likewise, as we commune with the Lord, meditating on and digesting His Word, the sweetness of His heavenly wisdom enters our spirit and permeates every fiber of our being. It becomes our very life and the substance of our existance.

5. If you find wisdom, what two things can you be assured of? (Prov. 24:14)
   a. _____
   b. _____

6. After feasting on this sweet heavenly wisdom, the maiden has received the spirit of wisdom and revelation in the knowledge of Him. Out of her fellowship and communion with her Lord, what three-fold vision has this maiden received? (Eph. 1:17-19)
   a. _____
   b. _____
   c. _____

7. In one exultant voice of praise, what does the maiden exclaim? (Song 5:16a)

   _____

   "He is wholly desirable," she cries out. It is to a Messianic prophecy given by Haggai that this phrase alludes. Jesus is referred to by that prophet as the *Desire of all nations*. (Hag. 2:7; see marginal reference in NAS). It is to this *Desired One*, which all nations and all ages have longed for, that we will now turn our attention.

8. What does the psalmist tell us the heavens are telling, declaring, and what do they reveal? (Ps. 19:1-4)

   a. _____

   b. _____

   c. _____

According to this passage, the heavens are revealing knowledge. In the starry expanse of the night sky, knowledge of God is revealed; it prophesies, telling of God's glory and sets forth His purposes and counsels.

9. Why did God create lights in the expanse of the heavens? (Gen. 1:14-16)

   a. _____ d. _____

   b. _____ e. _____

   c. _____ f. _____

We find that one reason for the lights in the heavens was for *signs* upon the earth.

10. Who named the stars? (Isa. 40:25-26; Ps. 147:4)

   _____

11. What are some of the names that the Lord gave the stars and constellations? (Job 38:31-32) Note in this scripture the word for constellation in the marginal reference is *Mazzaroth* which is the twelve signs of the Zodiac.

   _____

In the system of stars, where constellations and signs of the Zodiac form the night sky, we find recorded the gospel of Jesus Christ and the plan for the redemption of the ages. This is a system Satan has perverted, trying to hide what is written there. He caused men to worship the created things—the sun, moon and stars—rather than the Creator Himself, to whom they point. The Bible strictly forbids looking to astrologers, monthly prognosticators and the reading of the horoscopes, identifying it as a satanic religion. Those who practice such things will incur the wrath of God which is revealed against all those who suppress the truth in unrighteousness.

Even more than 2,500 years before the Bible was written, God's people were not left in ignorance or in darkness as to God's purposes and counsels, nor were they without hope as to the ultimate deliverance from all evil and the Evil One. Adam, who first heard that wonderous promise, repeated it, and gave it to his posterity as a most precious heritage. It became the ground of all their faith and the object of all their desire. Seth and Enoch carried this on as Enoch prophesied, "Behold the Lord cometh with ten thousand of His saints to execute judgment upon all." (Jude 14) The Holy Prophets, who according to Luke have been prophesying since the world began, recorded those ancient prophesies truthfully and powerfully in the heavens through the constellations and their interpretations.

In searching through ancient history, it has been discovered that in *all early civilizations* there was recorded a system of constellations which we know as the Zodiac. Each sign in the Zodiac has an identical counterpart in every other ancient astronomical record, as well as identical meaning. These records go back further than 2,000 B.C. in Chinese, Chaldean and Egyptian history. Ancient Persian and Arabian tradition ascribes the invention of this system to Adam, Seth and Enoch. The Bible is not silent concerning these constellations, their names or their meanings. It is the Holy One, He that inhabits eternity, who has named them, and it is His story that they tell.

It is to one of these constellations which we now refer. If you would like any more information on this subject, we refer you to two books—*The Gospel in the Stars* by Joseph A. Seiss, and *The Witness of the Stars* by E. W. Bullinger, D.D.—both published by Kregel Publications. These books are classics on the subject and were written approximately one hundred years ago. It is from the latter that the information recorded above and the star picture which we are about to discuss was taken.

We look now at the constellation *Comah* or *Kamah*, which is pictured by the most ancient star maps as a woman with a child in her arms. The name of the constellation *Comah* is Hebrew, meaning *the desired, the yearned for*, or *the longed for*. This word appears in Psalm 63:1 as David cries out:

O God, Thou art my God, I shall seek
Thee earnestly;
My soul thirsts for Thee, my flesh
yearns (Kamah) for Thee,
In a dry and weary land where there
is no water.

The Persians, Chaldeans, and Egyptians taught that the constellation Comah was a young woman whose Persian name denoted a pure virgin. She was sitting on a throne, nursing an infant boy. The boy, having a Hebrew name, is by some nations called *Ihesu* with the signification *Ieza*, which in Greek is called *Christios*. The ancient Egyptian name for this constellation was *Shes-nu*, or *the desired son*.

It was in all probability that it was from the constellation of Comah that the *star of Bethlehem* appeared. There was a traditional prophecy which was well known in the East, and carefully handed down which said that a new star would appear in this constellation when He of whom it foretold should be born. According to Abulfaragius, and Arab Christian historian of the 13th Century, Zoroaster the Persian, was a pupil of Daniel the prophet. Daniel predicted to the astronomers of Persia, known as the Magians, that a new star would one day appear in the constellation of Comah. This star was to notify them of the birth of a mysterious child whom they were to adore.

12. After Jesus was born in Bethlehem, Magi arrived from the East in Jerusalem. What were they saying?
     (Matt. 2:1-2)

     _____
     _____

And so, the Desired of all nations — the longed for, the One whom all creation yearned for and all nations sought for — was born.

Job, which is the oldest book in the Bible, perhaps the oldest book in the world, says:

And as for me, I know that my Redeemer
lives,
And at the last He will take His stand
on the earth. —
Job 19:25

And Zacharias, the father of John the Baptist, prophesied this as He was filled with the Holy Spirit:

Blessed be the Lord God of Israel;
For He hath visited and redeemed His
people,
And hath raised up a horn of salvation
for us in the house of His servant
David;
As He spake by the mouth of his Holy
prophets,
Which have been since the world began. —
Luke 1:68-70 KJV

It is this Redeemer, this Desired One, whom our maiden is proclaiming to the daughters of Jerusalem.

13. What is the cry of her heart? (Ps. 73:25)

     _____

This is the cry of those who have forsaken all to "follow the Lamb wheresoever He goeth."

14. What is the desire of her soul? (Isa. 26:8)

     _____

111.

15. At night, what is the desire of her soul and her spirit? (Isa. 26:9)

_____

16. What is the one thing that she, like the psalmist, has desired of the Lord? What has she set her heart to seek? (Ps. 27:4)

_____

_____

17. What figurative language does the psalmist use to describe this same desire of which the maiden speaks? (Ps. 42:1-2)

_____

_____

18. What did Jesus say about those who hunger and thirst after righteousness? (Matt. 5:6)

_____

19. What does the maiden call her Bridegroom? (Song 5:16)

_____

The maiden's glorious testimony of Jesus as her God, her beloved One, and her friend has inspired and created within those who heard her a great desire to seek Him also.

20. How did the daughters of Jerusalem who were listening to her testimony respond? (Song 6:1)

_____

21. What has the maiden done? (Matt. 5:16)

_____

22. What has she become? (Matt. 5:14)
    a. _____
    b. _____

23. Because she has not hidden her light but set it upon a lampstand, what has happened? (Matt. 5:15)

_____

24. What had God been pleased to do in this maiden's life as well as in the life of Paul and for what purpose? (Gal. 1:16)

_____

To preach Him is very different than preaching about Him, even though His person might be the subject. As the daughters of Jerusalem have been listening to the maiden preaching Him, they have seen God's glory and have heard the voice of the Spirit speaking unto their hearts.

25. What has the Spirit been speaking to their hearts? (Isa. 55:3, 6)

_____

26. As the maiden lifted up Jesus what happened? (John 12:32)

_____

27. What is the Lord's attitude toward the daughters? (Jer. 31:3)

_____

28. What ministry has the Lord committed unto the maiden? (II Cor. 5:18-20)

_____

Jesus did not come into the world to condemn or judge the world, but to reconcile the world to Himself. Likewise, He again appears by His Spirit in the life of this maiden, entreating and drawing men unto salvation and eternal life.

It was God personally present in Christ,
Reconciling and restoring the world to
favor with Himself...
And committing to us the message of
reconciliation of the restoration of
favor.
So we are Christ's ambassadors,
God making His appeal as it were through
us... —
II Cor. 5:19-20 Amplified Version

NOTES

NOTES

STUDY 22

FAITH AT ITS BEST

Now faith is the substance of things hoped for,
The evidence of things not seen.
For by it the elders obtained a good report. —
Heb. 11:1-2

As we recall from our previous studies, when the Lord appeared to the maiden He called her into total identification with His death. As we remember, she shrank back, not in the intent of her will but in the weakness of her flesh. As the Spirit of the Lord touched her heart, she put away her fears, choosing the path of sacrifice and total trust in Him. As she gave her consent, she entered into the dark night of the soul where all *feelings* of His presence were removed. It seemed that God had deserted her, hiding His face from her.

1. What did we discover that the Lord desired to teach her during this dark night of testing? (Isa. 50:10)

   _____

We found that the purpose of this testing was two-fold. First, to see if the maiden loved Him for the feelings and the blessings, or for Himself alone. Secondly, to teach her to trust and rely on God and His Word only, instead of on the sense of His presence or His blessing. This darkness came upon the maiden to teach her what true *faith* is all about, and to test her commitment and faithfulness unto God. It came upon her to test her — to see if she would serve God.

She arose to follow Him and began seeking that sense of His presence and blessing which she felt she had lost. As she was searching, she exclaimed that she was *sick* with love. In the former times, when she had been flowing in the stream of love with a great sense of His presence, she had spoken like this. But, to speak like this at a time of intense adversity, darkness and unsatisfied longing proved that she had learned to control her emotions. This lovesickness did not stem from having drunk and been full, but rather from a very deep hunger and thirst for Him. As she continued through that darkness to hold fast to her beloved Jesus by faith, and as she began to describe to the daughters of Jerusalem her glorious Savior, a new revelation of His glorious Person and a new enlightenment had come to her. (This dark night of the soul can last many days or many months. The Lord will not test you more than you are able to bear, and will remove the darkness from you when it has accomplished the full purpose for which He sent it.]

2. After she received a deeper revelation of Jesus, she received new enlightenment to His whereabouts. Where did she say her glorious Lord was? (Song 6:2)

   _____

This garden, as we discovered earlier, speaks figuratively of the soul of the believer and of her life in Christ. He was living in her own spiritual affections. She had already come to know the reality of His abiding presence within her in her earlier experiences. Yet, very suddenly, inner light had shone into her heart and had brought about a deeper understanding of the reality of His presence. Through the dark night of the soul which the maiden has just passed, the maiden has learned many spiritual lessons.

3. What was one truth that was made real to her here? (Prov. 3:5-6)
   a. _____
   b. _____
   c. _____
   d. _____

Instead of fretting because of a lack of a conscious feeling of God's presence, the maiden learned to lay hold upon His Word and the commitment she had made to the Lord. She trusted in and relied on Him and His faithfulness alone. She learned that, at God's appointed time, He will manifest His living presence and make her conscious of Himself.

4. Though her soul hungered and thirsted for Him, what did she still endeavor to do? As a result, what happened? (Isa. 58:10)

   a. _____

   b. _____

5. What else did the Lord do for her? (Isa. 58:11)

   a. _____

   b. _____

   c. _____

   d. _____

   e. _____

6. The garden represents the beauty of the New Creation life within and the fruits and blossoms that God has planted there. In what specific part of the garden did she say the Lord was? (Song 6;2)

   _____

7. What other reference do we have to the bed of balsam? (Song 5:13)

   _____

We found that the Lord's cheeks, which are described as a *bed of balsam*, represented His example of humility and obedience to the point of death that He has set before us. The maiden, then, is saying that she has followed Jesus' example of humility and obedience to the point of death. It is that quality of spirit which He is planting in His garden within her.

8. What does the maiden say that Jesus is doing there? (Song 6:2)

   _____

9. At the beginning of this song, what had the maiden requested of the King? (Song 1:7)

   _____

At first, the maiden had sought from the Lord to know the place where He pastured His flock and made them lie down at noon. We learned that the maiden was asking the Lord for the pathway to spiritual maturity. She desired to be on the path of rest with God in the fulness of His light, in divine union with His heart. As this new spiritual intelligence and enlightenment has begun to break upon her, we find that the maiden realizes that her life has become one of spiritual maturity. She has entered into that path of rest with God in the fulness of His light, in divine union with His heart. Her life has become one in which He can pasture His flocks in order to feed them spiritual food.

10. What is the Lord gathering in the garden of the maiden? (Song 6:2)

    _____

11. In the maiden's description of her glorious Lord, what did she describe as lilies? (Song 5:13)

    _____

We learned that the *lips as lilies* referred to *the Word of the Lord spoken to the spirit of the believer*. We found that the maiden's spirit was wrought with *lily work*. Worked into her spirit is the familiarity of that still small voice of the Lord which penetrates and graces her innermost being. She has become one who is able to follow the leading of that still small voice.

12. What statement of relationship does the Bride make concerning her beloved? (Song 6:3)

    _____

She has entered now her true center of rest. She trusts and relies on God and His Word alone. She is able to say with the Apostle John, "I am the disciple who Jesus loves." She has learned that, though feelings change, the covenant she has with Jesus is unchangeable. In the past she had declared, "My beloved is mine and I am His." (Song 2:16). Now, the focus of her life has moved from self to the person of Jesus the Lord. Her statement rests not on emotional feelings but solidly on faith. She rests upon the faithful God who changes not.

13. What has she come to realize? (Rom. 8:38-39)

_____

This is the secret of abiding with Christ. To run after Him suggests that He is separate from the soul, and yet to be known in oneness of life.

14. What has she come to understand in a deeper way? (Ps. 139:7-12; Acts 17:28)

_____

The maiden has truly come to realize that nothing can separate her from the love of God, that _in Him_ she lives, moves, and has her being. She has found that every particle of the atmosphere, every atom, every molecule is charged with His life and that He is always present. She has learned that every part of her spirit is charged with His power. She knows that she is truly one spirit with Him, and that her whole being is engulfed in Him.

She does not see her Lord as separate or standing apart from His creation; rather, she sees Him as the Spirit that contains the whole universe. She sees the earth and all that is within it — the universe itself — being pervaded by His eternal Spirit. And she knows all this not by feelings, nor by an overwhelming sense of His presence, but by _faith_: faith in who He is and the reality of His Word. _And this is faith at its best._ She has learned that when great feelings of God's presence pervade one's life, faith is not needed, for then one can feel God's reality. She has come to realize that true faith is, in actuality, the substance of things hoped for, the evidence of things not seen or felt. She has found that true faith is the leaning of the entire personality on God in absolute trust and confidence in His wisdom and goodness. And, _by this_, she has obtained favor with God, truly becoming His friend. She has proved that she loves Him for Himself alone.

15. Through this great testing, what did the maiden learn to hold fast to without wavering, and what did she learn about God? (Heb. 10:23)
    a. _____
    b. _____

16. Therefore what has she become careful not to do and what quality has been worked into her life? (Heb. 10:35-36)
    a. _____
    b. _____

17. What does the Lord desire of each one of His children and why? (Heb. 6:11)
    a. _____
    b. _____

18. Who are we to imitate? (Heb. 6:12)

_____

This maiden has set the example of diligently seeking the Lord, for she has held fast to Him by faith. So are we to follow the same example, as well as the example of all those who through faith and patience have inherited the promise of God.

The Amplified Version says it this way:

> But we do strongly and earnestly desire
> for each of you to show **the same
> diligence and sincerity all the way
> through**
> In realizing and enjoying the full assurance
> and development of your hope until
> the end,
> In order that **you may not grow disinterested**
> And **become spiritual sluggards** but imitators,
> Behaving as do those who **through faith,**

That is by their leaning of the entire
personality on God in Christ in
absolute trust and confidence in His
power, wisdom and goodness
And by **practice** *of* **patient endurance** *and*
waiting *are now inheriting the promises.*
Heb. 6:11-12

19. Abraham is an example to all of us who are diligently pursuing the One who made heaven and earth. What four things did Abraham do that we will do well to imitate? (Rom. 4:20-21)
    a. _____
    b. _____
    c. _____
    d. _____

20. As a result, what has been reckoned unto Abraham as well as this maiden and all those who her *type* represents? (Rom. 4:22-24)

    _____

My hope is built on nothing less
Than Jesus' blood and righteousness;
I dare not trust the sweetest frame,
But wholly lean on Jesus' name.

When darkness veils His lovely face,
I rest on His unchanging grace;
In every high and stormy gale,
My anchor holds within the veil.

His oath, His covenant, His blood,
Support me in the whelming flood;
When all around my soul gives way,
He, then, is all my hope and stay.

When He shall come with trumpet sound,
Oh, may I then in Him be found;
Dressed in His righteousness alone,
Faultless to stand before the throne.

On Christ the solid Rock, I stand
All other ground is sinking sand.
Edward Mote

NOTES

STUDY 23

THE HIDDEN LIFE WITHIN
THE VEIL

The two shall become one...
This is a great mystery...
With reference to Christ and His
Church. —
Eph. 5:31-32
The Bridegroom speaks again as the Soul rests in Him.

1. What three-fold description does He give of this maiden? (Song 6:4)
    a. _____
    b. _____
    c. _____

For the first time, Jesus calls her beautiful. *Beauty* in the scriptures signifies *holiness*. *Tirzah*, meaning *delight*, was the King's residence and corresponds to the Holy of Holies in heaven, which is God's abiding place.

2. How has this maiden walked before the Lord to cause Him to *delight* in her? (Prov. 11:20)
    _____

3. What befits the Lord's dwelling place? (Ps. 93:5)
    _____

4. Where does the Lord dwell and with whom? (Isa. 57:15)
    _____

5. How does the maiden become this holy place where the Lord can, in His holiness, make His dwelling place? (I Thes. 3:13)
    _____

Jesus sees the maiden as His Holy of Holies where He can, in a greater measure, begin to reveal Himself in His great and terrible holiness and glory. She has passed through the many waters in her fellowship with the Lord. They did not quench her love for Him. As a result of the brokenness that has resulted in her life, her spirit has been freed from much that kept her from a fuller knowledge of Him.

He will teach her now how to dwell with Him and will open to her the life which is within the veil. It is to *this* life which He has been drawing her since she first cried out, "Draw me after you and let us run together."

6. When she first began to trust in the Lord, He began drawing her to Himself. Where do we find the anchor of her soul? (Heb. 6:18-20)
    _____

7. What is that anchor? (Heb. 6:18-20; Col. 1:27; I John 3:2-3)
    _____

8. In comparing the maiden to the New Jerusalem, what does Jesus see in her? (Rev. 21:2)
    _____

Jesus already sees in her the marks of His Bride, the New Jerusalem. She is already reflecting the holiness and beauty of that day.

9. In comparing the maiden to the New Jerusalem, what type of believer is she? What has the Lord made her? (Rev. 3:12)
    _____

Consequently, she is no longer to go in and out of the Holiest place of all, into which the Spirit of God has not drawn her, but she is to remain in the Holiest with Him. For "like the light of dawn she will shine brighter and brighter until the full day." She is to grow up into maturity here. As in those silent years in which Jesus grew in wisdom and stature and favor with God and man before His presentation as a Son before the world, so also the Lord is preparing her, His Bride, for presentation to a lost and dying world. This is an individual as well as a corporate presentation.

10.   On that full day, what will happen? (Col. 3:4)

_____

The third part of the description of the Bride given to us by the Bridegroom is "awesome as an army with banners." The word *awesome* means a mixed feeling of reverence, fear and wonder. It is caused by something majestic and sublime, having the power to inspire intense fear.

11.   What does the banner denote? (Ps. 20:5)

_____

We find that the banner denotes *victory*. In a war it is important to have weapons; in time of victory it is important to have a banner to display. The enemy looks upon that banner with fear and respect for the army for which it stands. The maiden, then, was not only a serene and quiet sanctuary, but also the abode of the Holy God, the Lord of Hosts, the Man of War. Her life behind the veil was not meant to be lived only in the sanctuary of God's presence, but in the field of battle before the enemy.

12.   What is that banner which the Lord has given to those who fear Him to display? (Ps. 60:4)

_____

13.   What is truth? (John 17:17)

_____

14.   What is the truth able to do? (John 8:32)

_____

15.   What alienates us from the life of God? (Eph. 4:18)

_____

It is the ignorance of the truth that keeps us bound in many areas to the forces of darkness. During the *Dark Ages* — the period of man's history so called because of the ignorance and darkness of the minds of men — the Bible was a forbidden book. Only the Roman Catholic Church was allowed to interpret the Book; consequently, it was kept from the average man and not written in the language of the people.

During this period of man's history, there were no great inventions; poverty and disease ran rampant; man was at his lowest ebb. Martin Luther, a Roman monk at the time, found a copy of the Bible in Latin at a library. Because he could read Latin, he studied this new-found book. Later, Luther made a pilgrimage to Rome to walk up some *special* stairs that were supposed to have been miraculously transported to Rome from Jerusalem. These were supposed to be Pilot's judgment stairs which Jesus ascended at His trial. As Luther was climbing these stairs on his knees, in order to supposedly obtain special forgiveness for sins, the Spirit of God spoke to his heart a scripture that he had read from the Bible. The Lord said to him, "Get up from there, for the just shall live by faith." That one sentence of truth spoken to him by the Spirit of God started the Protestant Reformation, and broke the hold that Satan, through the guise of the Roman Catholic Church, had held on the minds of men.

The Bible began to be translated into the language of the people. Although many were martyred, the truth prevailed. Men's minds, becoming enlightened by the Word of God, could no longer be held in bondage by the lies of the enemy. History moved upward as the Renaissance began. The Renaissance — the rebirth or revival of learning — took place in all areas of religion, the arts, and the sciences.

Martin Luther, as well as his contemporaries, was like a man who had just stepped out of a dark cave. Knowing their eyes could not take the light of the noonday sun, the Lord brought them into the twilight of a new day. Since that time, the Lord of Glory has been restoring and revealing His truth that Satan for so long had tried to hide. As the truth is learned, the shackles of the enemy are broken and men rise up to take the position which Jesus won for them through His death and resurrection.

The revelation of that truth will continue until men emerge into the full light of the noonday sun.

16. During the reign of that antichrist-system, how did the Lord break the yoke of the enemy? (II Thes. 2:8)

_____

17. Whenever the truths of the scripture are not known, what happens to the unbelieving? (II Cor. 4:4)

_____

This gospel is described as the "gospel of the glory of Jesus Christ." He is the image of God. It is the right and privilege of every blood-bought believer to be transformed into that same image and to walk in that same glorious freedom that Jesus had while He was on earth. It is the privilege of the New Creation man to take what is his under the new covenant and deliver death blows to the enemy through believing the truth.

18. How is the new victorious self put on? (Eph. 4:23-24)

_____

19. Consequently, what should be our attitude toward the truth? (Prov. 23:23)

_____

It is this *banner of truth* that the Lord of glory has given to this maiden. It is this banner unfurled in the face of the enemy that causes hell to tremble and demons to flee in His name. It is the banner of truth unfurled and practiced, stood upon and carried throughout the world, that will bring Satan's ultimate downfall and usher in the new age of the Kingdom of God.

20. What has the Lord called and appointed this maiden for? (Isa. 42:6-7)
    a. _____
    b. _____
    c. _____
    d. _____
    e. _____

21. How will the Lord respond to the proclamation of His truth? (Isa. 42:13)
    a. _____
    b. _____
    c. _____
    d. _____

This is His beloved Bride, as beautiful as Tirzah, as lovely as Jerusalem, and as awesome as an army with banners. She is maintaining a holy character and a victorious warfare, holding up the banner of truth unfurled, uncompromised, and boldly proclaimed in the face of man and devil. The maiden witnesses the retreat of the enemy for the hosts of the opposition move back and dare not advance.

Let us all, through the Word of truth and the renewing of the Spirit, become both the lovely abode of the Holy God and become awesome and terrible to man and devil.

O send out Thy light and Thy truth,
Let them lead me.
Let them bring me to Thy holy hill
and to Thy dwelling places.
Then I will go to the altar of God,
To God my exceeding joy. —
Ps. 43:3-4

STUDY 24

THE EYES OF LOVE

*A friend loves at all times
And a brother is born for
adversity. —
Prov. 17:17*

Following the comparison of the maiden to the City of the King, we find that the Bridegroom repeats some characteristics of the New Creation life given earlier in the Song. Some changes and omissions in using the same types and shadows show us that the maiden is reaching full growth. She is now of the ripe age to receive the fulness of Christ more fully by Him so that she may be able to accomplish all His will.

1. What did the Lord say earlier about the maiden's eyes ? (Song 1:15)

The first time the King spoke of His redeemed one's eyes, He saw the Holy Dove shining through her eyes, which are the windows of her soul.

2. How does the King now view His beloved's eyes? (Song 6:5)

The word *confused* in the NAS is translated *overcome* in the KJV and other translations. "Turn away your eyes for they have overcome me," says the Lord. We find that this is a poetic expression meaning that her strong love for Him has overwhelmed Him. It does not mean that He is refusing her love or rejecting it.

3. What similar instance do we see of this seeming rejection by the Lord? (Ex. 32:10; Gen. 32:24-26; John 11:3-6)
    a. _____
    b. _____
    c. _____

4. As the result of Moses' intercession with the Lord, what did God say to him? (Ex. 32:10-14)

5. As a result of Jacob's wrestling with the Lord, what did God say to him? (Gen. 32:26-28)

6. In these instances the Lord seems to convey the idea that He wants to turn away. Why? (Matt. 7:6; Heb. 11:6; II Chron. 15:2) (Summarize briefly).

This move is designed to challenge a return expression of love from the believer. The Lord continues to test the hearts and try the motives of those whose hearts are completely His. Do they love Him for Himself alone? He tests them that, by their reaction, His heart may be satisfied with their love.

We find an example of this *contrasted* in the stories of Jacob and Moses.

7. As Jacob wrestled with God and prevailed, what was it that he desired of the Lord? (Gen. 32:26)

8. After God had blessed Jacob, Jacob continued to seek after God, asking Him, "What is your name?" What did the Lord answer him and what was Jacob's response? (Gen. 32:26-30)

We find that Jacob's interest was in personal blessing. When the Lord challenged Jacob as to the reason that Jacob was seeking to know Him, Jacob did not respond. This challenge was designed to spark a return expression of love and desire from Jacob. The Lord tested Jacob's heart and found him lacking in desire.

9. In contrast, let us look at the Lord's conversation with Moses. What was it that Moses desired from the Lord? (Ex. 33:11-13)

_____

10. What was the Lord's response to Moses? (Ex. 33:14)

_____

11. What was Moses' response to the Lord's answer? (Ex. 33:15)

_____

Moses, by this reponse, reveals that he desires God's *presence* more than God's *promises*.

12. Did God grant Moses his request? (Ex. 33:17)

_____

13. Again, what was Moses' response to God's answer? (Ex. 33:18)

_____

Again Moses presses into God, continuing to request further revelation knowledge of God.

14. What was God's answer? (Ex. 33:19-23) (Summarize briefly).

_____

15. Why did God reveal Himself to Moses to such a great extent, but did not give this revelation to Jacob? (Jer. 29:13)

_____

We find that Jacob lacked that desire of a diligent seeker. His life as far as personal revelation and knowledge of God was very shallow.

In the story of Mary, Martha and Lazarus, we again find the Lord appearing to reject Mary and Martha's cry for help.

16. What was Jesus' relationship to Mary, Martha and Lazarus? (John 11:1-6)

_____

We discover that Jesus delayed His visit to them to test the strength of their love and their belief in Him.

17. When he finally came to Bethany, Martha went out to meet Him. What did she say to Him? (John 11:21-22)

_____

Martha did not see her brother's situation as hopeless; seeing the Lord reaffirmed her faith and belief in Him.

18. What did Jesus ask her? (John 11:25-26)

_____

_____

19. What was her response? (John 11:27)

_____

_____

Jesus, in His teachings, had said, "To those who love Me, I will make Myself known unto them." In light of the revelation that Martha had of who Jesus was, we can perceive the depth of love that she had for Him.

20. In Mary we see an even deeper love displayed for Jesus. She had waited quietly in the house until the Lord had called for her? What did she do when she saw Jesus? (John 11:32)

_____

Notice that Mary fell at Jesus' feet; this is a sign of her worship, devotion, and submission to His Lordship. Jews were to worship the Holy One of Israel, the true and living God.

21. When Jesus saw her act of devotion and her weeping, what happened? (John 11:23)

_____

Mary was one of those of whom it is written "turn away your eyes from me, for they have overcome me." Jesus, being overwhelmed by her love and devotion to Him, was deeply touched by her grief and was moved in His Spirit. It is this type of believer who can move the heart of God to action and who can prevail with Him in prayer. It is the same kind of love and devotion that Moses had displayed as he pleaded with God on behalf of Israel.

22. Let us look at another believer, Mary Magdalene, who also is represented by the maiden of our Song. Where do we find this Mary? (John 19:25-26)

_____

Of all who followed Jesus, there were only four people who stood at the foot of the cross with Jesus as He was crucified: Jesus' mother, His mother's sister, Mary Magdalene, and John His disciple. To so identify with a crucified man could mean certain death. The rest of the disciples stood at a distance as they feared for their lives. But these four did not count their lives as dear. As Jesus had taught, "greater love has no man than this, that he would lay down his life for his friends." (John 15:13) These four showed that *greater* love and the heart of Jesus was deeply moved by their devotion. These are those of whom it is written, "turn away your eyes from me for they have overcome me."

Of the remaining disciples, John was the only one who did not die a martyr's death; for, standing at the foot of the cross, he had already counted his life as nothing.

23. Where do we find Mary Magdalene after His crucifixion? (John 20:1)

_____

She ran to get Peter and John. When the men came to the tomb and saw that the body of Jesus was gone, they returned again to their own home.

24. What did Mary do? (John 20:11-13)

_____

25. Mary Magdalene remained at the tomb, still seeking the Lord out of her love for Him. As a result, what happened? (John 20:14-18)

_____

Mary Magdalene was the first person Jesus revealed Himself to after the resurrection. It was by her that He first sent Word to His disciples of His victory over death. Most of the disciples were in hiding because they feared for their lives. The beloved John had come; Peter, who being deeply repentant because of his recent denial of the Master, had come also. John records of himself that, when he saw that the body was gone, he believed. This reveals to us the depth of understanding John had concerning who Jesus was. Both men returned home. Mary alone remained, deeply grieved, seeking to find His body.

As a result of her love for Him, Jesus chose her as the first to behold His glory. Jesus was irresistably overcome by the strength of her love for Him. Mary Magdalene was one of those believers of whom it is written, "turn away your eyes from me for they have overcome me."

Finally, in a story about David, we see a different facet of this kind of love which those *eyes* of the maiden represent. Read II Samuel 23:13-17. Now this account is a parable. In this passage, David is a *type* of Jesus.

26. Who came to David in the cave of Adullam? (II Sam. 23:13)

_____

30 = the number of full stature or maturity for ministry

Jesus was 30 when He began to minister.
Joseph was 30 when he began to rule in Egypt.
David was 30 when he began to reign as king.

3 = fulness of God.

Three of the 30 chief men represent those who were filled with the fulness of God from among those who had grown to full stature and maturity for ministry. These three men represent those of the same quality of life as the maiden of our Song.

27. At what time did they come to David? (II Sam. 23:13)

_____

The *harvest* time represents the *end or consummation of the age*, according to Matt. 13:39.

28. What was the political situation at the time? (II Sam. 23:13-14)

_____

29. What did the three mighty men do when they heard David speak his desire? (II Sam. 23:15-16)

_____

This was a mighty demonstration of love on the part of these men toward David. Having overheard David express his desire for this water, these three set out to bring to him that which his heart desired. David, who represents Jesus here, had not commanded them to go and get this water. He had not even thought of sending them for it. Yet these three men, in their love for David, wanted to do whatever they could to serve him. They were willing to risk their life's blood to meet not only his needs but also to fulfill all his heart's desire.

On their own initiative these three mighty men waited until night, broke through the enemy's camp, and then went into Bethlehem. There they broke through the garrison of Philistines who were guarding the city. They went to the well of Bethlehem and drew water from the well. Breaking back through the garrison of soldiers and the camp of Philistines, they returned to David's stronghold. When they arrived there they poured a cup of cool water from that well and presented it to David saying, "Here David, here is our love gift to you, the cup of cool water from the well of Bethlehem which you desired."

30. What was David's response? (II Sam. 23:16-17)

_____

David's heart was so moved and he was so overwhelmed by such a demonstration of love that he poured the water out on the ground as a holy offering unto the Lord. The cup of water represented to David the life blood of these men.

These three mighty men of David represent those believers of whom it is written, "Turn away your eyes from me for they have overcome me." The quality and strength of that love demonstrated by these men represent those believers who have such a strong love for the Lord that they are doing more than serving Him. They are listening to the desires of His heart and are waiting to fulfill them. They are seeking on their own to do whatever is pleasing in His sight.

STUDY 25

THE WIFE OF THE KING OF LIGHT

*And by common confession great is the
mystery of godliness. —
I Tim. 3:16*

1. How is the hair of the maiden described? (Song 6:5)

   _____

2. What does the hair signify as we learned earlier? (Num. 6:1-5)

   _____

We find the same description of the maiden's hair that we found earlier. This signifies that the strength of the New Creation is the same in maturity as in childhood. The secret of her ever-growing life and relationship with the Lord lies in her separation unto God.

3. Describe the maiden's teeth. (Song 6:6)

   _____

4. What is omitted from this description of the teeth in comparison to the description given earlier? (Song 4:2)

   _____

Again, we find an almost identical description of the *teeth* as in the maiden's childhood. We established earlier that the teeth signified the *mind*. We discovered that the mind of the Bride had been washed in the water of the Word, becoming transformed, sanctified, and cleansed. The *newly shorn ewe*, which represented the *mind* of the new believer, had been *newly shorn of the wisdom of this world* and *the curses of this earth*. In chapter six, *newly shorn* has been *omitted*, signifying that the maiden has been separated from these things and has gone on to *maturity*. The *twins* signify *the balance of wisdom and maturity*. As in childhood, so it is in maturity: the understanding has needed a continuous separation from the wisdom of the world that it might be taught the wisdom of God. Therefore, it is said to have come up from the washing of the Word.

5. Consequently, what is the maiden's mind filled with? (Col. 1:9)

   _____

6. As a result, how does she walk before God? (Col. 1:10)
   a. _____
   b. _____
   c. _____
   d. _____

7. What description is given of her temples? (Song 6:7)

   _____

Again the exact description is given as earlier in our Song. We established previously that the *temples* represent the *seat of man's thoughts*. In describing the temples as a *sliced* pomegranate, we see that the thoughts of the Bride are opened and exposed before God, but veiled from the outward world. It is in the same way that the beautiful interior of the pomegranate is hidden by its skin, except when it is cut and laid open.

8. When shall the world view the glorious work which God has done in her life? (Col.3:4)

   _____

Although all these characteristics were present at the beginning of the New Creation life, a more profound depth of experience has been worked into her life in each area. Spiritual lessons are taught over and over by the Spirit at each level of our growth in the Lord, and each time they are taught they become more profound and perfect than when they were taught at an earlier stage of development.

9. What did Jesus know about Himself, yet what was He able to do? (John 13:3-5)

_____

The maiden, in her soul-life, is seeking to be conformed into His image. By the power of the indwelling Christ, unconsciously and habitually, she is able to humble herself and take the lowest place. All outward veneer passes away because transparency desires no cover. She is as comfortable in Him addressing the masses as in doing the most menial task. All is the same to her, because she does all things unto Him for His glory. So it is with the life that is in union with the Lord Jesus. As she dwells in Him, she trusts Him to manifest Himself through her spontaneously and naturally.

10. What four types of believers are mentioned here? (Song 6:8-9)
   a. _____
   b. _____
   c. _____
   d. _____

In a previous study, we have discussed at length the different types of believers listed here and their varying degrees of relationships and intimate fellowship with the Lord. Consequently, we will now discuss only the believer that displays the Bride spirit, of which group the maiden of our Song is a part.

11. Describe the believers who have the Bride spirit. (Song 6:9)
   a. _____
   b. _____
   c. _____
   d. _____
   e. _____

12. In describing His Bride as His *perfect one*, His language corresponds to the words which he expressed just before surrendering Himself to the cross. In these words He expressed the supreme desire of His heart. What was that desire? (John 17:22-23)

_____

The heavenly Bride will consist of many believers brought into oneness of life and Spirit with Jesus. In speaking of His Bride as His *perfect one*, the Lord is prophetically speaking of those who will come unto a perfect man, unto the measure of the stature of the fulness of Christ. By the Spirit, He has already seen the Church as being one. We will now look into this fulness of stature and this perfection.

13. What were the law and sacrifices not able to do? (Heb. 10:1)

_____

14. What is the blood of Jesus able to do? (Heb. 10:14)

_____

15. What is it impossible for the blood of bulls and goats to do? (Heb. 10:4)

_____

The blood sacrifice under the old covenant provided a covering for sin.

16. What did John the Baptist say prophetically of Jesus? (John 1:29)

_____

17. What type of church is Jesus coming for? (Eph. 5:27)
    a. _____
    b. _____
    c. _____

18. How will Jesus sanctify and cleanse her? (Eph. 5:26)
    _____

19. Describe the three-fold power of the overcoming church for which Jesus is coming? (Rev. 12:11)
    a. _____
    b. _____
    c. _____

20. To whom will the Lord reveal Himself, and to whom will He appear the second time? (John 14:21; Heb. 9:28)
    a. _____
    b. _____

The verse from Hebrews appears as follows in the Amplified:

> *Christ having been offered to take upon*
> *Himself and bear as a burden the sins*
> *of many, once and once for all,*
> *Will appear a second time,*
> *Not carrying any burden of sin nor to*
> *deal with sin,*
> *But to bring to full salvation those who*
> *are eagerly, constantly and patiently*
> *waiting for and expecting Him.*

It is this *full* salvation — *perfection* made possible *through His blood* — that Jesus will bring when He appears a second time. He will not bring it to just *any* believers, but He will bring it to those who are patiently waiting for and expecting Him. This full salvation will be brought not to a defeated band of slaves, but to an *overcoming church* who have laid aside the deeds of darkness and who are dealing with and overcoming sin in their lives. He will bring to full salvation those who are being washed and cleansed in the Word daily, and those who through their testimony are overcoming the evil one. He will bring to full salvation and perfection those who are believing in the blood of Jesus to totally wash and perfect them forever — those who are looking for and expecting and waiting patiently for this perfecting atonement. The maiden of our Song is one of this company.

21. To whom can we liken these believers? (Matt. 25:1-13)
    _____

The Day of Atonement, preceding the Feast of Tabernacles, offers us a type of the full salvation and perfection that is to be wrought in the overcoming church through the blood of Jesus. The Day of Atonement and the last feast await their spiritual fulfillment in the Church. The preceding feasts of Passover and Pentecost have been fulfilled historically and experientially in the lives of the believers in the Church. But, it must be admitted that the last and greatest Feast of Tabernacles, which is preceded by the great Day of Atonement, has not yet been fulfilled historically and experientially in God's people.

The Day of Atonement took place during the seventh month on the tenth day of the month. At that time the High Priest went into the Holy of Holies to make atonement upon the mercy seat with blood for the sins of Israel. These sins, which had been covered during the year with the daily blood sacrifices upon the golden altar in the outer court, were no longer simply covered but completely removed and separated from Israel.

What then, we ask ourselves, did the blood of atonement do for Israel that has not yet been experienced by the Church? The blood of atonement will bring the overcoming church into sinless perfection. For it is a perfect and a sinless bride—not only by faith but in experience—that Jesus is returning for.

It is the characteristics of this perfect and complete one that Jesus sees in this maiden.

22. What did the virgins, queens and concubines say of that perfect one? What four-fold description did they give of her? (Song 6:10) Note: the number 4 signifies the completion of the New Creation.
    a. _____
    b. _____
    c. _____
    d. _____

23. When the nations look upon those who possess the Bride spirit, what will they acknowledge? (Isa. 61:9)

    _____

It is a testimony of heavenly light and glory that is given by those who behold the Bride. Because the glorified Lamb has been revealed in such depth to the Bridal Soul, and because she has been in such deep fellowship and communion with Him in the Holiest Place, she has come forth with the light of God upon her. That light causes those around her to break out into a glorious description of her as they see her in Christ.

Let us briefly look into this heavenly glory and radiance.

24. When Moses was in communion with God upon Mount Sinai, after receiving the Ten Commandments, how did his countenance appear? (Ex. 34:29-35)

    _____

The actual meaning of this passage was that Moses' face shone with *lightning bolts of glory shooting forth*. Now the skin of Moses' face shone whenever he would talk with the Lord. But, that glory that was upon his face faded after a time until he again spoke with the Lord face to face.

Because of Israel's tendency to rebel continuously against God's appointed leadership, Moses had to put a veil over his face to keep the sons of Israel from looking upon this vanishing splendor and mistakenly think that God had removed His anointing from Moses. That glory, as powerful as it was, was old covenant glory.

25. What shall accompany the ministry of the Spirit under the new covenant? (II Cor. 3:7-8)

    _____

26. Describe the glory which accompanies the ministry of the Spirit under the new covenant in comparison to the old covenant. (II Cor. 3:9-11)
    a. _____
    b. _____
    c. _____

27. How do we under the new covenant behold the glory of the Lord and what are we being transformed into? (II Cor. 3:18)
    a. _____
    b. _____
    c. _____

We, under the new covenant, do not have a radiance that is fading or temporary, nor do we have to veil our face because the glory fades. Neither do we have a glory that illumines our face from time to time. Rather, under the new covenant, we are totally new creatures who have hidden deep within our spirits that same shekinah glory which illuminated Moses. As we meditate upon and gaze into the Word of God, that radiance which lies within us begins to break forth, transforming our souls from glory to glory in ever increasing splendor. The outraying of the divine life within in the early stages of the New Creation life is but a mere seed of that which in maturity will reveal His very image and likeness. This radiance is manifested in the life of believers in different degrees of glory depending upon their stage of growth and development in the Lord.

28. As our maiden beholds the glory of the Lord through the Word and her intimate communion with Him, what happens? (Ecc. 8:1)

_____

29. Who will shine like the stars and the brightness of the expanse of heaven? (Dan. 12:3)
    a. _____
    b. _____

30. What is the path of the righteous like? (Prov. 4:18)

_____

So it is with the maiden of our Song, for she is said to "grow as the dawn." She represents the righteous man who continually gazes into that perfect law of liberty. Beholding God's glory, her path is like the light of dawn, continuing to grow brighter and brighter until the full day. Those who have the Bride spirit will settle for nothing less than being transformed into His very image and likeness. Although the maiden of our Song has not yet come to the full light of high noon, her life is like the womb of the morning. Her hopes shine with the brightness of day break, for the whole purpose of her being is to shine forth with brightness of the noonday sun.

Secondly, those with the Bride spirit are said to be as beautiful as the _full moon_. (In scripture, the moon always represents the Church). The moon takes its light from the sun and reflects it. Notice that the moon seen here is not seen as waxing or waning with the shadow of earth cast upon it. Rather, the moon is seen here in its fulness with no shadow of earth standing between her and her _sun_. This full moon represents the Church in its purity, free from worldliness or any spot or shadow that the earth would cast upon it.

Psalm 89:37 tells us that the moon is a _faithful witness_ in heaven. Genesis 1:14 tells us that the lights in the sky were put there NOT only to provide light, but also for the signs in the earth. Twelve times a year the moon gives forth her testimony. Twelve times a year the moon shines forth in its fulness. Twelve is the number of _divine government_. What does the moon proclaim? When the Church, corporately as well as individually, comes under the divine government of Almighty God and under His total Lordship, and when she is completely led and governed by His Holy Spirit, no shadow of earth can be cast upon her to mar or detract from her beauty and brilliance. She will stand unhindered to radiate the light of the sun of God and its light will not be hidden.

31. Because of the holiness and purity in the life of our maiden, what is she able to teach the people? (Ezk. 44:23)
    a. _____
    b. _____

32. Because of this holiness and purity, what is she able to do in a dispute? (Ezk. 44:24)

_____

33. Because of her purity and holiness, describe what type of priest she has become. (Mal. 2:7)
    a. _____
    b. _____
    c. _____

Thirdly, our maiden is said to be as _pure as the sun_.

34. What are those who love Him to be like? (Judges 5:31)

_____

Therefore, our maiden is recognized to be one of those who love Him, for she is seen by those who behold her as the sun rising in its strength.

35. What is the Lord our God? (Ps. 84:11)

_____

36. When Jesus was transfigured before Peter, James, and John, how did He appear? (Matt. 17:2)

_____

37. In Revelation, we see a picture of the resurrected Christ. How does His countenance appear? (Rev. 1:16)

_____

The sun, then, represents Jesus who is the glory of God in all its fulness. God is light and in Him is no darkness at all.

38. What picture do we see in Revelation 12:1? Describe. (Rev. 12:1)

_____

Here we see a picture of the wife of the King of Light. In that this is a *sign*, it is symbolic and points to its fulfillment. This *sign* will find its fulfillment in the Bride of Christ, the wife of the Lamb. This passage will be fulfilled in the life of all those of the Bride spirit. The fact that the moon was her footstool signifies that she has been built upon the foundation of all those *faithful witnesses* that have gone before her. (Ps. 89:37; Heb. 12:1) The crown of twelve stars represents the dominion and authority of God over her life (twelve being the number of divine government). The woman, which is His Bride, no longer reflects His light, but is transformed and transfigured into His same glorious image, *clothed* as it were *with the sun*. Now He who has prepared us for this same purpose is God.

39. What will happen to the righteous? (Matt. 13:43)

_____

Fourthly, the maiden is seen by those looking upon her as being as awesome as an army with banners. Not only is the maiden seen as one who is full of light, and full of the life of Christ, but also one who is full of victory.

We find a description of this great army of which our maiden is a part given by Joel. Read Joel 2:1-11. Now this is a description of God's great army of overcomers. We will look into a few of the verses given here.

40. What is this great and mighty people compared to that is similar to what is said about our maiden? (Joel 2:2)

_____

41. What is the land like before them? (Joel 2:3)

_____

Notice that there is fire behind them and before them. This great army of God, of which our maiden is a part, has come through much fire, purging, and testing. And there are more testings to go through before they come back into the garden of Eden. Behind them is a desolate wilderness, for there is nothing to turn back to. Before them is Eden, for their faces are set toward a return to that garden and their hearts are set on complete restoration.

42. Describe those men who come face to face with this great army. (Joel 2:6)

_____

Here we see people gripped with conviction and anguish as they meet God's terrible holiness in His people. The thoughts and intentions of those with convicted hearts are laid bare as they are faced with a decision and are challenged to forsake all to follow the Lamb.

43. Describe their submission and commitment to one another. (Joel 2:7b-8)

    a. _____

    b. _____

    c. _____

    d. _____

    e. _____

This is a description of an army that is under authority. Each man knows his own calling and cooperates with his comrades. As it is written in Eph. 4:15-16, they have grown up

> in all aspects into Him, who is the head,
> even Christ, from whom the whole body,
> Being fitted and held together by that
> which every joint supplies, according
> to the proper working of each individual
> part,
> Causes the growth of the body for the
> building up of itself in love.

This is the army that God is preparing for His Great Day.

44. Though she has been so gloriously praised by those who behold her, notice that the maiden does not linger to bask in all this praise. This reveals her humility, for the affections of her heart lie in something else. To what did she turn her attention? (Song 6:11)

    a. _____

    b. _____

    c. _____

    d. _____

45. This relates to the experience of James, Peter and John on the Mount of Transfiguration. After that glorious revelation the disciples said, "let us stay here and build tabernacles." But Jesus did not intend for them to camp around that revelation; instead, He had work for them in the valley which the revelation of His glory had equipped them to do. When they came down from the mountain, what did they find? (Mark 9:14-18)

_____

We see then that the disciples found people below that needed ministry and who were desiring to see Jesus.

Our maiden manifests this same Christ-like Spirit. She did not bask in praise and revelation but rather went down to inspect the orchard. The *orchard of nut trees* speaks to us of the multitude of humanity that are desiring ministry from Jesus. Our maiden and those who have the Bride spirit do not desire to be shut up to the Lord alone, but rather desire to be His hand extended to the world. Our maiden has become a more illuminated vessel of clay in order that the Lord might show Himself again through her to weary hearts who are lying in darkness and the shadow of death.

46. What did Jesus ask those who love Him to do? (John 21:15-17)

_____

Secondly, we found that our maiden was checking to see if the vine had budded. The vine in scripture always represents the Church of which Jesus is the inseparable head. The *budding* of that vine is a reference to *Aaron's rod that budded*. Rod signifies *authority*. Aaron's rod budded, grew blossoms, and produced almonds, thus signifying that he was the chosen vessel in whom God had invested His authority.

Our maiden, then, goes down into the valley not only to minister to the needs of humanity but also to examine the Church—to see that God's authority and life is coming forth in it. Likewise, as Jesus came down the mountain, He found His disciples trying to cast out a demon. He then instructed them, showing them how to use his authority. His disciples were as vines bringing forth their tender buds, but they had not yet produced almonds, or come to full maturity in their authority. Jesus cultivated that authority through instruction.

Thus, our maiden represents that company of people who are discipling others for their ministry, encouraging them to launch out in the Spirit and to rise up and take the authority that Jesus has given to His Church.

Thirdly, we found the maiden checking to see if the pomegranates have blossomed. We have learned earlier that pomegranates symbolize pure and godly thoughts. Again we find a parallel to this from our passage in Mark. After Jesus had come down from the mountain, reached out to the multitudes and instructed His disciples, he began to mininster to the disciples concerning their character. He desired that their minds be renewed and their thoughts become pure.

47.   What did Jesus question His disciples about and why? (Mark 9:33-37)

_____

Jesus, knowing that in their thoughts they desired to exalt themselves, began to teach them a parable that would instill in them the right motives.

Likewise, our maiden checks to see if the pomegranates have blossomed. She gives attention to those whom the Lord has given her to shepherd and disciple so that she might instruct them in the way of purity and godliness.

48.   While our maiden was engrossed in her work in the Lord's vineyard, what happened to her personally? (Song 6:12)

_____

The word for *over* here can also be translated *among*, and can be read *among the chariots*. The word *Ammi-nadeb* (see marginal reference) is translated *my noble people*. This can also be translated *my people of a willing heart*. Thus this passage may also read, *My soul set me among the chariots of my people of a willing heart.*

49.   In the Day of God's power, what will He have? (Ps. 110:3)

_____

We see now another group besides these whom our maiden is laboring among. These are her contemporaries, who are *those of a willing heart*, that walk in holiness and volunteer freely to do God's will and to finish His work. The word *chariot* suggests a *vehicle for movement*. As she had manifested a selfless existence, the burden of her heart being the work of the Lord, she found that she had become a chariot for her Beloved. She carries Him across the fields of the earth, that through her He is again able to show Himself mighty in behalf of those in need of Him.

Their personal chariot was accompanied by others, all of which are spoken of as the chariots of *My people of a willing heart.* Her companions, those who also had the Bride spirit, had also risen up freely to be a chariot unto the Lord, that they might be unto Him a vehicle for swift movement in the earth. This again does not represent all believers, but only those who have a heart for His work. These are the *noble people* who are our maiden's contemporaries. It is of these noble ones that the following Song was written.

> *Lead on, O King Eternal*
> *The day of march has come;*
> *Hence forth in fields of conquest*
> *Thy tents shall be our home.*
> *Through days of preparation*
> *Thy grace has made us strong*
> *And now, O King Eternal,*
> *We lift our battle song.*

Lead on, O King Eternal
Till sin's fierce war shall cease
And holiness shall whisper
The sweet amen of peace;
For not with swords loud clashing,
Nor roll of stirring drums,
With deeds of love and mercy
Thy heavenly Kingdom comes.

Lead on, O King Eternal,
We follow, not with fears;
For gladness breaks like morning,
Wherever thy face appears;

Thy cross is lifted o're us
We journey in its light
The crown awaits the conquest;
Lead on, O God of might. —

Ernest Shurtleff
(1862-1917)

NOTES

NOTES

STUDY 26

A TESTIMONY IN THE DANCE
OF VICTORY:
THE DANCE OF MAHANAIM

Again you shall take up your tambourines,
And go forth to the dances of the merry-
makers.
And they shall come and shout for joy in
the height of Zion,
And they shall be radiant over the bounty
of the Lord —
The virgin shall rejoice in the dance,
And the young men and the old, together,
For I will turn their mourning into joy,
And I will comfort them
And give them joy for their sorrow. —
Jer. 31:4, 12-13

1. What request is made of our maiden by those who look upon her? (Song 6:13a)

   _____

This request is prompted by the Holy Spirit of God. It is a call for the Shulamite, the true person of peace, those who are in inseparable union and identity with Him to come forth in these last days so that others who are less mature spiritually and those who are hungering and thirsting after righteousness might look upon her, observe her life and ways, and learn the secret of her progress in the Lord. This desire comes forth from those who have a genuine quest for the mature spiritual relationship they see demonstrated in our maiden and from those who want to know how to attain to the victory which she possesses.

The next sentence contains a question and then an answer. Most translations put it this way:

What will you see in the Shulamite?
As it were the dance of two companies. —
Song 6:13b

This question is engineered by the Holy Spirit to provoke a response from those who are desiring to gaze upon her and study the life of the Shulamite. They are asked to tell what they see in the maiden that they desire, and they respond in a seemingly strange way. They see in her the dance of two companies. Let us look into this a little further.

2. The word for two companies is *Mahanaim* (see marginal reference). What does this refer to? (Gen. 32:1-2)

   _____

They respond by saying that they are as Jacob when he met the angels of God along the way. They see her as a place where God encamps.

3. Notice that they refer to the Shulamite as the *dance* of Mahanaim. What does the *dance* represent in the scripture? (Ex. 15:19-21; I Sam. 18:6-7)

   _____

At this point, the onlookers, who have an earnest desire to gaze at the Shulamite and to study her life and her walk with the Lord, break forth into a testimonial dance of her victory. The words of this dance are given to us in the first five verses of chapter seven.

In the words of this dance we find written the effect that the Shulamite's ministry is having upon those who sit in the land of darkness and the shadow of death, and we see just what that ministry means to them. Here we see the *desire of those who wait* to be harvested. Upon seeing the Shulamite maiden of our Song, their spirits rise up to greet her as a welcomed guest.

4. What is the first thing that those who have seen the glory of God shining through the Shulamite say about her feet? (Song 7:1)

   _____

5. What has this Shulamite maiden been doing which causes those who look upon her to be blessed by her feet? (Isa. 52:7)
   a. _____
   b. _____
   c. _____
   d. _____
   e. _____

6. Describe the reaction of those who sit in darkness with open hearts toward God as they wait to hear the gospel that the Shulamite maiden brings. (Isa. 9:2-3)
   a. _____
   b. _____
   c. _____

7. What shall the Lord do for them through the Shulamite? (Isa. 9:4)

   _____

Thus they are released from the burden of guilt and sin, and they are delivered from the authority, rule, and guidance of Satan in their lives.

8. In short, what has the Lord done for them through the testimony of the Shulamite? (Col. 1:13)

   _____

Therefore, they rejoice as men who divide great spoil. Their hearts thrill and rejoice. They dance the Mahanaim, the dance of victory over their enemies, giving thanks to God who has sent the Shulamite to minister to them the gospel of His glorious Kingdom.

9. In referring to the beautiful feet of those who preach the gospel, what heart-searching questions does Paul ask us? (Rom. 10:14-15)
   a. _____
   b. _____
   c. _____
   d. _____

We have said earlier that this Shulamite had become a chariot for the Lord of hosts. She has become a vehicle for His movement in the earth among the harvest fields, along with her contemporaries who were called *my noble people* or *my people of a willing heart*. To be a part of this glorious Shulamite company we must have a willingness for the work. Are you willing to be that preacher, to go to those who have not heard, to be sent to announce salvation and glad tidings to those who sit in darkness?

10. For all those who have the Bride spirit, what desire burns upon their hearts as it did upon the heart of their Savior? (Luke 19:10)

    _____

11. Describe her hips. (Song 7:1)

    _____

The word *hip* here can also mean the leg, limb or thigh. Thighs or hips symbolize *strength* and speak of the strength of her witness for Christ and ability to do His work. This strength had to come to her through great training and discipline of the Holy Spirit.

12. What do the jewels represent? (Prov. 20:15; Prov. 8:11)

_____

We find that the strength of her ministry to others lies in the spiritual wisdom and knowledge which she had received from God, rather than in the strength and zeal of her flesh.

Jesus, Himself, mininstered to others out of this same spiritual wisdom and knowledge. To one woman He spoke a word of knowledge that laid bare her heart and caused her to say, you are the Christ. To another He brought healing. To others He brought deliverance. The Shulamite herself followed Jesus' example. Through the spiritual wisdom and knowledge that had developed in her life she was able to bring the desired ministry to the needs of those whom she was sent. Notice that this attribute was recognized as the work of an artist. So the spiritual beauty of the New Creation man is the work of the Great Creator.

13. In what six ways does the Spirit of the Lord rest upon the Shulamite? (Isa. 11:1-2) Notice that Jesus said that we are the *branch*. We bear fruit from His roots.
     a. _____
     b. _____
     c. _____
     d. _____
     e. _____
     f. _____

14. Describe the navel of the Shulamite. (Song 7:2)

_____

15. When the 120 had received the Baptism of the Holy Spirit on the Day of Pentecost, what were they accused of? (Acts 2:13; 15-17)

_____

16. What did Jesus say would flow from the belly or innermost being of those who believe in Him? (John 7:37-38)

_____

In the navel that never lacked mixed wine, we find that the Shulamite was a vessel from which the Holy Spirit of God continuously flowed out to others.

17. Ezekiel also spoke of this belly which never lacked mixed wine. This is the life from which flows the living waters of the Spirit. What did he say would happen wherever the waters of this river went? (Ezk. 47:9) *Fish* in the scriptures represent *men*; as Jesus said, "Follow Me, and I will make you fishers of men."
     a. _____
     b. _____

The living water which pours forth from the maiden's belly is filling men with the life of Jesus. Many men enter the Kingdom of God through her witness, life, and testimony. Those who have drunk of her wine of the Spirit are rejoicing and giving praise to God in the dance of Mahanaim.

18. Describe the belly of the Shulamite. (Song 7:2b)

_____

19. Wheat is the source of bread and is called the staff of life. What is the bread of God able to do? (John 6:33)

_____

20. What did Jesus say about Himself? (John 6:51)

_____

21. What did Peter say of Jesus? (John 6:68)

_____

So likewise, that which flows from the belly or innermost being of the Shulamite is said to be wheat—the bread of God. She has within her the Words of eternal life which give life to the world. Truly our maiden has become God's chariot. Through her life Jesus spiritually moves through the earth, feeding and giving life to the world.

22. What has the Shulamite's food become? (John 4:32-34)

_____

23. From what has the maiden been partaking? (Rev. 2:17)

_____

We will recall that the Shulamite's belly was said to be a heap of wheat which was *fenced about with lilies.* As we learned in a previous study, the *lily* represents *the spiritual thoughts and spiritual words imparted to the spirit of man.* The *lily work,* so to speak, appearing on the Shulamite's belly or her innermost being, represents the *ability* to hear and receive those spiritual thoughts and words. She has this ability because of the familiarity of the voice of the Spirit which has been developed within her heart. Those hungering and thirsting after righteousness look upon her and exclaim, "Truly Solomon, in all his glory, his wisdom, very great discernment, and breadth of mind, was not arrayed like one of these."

24. Describe the breasts of the Shulamite. (Song 7:3)

_____

This statement is a repetition of a quality that the Lord Himself had recognized in the maiden in Song 4:5. In that previous study we went into great detail about this particular feature of our maiden. In summary, we found that the two breasts signify the spiritual capacity for feeding others; they also represent the breastplate of our spiritual armor. In this breastplate we found four spiritual qualities. They were faith, love, righteousness and judgment. We found that faith within produces righteousness (right standing with God), for it is written that Abraham believed God and it was accounted to him as righteousness. The result of the inward quality of love produces the ability to judge with righteous judgment. Also it is the love of God that causes judgment to come upon the Church and the world, for it is written in Hebrews, "if we are without correction, we are bastards and not sons." (Heb. 12:8) The two breasts on the breastplate of the Shulamite could be diagrammed as follows:

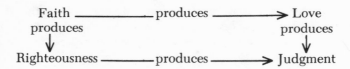

We noticed the progression in the development of the breasts as well as the balance. Therefore, it was written that they are *twins* because they balance one another. We found also that through diligent study of the Word of God, the Shulamite became skilled in the Word of righteousness. By reason of use her senses became exercised to discern both good and evil. We also found that inside the breastplate of the High Priest (who symbolizes us as believers who are priests unto God), were two stones, the Urim and the Thummim, by which the Lord made known His counsel and His will.

The *Urim,* we discovered, means *lights* and represents the *supernatural revelation* of the Word of God. We found that revelation was deeper than faith knowledge. Faith knowledge was comparative to understanding the basic mathematic equations: multiplication, subtraction, addition, etc. Revelation knowledge, however, is like understanding geometry. Unless there has been line upon line understanding of basic math, geometry can never be understood; so it is with the Word of God. Thus we can diagram the progression of development in the breasts of the Shulamite as follows:

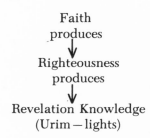

Faith
produces
↓
Righteousness
produces
↓
Revelation Knowledge
(Urim — lights)

We also found that the twin of the Urim was the Thummim. The Thummim we learned means *perfections* and represents that *perfect measurement* by which the believer is being judged, as well as the measurement by which he judges others. We discovered that this measurement was the stature which belongs to the fulness of Christ — His image and His likeness. We also noted that as we submit to the love of God, He judges our life, corrects us, instructs us in righteousness, washes us in the Word and finally brings us into perfection.

Therefore, we had the development of the breast:

Love
produces
↓
Judgment
produces
↓
Perfection
(Thummim — perfections)

Therefore, we found that the breasts of the mature believer should look like this:

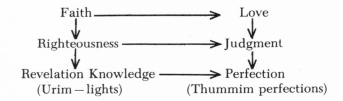

Faith ——————————→ Love
↓ ↓
Righteousness ——————→ Judgment
↓ ↓
Revelation Knowledge ———→ Perfection
(Urim — lights) (Thummim perfections)

We noted that the breasts of the Bride were compared to a *fawn*. A fawn is a very *sensitive* creature as are all these qualities of the Spirit. In that these fawns are said to be twins of a gazelle, we noted that the *gazelle* represented the *victory of the resurrection life*. These qualities of the Spirit, then, are a product of that victorious resurrection life.

Earlier in our Song we noted that these fawns were feeding among lilies so that they might become fully developed. Here we find that the fawns of the Shulamite are feeding no longer, but rather have grown to a maturity of life by which she is able to feed and sustain others.

25. Those who gaze upon the Shulamite — the beautiful Bride of Christ — are rejoicing over her in the dance. What exhortation does Isaiah the prophet give that supports their joy? (Isa. 66:10-11)
    a. _____
    b. _____
    c. _____

26. What shall happen to those who receive the ministry of the Shulamite? (Isa. 66:13-14)
    a. _____
    b. _____
    c. _____
    d. _____

Upon the high hilltops of Zion
The handmaidens came to laud
For the grain and the wine,
The oil and the herds,
And the plenteous goodness of God.

No more did they suffer in sadness
Since the Lord heard their
mourning and cries.
Set free from the sackcloth
and ashen rags,
Their music and song filled the
skies.

The stars in their heaven were singing!
There came great applause from
the trees.
Streams in staccato,
Crescending waves
Were rolling with praise
From the seas.

The radiant children of Beulah
Were laughing and leaping to start,
Twirling their skirts
And their colorful coats,
Then dancing, each one
From his heart.

Their faces and hands were uplifted
And their spirits were
Bursting with praise,
They ached to have more than
Just feet, hands and head
To worship the Ancient of Days.

"Your lives will be full as a
garden,
Your iniquities white like
the snow,
The young and the old
Will be merry and glad,
You'll not languish,
Nor ever have woe."

"In dancing you offer Me praises!
In singing your heart is outpoured!
The soul that dances
Before Me with love
Makes Me happy," saith the Lord. —

In Dancing You Offer Me Praises
by Laurie Masten

142.

THE DANCE OF MAHANAIM:
THE SUBMISSIVE WILL, LIVING WATER
AND HER GREAT PEACE

The people who walk in darkness
Will see a great light;
Those who live in a dark land,
The light will shine on them. —
Isa. 9:2

We continue with our study of the dance of Mahanaim which is the testimonial of the ministry of the Shulamite maiden on behalf of those who are desiring to know God.

1.   How is the neck of the Shulamite described? (Song 7:4a)

_____

We have learned from previous studies that the *neck* represents *the will*. We have found that *ivory* represents the *King's throne*. Therefore, those who are being ministered to by the Shulamite maiden see her as one whose will is completely submissive to King Jesus. Her will and God's will are one in the same.

2.   What can we say of the Shulamite which Jesus also said of Himself? (Heb. 10:7)

_____

3.   What did David say about himself that the Shulamite can also testify to? (Ps. 40:8)

_____

The Shulamite's neck, which represents her will which is under complete submission to Jesus her King, is said to be a *tower*. We discovered that a *tower* represents a place of refuge and a stronghold of strength against the enemy. Our maiden has become, to those who seek ministry from her, as a refuge and strength against the enemy. She has become a shadow of a mighty rock within a weary land.

4.   What will be given to those who are as the tower of the flock? (Micah 4:8)

_____

Those whose will are one with the will of God — and who are as a tower of strength — will receive the former dominion which Adam lost.

5.   How do the onlookers describe the eyes of the Shulamite? (Song 7:4)

_____

As pools of water are clear and still, so the inner life of the Shulamite is one from which exudes great peace and a very deep calm.

6.   As those who look upon the Shulamite dance and describe her as pools of water, what have they found in her personally? (Isa. 41:17-18)

_____

7.   Who has sent the Shulamite their way to quench their thirst? (Isa. 41:17-18)

_____

The Lord, Himself, has prepared this corporate Shulamite maiden to be a pool of water to those who are hungering and thirsting after righteousness. The Lord has sent her forth. Those who behold her eyes have seen a deep spiritual pool and have drunk their fill of the water of the living God.

8. What did Jesus say to the woman He met at the well? (John 4:10)

_____

_____

Those whose spirits have risen up to greet the Shulamite have looked into her eyes and have seen the gift of God. They have found her to be as one who possessed the living water.

These pools are said to be in *Heshbon*, meaning *stronghold*, and by the gate of *Bath-rabbim*, meaning *daughter of many*. Again, she is seen as a *stronghold* for the Lord and as a *unique daughter* among many.

9. Of what covenant has she partaken? (Isa. 55:10)

_____

10. How did she learn this great peace and very deep calm which has caused her eyes to appear as pools? (Ps. 119:165; Prov. 3:1-2)

11. As those who receive her ministry see her as one with beautiful feet announcing salvation and bringing good news of happiness, what else do they see her as announcing? (Isa. 52:7)

_____

12. She, whose very name means *person of peace*, is seen as one who reflects the life and light of her King. In a prophecy given about Jesus by Isaiah the prophet, list His four names. (Isa. 9:6-7)
    a. _____
    b. _____
    c. _____
    d. _____

13. What did Isaiah prophesy that there would be no end to? (Isa. 9:7)

_____

14. Before Jesus' birth, what did Zacharias, the father of John the Baptist, prophesy concerning Him? (Luke 1:78-79)

_____

15. What did Jesus say of Himself? (John 14:27)

_____

16. What did He exhort those who love Him to do? (John 14:27)
    a. _____
    b. _____

17. When Jesus died upon the cross, what fell upon Him? Notice marginal reference says *well being* literally means *peace*.

_____

18. After Jesus' resurrection, with what first words did He greet His disciples? (John 20:19-21)

_____

The reign of the Prince of Peace is seen shining through the eyes of the Shulamite who has beheld for herself the glory of the resurrected Lord. Her heart is not troubled, neither is it afraid. She has received and is experiencing the peace that Jesus bought at Calvary. She has loved God's Word and kept and pondered it in her heart.

The deep calm and peace that exudes from her spirit, a peace that is seen radiating from her eyes, has captivated the desire of those who exalt her in the dance of Mahanaim. She is one in whom God encamps. She has become to them as one who announces salvation, who announces peace, and who says unto Zion, your God reigns.

19. As she dwells in the shelter of the Most High, what has brought about her freedom from fear? (Ps. 91:1-7)

_____

As the mind of the Shulamite is wholly fixed on the Lord her God, she has freedom from fear or anything else that would trouble her heart.

20. What else has quieted all fears in her heart? (I John 4:15-18)

_____

The Amplified Version records it this way:

> *In this union and communion with Him,*
> *Love is brought to completion and attains*
> *perfection with us that we may have*
> *confidence for the day of judgment,*
> *With assurance and boldness to face Him,*
> *Because as He is, so are we in this world.*
> *There is no fear in love — dread does not*
> *exist;*
> *But full-grown, complete, perfect love,*
> *Turns fear out of doors and expels every*
> *trace of terror!*
> *For fear brings with it the thought of*
> *punishment,*
> *And so he who is afraid has not reached*
> *the full maturity of love —*
> *Is not yet grown into love's complete*
> *perfection. —*
> *I John 4:17-18*

This, then, is the center of the Shulamite's rest and peace. Through her union and communion with her glorious Lord, she has come into full grown, complete, and perfect love for the Lord her God. She can face Him with full assurance and boldness. The full maturity of the love they share has turned fear out the doors.

Through the maturity of love, she has come to know, experience, and believe in this great love that God has for her. And through this, the peace of God reigns in her heart, pervades her inner being, exudes from her spirit, and radiates into the world. Thus, those who look upon her cry out, "Your eyes are as pools of water, still, calm, and very clear into their depths; great peace have you O Prince's daughter."

Truly her life demonstrates that peace which Jesus bought with His own blood for His Holy Bride.

NOTES

STUDY 28

THE DANCE OF MAHANAIM:
HER STRONG DISCERNMENT, THE HIGHWAY OF HOLINESS,
AND THE CAPTIVATED HEART

Yes, let them rejoice with gladness.
Sing to God, sing praises to His name;
Cast up a highway for Him who rides
through the deserts,
Whose name is the Lord,
And exult before Him. —
Ps. 68:3b-4

1. How do those who celebrate the life of the Shulamite in the Dance of Mahanaim describe her nose? (Song 7:4)

The reference to the nose points to the maiden's sense of smell and her quickness of scent.

2. What spiritual capacity does the nose suggest? (Heb. 5:14)

Our maiden is one of great discernment, having her senses exercised to discern good and evil. We will remember at the beginning of our Song that the Lord brought her to His banqueting table. We studied the strong meat that was found on King Solomon's table (I Kings 4:22-23), and discussed that spiritually the meat signified the strong meat of the Word. As our maiden has been feasting upon the strong meat of the Word in her communion with the Lord, her *nose* or sense of smell or *discernment* has grown to full maturity.

3. What has been her attitude? (Ps. 119:97-104)

4. As a result, what has happened in her life? (Ps. 119:97-104)
   a. (v. 98) _____
   b. (v. 99) _____
   c. (v. 100) _____
   d. (v. 104) _____

From this we see how her spiritual *nose*, her *discernment*, has developed and come to maturity. Not only has she loved and meditated on God's Word, but she has acted upon it. Thus her senses have become exercised to discern both good and evil.

5. How does she make a judgment? (Isa. 11:3)

6. When Moses chose wise, discerning, and experienced men to help him judge Israel, what instructions did he give them for judgment? (Deut. 1:16-17)
   a. _____
   b. _____
   c. _____
   d. _____

7. What did Jesus say about the judgment or word he spoke? John 12:48-50)
   a. _____
   b. _____
   c. _____

We find that the keen sense of discernment exercised by the Shulamite has been developed by judging things according to the Word of God. This discernment transcends things seen and heard and is able to distinguish and discriminate between things which are of God, man, or devil. This discernment is not logic subject to natural reasoning, but an awareness that is spontaneous and precise. It brings an immediate witness to the spirit as to whether a thing is born in heaven or not.

8. We find an example of this very great discernment in King Solomon. What did he desire from the Lord? (I Kings 3:9)

    _____

9. We see an example of this discernment given in a situation in which two women were claiming to be the mother of one baby. What judgment and discernment was handed down by the King and what was the result? (I Kings 3:16-28)

    _____

Now this judgment was a discernment from the Lord, for there were no witnesses to prove who the true mother was. God gave Solomon a word of wisdom that was designed to lay bare the true intent of the heart. It was not wisdom that was natural nor reasonable, but it brought about the desired results and caused the truth to be made manifest.

Likewise, it was this same discernment which caused Jesus to know what was in the heart of a man and to be able to read their thoughts before they were ever spoken.

10. The Shulamite's nose is said to be like the tower of Lebanon. We have said earlier that *tower* signifies *strength*. What does *Lebanon* represent? (Isa. 60:13; Isa. 35:2)

    _____

Lebanon then signifies *God's glory* and *His majesty*. The maiden's *discernment*, that appears as the *tower of Lebanon*, is the *strength of God's glory and majesty*. Through it God is able to bring forth His righteousness and glory in the earth.

Now her *nose*, her strength of discernment, was said to face toward *Damascus*. Damascus is said to be the oldest city in the East. Damascus owes her importance and stability to the fact that she is situated on the natural highway from east to west. Three great roads go forth from her to the west, south, and east. It is to *that great highway* that runs through *Damascus* that the Lord, by His Spirit, is pointing to.

11. What is this highway? (Isa. 35:8)

    _____

12. Who will *not* walk on that highway? (Isa. 35:8-9)
    a. _____
    b. _____
    c. _____
    d. _____

13. Who will travel on it? (Isa. 35:8-10)

    _____

14. What is the highway of the upright? (Prov. 16:17)

    _____

This strong discernment is given to the Shulamite to point people toward the highway of holiness, without which no man will see the Lord.

15. As a result of this strong discernment, what ministry has the Lord given to the Shulamite? (Ezk. 44:23)

    _____

16. What has the Shulamite become to all those who look upon her? (Isa. 40:3)

_____

17. What type of church is Jesus coming for? (Eph. 5:26-27)

_____

This Shulamite has joined with the Lord in His cleansing ministry of preparing for Himself a holy and blameless Bride. By extracting the precious from the worthless in the lives of those whom she ministers to through the strong sense of discernment which the Lord has developed in her life, she points them to the way of holiness.

18. What is said of the Shulamite's head? (Song 7:5)

_____

19. What happened on Mt. Carmel? (I Kings 18:17-24) Summarize briefly.

_____
_____
_____

It was at Carmel that Elijah's mighty prayers were heard by God and answered by fire. Having a head like Carmel, the Shulamite's whole mind and heart is anointed with the ability and power to bring wayward people back to God. The _crown_ symbolizes dominion. It was the _dominion_ of Carmel that the Shulamite possessed, having power with God and prevailing with men.

20. We see Jesus crowned with this same dominion and power at the resurrection of Lazarus. In His Words is revealed the key to entering into this kind of relationship with the Father God. What did he say? (John 11:41-43)

_____

Here lies the secret of those who have power with God and prevail with men—"Father, I know that You hear Me always." Jesus left us His example that we may follow in His steps.

21. What is the confidence that the Shulamite possesses? (I John 5:14-15)
    a. _____
    b. _____

22. How did she develop this confidence before God that both Elijah and Jesus displayed? (I John 3:21)

_____

23. Why does her heart not condemn her? (I John 3:22)
    a. _____
    b. _____

24. What promise did Jesus give to those who love Him? (John 14:13-14)

_____

The Shulamite is one who has come to _believe_ the love that God has for her. She is one who has come to believe in, trust in and act upon His Word. She does not represent the new believer who sometimes looks at God as a _Santa Claus_ with a bag full of blessings. She represents those mature believers who through a deep relationship with the Father have come _to know_ and realize with their whole beings that the Father always hears them and grants what they have requested.

Jesus said, "Father, I _know_ that You hear Me." This is the confidence that causes those who look upon the Shulamite to exclaim, "Your power with God in prayer crowns you like Carmel, for you are one who speaks to God in prayer and whom He answers with fire. You are one who knows that the Father hears you."

25. Describe the Shulamite's hair. (Song 7:5b)

_____

The hair once again signifies separation unto God. But here we see that this separation and complete dedication unto God has the potential of captivating and holding the King in its tresses. In earlier stages of spiritual life, she could not be entrusted with such power; but now in maturity this was made possible because she was completely delivered from the motivations of selfish interests.

When her dedication, devotion, and capacity for obedience had reached maturity, her mind had become so filled with the understanding of her Bridegroom's glory, that her hair turned _purple_. The color of purple represents _throne_ or _royal authority_.

26. What does the color of purple seen in the Bride's separation unto God signify here? (I Peter 2:9)

_____

Here we see her ministry of king and priest unto God. She now in maturity has learned how to exercise throne authority. Jesus is captivated by her because her spiritual affections are wholly for Him and her only desire is to see His will performed in the earth.

27. We see a type of this captivating intercession in the prayers of Moses. What was Moses' burning desire? (Num. 14:11-21)

_____

28. What does verse 11 tell us about Moses' relationship with the Lord? (Num. 14:11)

_____

Moses was so close to the heart of God that the Lord felt a liberty to share His heart with this degree of intimacy.

29. For those who are able to share in the Lord's sufferings, what authority and power are they given? (Luke 22:28-30; II Tim. 2:12)

_____

30. What exhortation has the Lord given to those who have captivated His heart? (Isa. 62:6-7)

_____

STUDY 29

THE DANCE OF MAHANAIM:
THE FULNESS OF HIS STATURE, THE HEART OF A SHEPHERD,
AND THE WINE OF MILLENNIAL DELIGHT

The Lord Thy God in the midst of you
is mighty!
He will sing, He will rejoice over you
with joy! —
Zeph. 3:17

Suddenly, Jesus Himself spontaneously burst into the song of the dance of testimony, pronouncing His agreement to the spiritual delights with which the life of the maiden is now enriched.

1. How does Jesus describe her stature? (Song 7:7)

2. In speaking of her stature, what does Jesus see her as growing up into? (Eph. 4:13)

In earlier stages there was no stature mentioned because there had not been that much growth and progress. But now, in the eyes of the Lord, her spiritual stature begins to come into view. In maturity she is beginning to come into that measure of the stature of the fulness of Christ.

3. What does the palm tree represent? (Ps. 92:12-15)

4. We will now look at the metaphor of the palm tree to see exactly what this stature to which she has attained is all about.

METAPHOR	PARALLEL
1. The palm tree is a very tall tree. Its branches do not grow from its sides as in other trees.	1. Col. 3:1-2
2. The roots of the palm tree are in touch with a deep fountain of living waters. Though exposed to hot tropical sunshine, its leaves and fruit grow without hindrance.	2. Rev. 22:1-3; Ps. 1:1-3
3. The palm tree is one of those trees that is always green; they never cast their leaves, neither do they fade or wither. It is also a tree that is full of fruits, namely dates and coconuts.	3. Ezk. 47:12; Rev. 22:2; Ps. 92:14; Ps. 1:3
4. The palm tree is a very weak plant when it stands alone, but if three or four are planted together, they strengthen one another and stand fast. By growing together, they join and grow one to another, becoming strong and flourishing.	4. Eph. 4:11-16; Ex. 17:9-13

5. The palm tree will thrive under heavy pressures and weights that are upon it. It grows the highest when the heaviest pressure is upon it. The burden will not make it crooked.

5. I Peter 4:12-14; James 1:2-4, 12

_____

_____

_____

6. The palm tree grows in the purest soil; it will not grow in filthy soil but rather spreads its roots by a river. It does not like dungy soil as other trees do.

6. Ps. 1:1-3; Ps. 93:5; II Cor. 6:14-18

_____

_____

_____

Conclusion:

As the stately palm, the Shulamite does not go to the right or the left, but grows upward. Her affections are set on the things above and her top reaches up into the heights of heaven where Christ is seated at the right hand of God. She keeps seeking those things which are above.

The roots of the Shulamite are in touch with the river of the water of life which flows from the throne of God and His Lordship in her life. Her hidden union with Jesus causes her to bring forth fruit without being affected by the circumstances or influences of the desert world around her. Because of the ever-greenness of that eternal life that is within, her spiritual beauty never fades or withers but rather goes from glory to glory. She is full of sap because she is a branch of the Living Vine, Jesus. His Spirit within her is a fountain which springs up to apprehend eternal life and immortality.

As a palm tree, she has become strong and flourishing because of her supportive relationships and union with other members of the body of Christ; she, as well as those with whom she is joined in the body, are growing up together into that full stature of Christ.

All trials, testings, and pressures that have come upon the Shulamite have caused her to grow up even higher. For those who are walking in this degree of maturity, there is no where to go except upward and onward into higher heights and deeper depths with the Lord their God. Having separated herself from the dunghills of this world and anything that would defile her walk with the Lord, she is planted in soils of holiness and purity. She is flourishing unto every good work.

5. What are her breasts likened to?

_____

Thus the Lord points to not only her capacity of feeding others milk, but also to her ability to feed them on the sweet fruit which comes from a life of maturity.

6. What did the Lord say He would do? (Song 7:8a)

_____

The fruit stalks or palm branches were broken off, waved, and used as signs of victory and rejoicing when the people, during Bible times, would express their great joy. The believer who has reached this stage of maturity is a branch in Jesus' hand — a sign of that glorious victory that He has obtained over the world, death, hell and the devil.

This passage also implies that, in the Lord's desire to take hold of her branches, He had something to personally take hold of for Himself in the life of this mature one. The Lord purposes to have fellowship with believers, and here it appears that He is the one in search of this love.

7. What do the eyes of the Lord search for? (II Chron. 16:9)

_____

The eyes of the Lord search with great desire for a believer whose heart is completely His. He looks for those whose total affections, emotions, mind and will are set upon Him.

8. Jesus mentions three aspects of the Shulamite's mature life that are particularly satisfying to Him. What are they? (Song 7:8b, 9a)

   a. _____

   b. _____

   c. _____

The breasts which are likened to the clusters of the vine signify the Lord's delight in the ability of His Bride to feed others.

9. What did Jesus say would be the activity of those who greatly love Him? (John 21:15-17)

   _____

10. What is one of the great offices and activities of Jesus? (Isa. 40:11)

   _____

The mature Shulamite — His Beloved, His Bride — has become His arm, as she gathers His lambs. She has become as His bosom, the seat and place where God has set His heart. Here she carries the lambs of His pasture. Through the guidance of His Spirit, she gently and tenderly leads the nursing ewes who are still in need of the milk of the Word.

11. What attitude and relationship toward His sheep does Jesus see reflected in the maturity of His Bride? (John 10:14-15)

   a. _____

   b. _____

Her capacity for feeding and leading others is patterned after the Great Shepherd. Thus, her breasts appear as clusters of the Great Vine, flowing with His life and feeding that life to all those whom the Father has put in her charge.

Secondly, it pleases the Lord that the fragrance of her breath is like apples.

12. What does the breath signify in scripture? (Gen. 2:7)

   _____

The *breath*, then, represents *that which makes man a living being*, in regard to man's life, walk, and relationship to this earth and other people around him. A man with breath is able to communicate with other living beings, while a man without breath is a corpse and has no ability to communicate because he is dead.

Earlier in our Song, the maiden saw the Lord as an apple tree among the other trees of the woods. Jesus smells or senses in her *earth walk* the fragrance of Himself. She is an aroma of Christ unto God.

13. What does Jesus compare the mouth of the bride to? (Song 7:9)

   _____

14. What is this a reference to? (John 2:10)

   _____

Let us now examine the parable of the wedding feast at Cana and Jesus' first miracle of turning water into the best wine. It is the truth that this parable sets forth that Jesus is now referring to. Read John 2:1-11.

15. What does the wedding feast speak to us about? (Rev. 19:7-9)

   _____

16. On what day was the wedding feast? (John 2:1)

   _____

The number three represents the perfection or fulness of God.

17. What did Jesus say would happen on the third day? (Luke 13:32) Notice that in the marginal reference, this verse can also be translated, "I am perfected".

_____

The third day of which this parable foretells is the day when Jesus shall reach His goal, His perfection. It is on this day that His Bride shall be filled with all the fulness of God and shall come into her own. This is the Great Day of the Lord spoken of by all the prophets.

18. Who does the mother represent? (Matt. 12:48-50)

_____

19. In answer to His mother's request, what is Jesus' response? (John 2:3-4)

_____

This response from Jesus seems to be a rejection, but as we have learned previously, this type of response to those who are the closest to His heart is designed to produce a response of faith and love returned.

20. What was the response of His mother? (John 2:5)

_____

This is her response of faith. As Jesus said to the Father, I _know_ that You hear Me. So also His mother responds with the assurance that He has heard her request and will act just as she instructs the other servants to "do whatever He tells you." She also is one who does all His will and not her own.

21. How many water pots were there, for what were they used, and how many gallons of water did each contain? (John 2:6)
    a. _____
    b. _____
    c. _____

Six is the number of man.
Twenty is the number of expectancy.
Thirty is the number of maturity for ministry.

The six stone waterpots represent the earthen vessels of man. The water that they contained represents the Word of God in which men may wash and be purified and cleansed. The fact that some were filled with thirty gallons of water and some with twenty speaks to us that these men, as vessels of the Lord, had come to a place of maturity for ministry and were waiting expectantly.

22. For what do those who have come to maturity for ministry expectantly wait for? (Rom. 8:19-23; Heb. 9:28)
    a. (v. 19) _____
    b. (v. 23) _____
    c. (v. 28) _____

This full salvation for which they eagerly await is that total removing of all sin, in which they will experientially enter into the Day of Atonement and be revealed unto the world as God's sons, going forth into the earth as He went forth. This will inevitably bring about the total redemption of the Body, for when there is no sin, the appointment with death is annulled and the law of sin and death is broken. They will then live for 1,000 years in a sinless Body, ruling and reigning with Christ upon the earth and finishing His work. This is the great Marriage Supper of the Lamb. It is not a literal dinner of steaks, pies etc.—it is greater than that. Jesus said, "My _meat is to do the will of God and finish His work._" So also those who are invited to that great Marriage Supper will partake of this _His meat._ This is the hour that Jesus spoke of that had not yet come; this is the hour when His glory would be revealed upon the earth. This, the hour when

God's sons come into their own, has been one which overcomers of every generation have expectantly waited for and desired earnestly to be a part of. It is the day of the *best wine*.

23. What were those overcomers who had come to maturity and were expectantly awaiting the revelation of God's glory in the earth able to do? (Heb. 11:33-34)
    a. _____
    b. _____
    c. _____
    d. _____
    e. _____
    f. _____
    g. _____
    h. _____
    i. _____

24. Although these gained approval through their faith, why did they not receive what was promised? (Heb. 11:39-40)
    _____

It is the *best wine* of the Millennial delights that the overcomers of all generations have longed to partake. They desire to enter into that perfection, not through death, for death has *never* made anyone, saint or sinner, perfect; but, through the power of that atoning blood they will be made perfect to go forth in the earth conquering and to conquer. Paul said, "not that I have already attained or were already made perfect, but I press on toward the goal."

As Jesus beholds the Shulamite, He sees within her the marks of His Bride, of those whose *mouth is like the best wine*.

25. What does the mouth represent? (Matt. 12:34)
    _____

Jesus finds in the Shulamite the very passion of His own soul, for from the abundance of her heart flows forth the cry for the Best Wine, as everything within her presses toward the goal and the mark of the high and upward call of God in Christ Jesus.

26. What is said about this *best wine*, this passionate desire that flows from the abundance of her heart and that for which she expectantly waits? (Song 7:9b)
    _____
    _____

The King James Version says it this way:

> ...that goeth down sweetly, causing
> the lips of those that are asleep to speak.

The dead are spoken of in scripture as those who have fallen asleep.

27. When will those lips of the dead speak again? (I Thes. 4:13-17)
    _____

Yes, the *best wine*, is that which will be the beginning of the manifestation of Jesus' glory in the earth. When it is given, it will cause the dead to be raised and cause the lips of those who are asleep to speak again. For the overcomers of every generation will make up that perfect Bride, the wife of the Lamb, and will take part in the Great Marriage supper—the 1,000 year reign of Christ and His Bride.

28. Who will take part in the first resurrection? (Rev. 20:4-6)
    a. _____
    b. _____
    c. _____
    d. _____

History and life itself can be considered a relay race. The overcomers of every generation ran the race of life with great passion, commitment and dedication to the Lord of glory. Each ran the race of life with their heart fixed to do God's will and to demonstrate His glory. When their course of life was finished and their portion of that great race was completed, they passed the baton on to the next generation of runners who had their eyes fixed on the goal and their hearts set on doing God's will above their own. Generation after generation has run their race and passed their baton on to others. The race is yet to be finished as the righteous and the committed of the years gone by are looking upon their teammates, cheering them on with great passion and love.

When that generation of overcomers, those to whom the baton has been passed for the last time, cross the finish line and reach that goal, then their teammates of past generations will also partake of the prize. For, as the scripture says, apart from us, the finishers, they could not be made perfect. Yes, the lips of those who are asleep will speak as they arise to rule and reign with Christ for a thousand years upon the earth and to finish His work. Those who finish the race, who are alive and remain, will not see death but their bodies will be changed also into the likeness of the body of His glory. Now the resurrected will be real people once again with bodies of flesh and bone, like the body of His resurrection. They will be able to eat, talk, and fellowship with man and yet at the same time not be limited by time and space. They will be made after the likeness of Him who has an endless life.

29. Since we have such a great cloud of witnesses surrounding us and cheering us onward and upward, what are we exhorted to do? (Heb. 12:1-2)
    a. _____
    b. _____
    c. _____

30. Lest we grow weary of the race, what should we remember and consider earnestly? (Heb. 12:3-4)
    a. _____
    b. _____

Forgetting all that lies behind,
I press toward the mark of the prize.
That high calling to be like Him,
And on this one thing I set my eyes!

But this hope we have within,
The promise that we shall be like Him.
The race is laid for us to run,
As everyone looks to see who will win.

The race is not for those who are swift,
and neither for the strong.
This race shall be won trading your
weakness for His strength,
With nothing but your faith to push you on.

Forgetting all that lies behind,
I press toward the mark of the prize.
That high calling to be like Him,
And on this one thing I set my eyes! —

Michael Powell

STUDY 30

GOD'S DESIRE FOR MANY SONS
IN HIS IMAGE

... for this reason He is not ashamed
to call them brethren. —
Heb. 2:11

Chapter 8 of our Song begins with our maiden's heart cry as she labors in the harvest.

1. What is the heart cry? (Song 8:1)

    _____

    _____

2. Who, again, did Jesus say were His mother, His brothers, His sisters? (Matt. 12:49-50)

    _____

As those with the bridal soul labor in the harvest, their hearts cry out for those of like precious faith—of like desire. They cry out for those who would be their true brothers in the Lord and whose utmost desire would be to do the will of the Father!

In ancient Israel, public kissing between men and women, even husband and wife, was forbidden and despised. The only exception was between blood-relatives such as brother and sister. Earlier in our Song her cry had been "let Him kiss me with the kisses of His mouth." Thus her heart cry was to be brought into intimate fellowship and union with the King. Now, her heart cry is to find one like a brother to her and to kiss him.

3. What is her heart crying out for? (John 17:21-23)

    _____

    _____

    _____

    _____

Her heart desires that unity and oneness of Spirit with her brother that Jesus cried out for in Gethsemane before His crucifixion.

4. As one who desires full maturity, what does her heart long to see? [Eph. 4:13]

    _____

The psalmist prophesied concerning this unity which is the desire of her soul.

5. How does David describe this unity? (Ps. 133)
    a. _____
    b. _____
    c. _____
       _____
    d. _____
    e. _____

In this longed-for unity, the anointing will be poured out upon that one mature man, the great high priest of God [represented by Aaron and his beard]. When this unity is achieved, God will command the blessing—life forever—which is the transformation of the saints and the resurrection of the Body. This unity is not only good and pleasant, but is to become one in which fellow believers enter into that same oneness with each other as they have with the Lord. It is this for which the bridal soul cries out.

6. When the bridal soul found one in the harvest who was a brother to her, what did she desire to give or impart to him? (Song 8:2)

_____

As we have said earlier pomegranates signify the pure and godly thoughts of the mind which has been renewed through intimate fellowship with the Lord of Glory. She desires to give her *brother* a piece of her mind, so to speak. She desires to impart to him the life and the godly thoughts that have made her what she is in Him. She desires to help perfect Him in the ways of the Lord.

7. We see a picture of this bridal soul in Proverbs. As this maiden has become filled with the wisdom of God, what invitation does she extend to mankind? (Prov. 9:1-6)

_____

_____

So, likewise, the bridal soul stands as that faithful servant who is prepared to give the strong meat and wine of the Lord's table to those who lack it. "Blessed is that servant who the master finds so doing when he comes. Truly he shall be put in charge of all his possessions." (Matt. 24:45-46)

8. What is the maiden's source of strength and support? (Song 8:3; Deut. 33:26-29)

_____

9. What do we find the Lord doing in Song 8:4?

_____

_____

Through this, we see Jesus as a God of providence who is behind the scenes watching over His own and ordering the events and circumstances of every day living that touch the lives of those who have entrusted themselves into His care.

10. As the bridal soul comes up from her labor in the wilderness of this world, among the crooked and perverse of this generation, who is she leaning upon for support and strength? (Song 8:5a)
    a. _____
    b. _____
    c. _____

11. What is her position of faith? (Prov. 3:5-6)
    a. _____
    b. _____
    c. _____

12. Therefore, what will her Lord do for her? (Prov. 3:6)

_____

13. What picture do we see of this in the following passage? (Num. 9:15-23) Give only the spiritual principle that is found here.

_____

_____

_____

We find a beautiful picture here of one who is not going to and fro at will, but one who is watching the cloud and being sensitive to the leading of His Holy Spirit. This is one who leans completely upon Him, moving only when He moves and stopping only when He stops. Such is the path of those who are pressing on into maturity. This is the path of the Sons of God.

In verses 5b-7 we find the Bridegroom speaking to those precious blood-bought ones whom His Bride has been laboring over in His harvest fields.

14. What did He tell them happened beneath the *apple tree*? (Which as we learned earlier, represents Jesus and the fulness of His love). (Song 8:5b)

_____

_____

We found that the *mother* represents those who *do the will of God*.

15. How did their spiritual mother give these blood-bought ones their spiritual birth? (Song 8:5b; Gal. 4:19)

_____

16. What happens when Zion—those who trust in the Lord—are in labor and travail through intercession? (Isa. 66:8)

_____

17. In Revelation 12, we see a picture of the wife of the King of Light. In what condition do we find that Bride company? (Rev. 12:1-2)

_____

18. As the birth pangs of intercession and travail gripped her spirit, what did she give birth to? (Rev. 12:5)

_____

The bride company birthed the spiritual overcomers, who together were to rule and reign with Jesus upon the earth.

As our maiden, His Bride, has gone forth into the harvest fields, she has been great with child and has been in pain to give birth. She travailed and brought forth her children—those in her likeness and image. It is these that Jesus awakened, giving them spiritual eyesight. It is of these that Jesus now speaks.

19. What does he instruct them to do? (Song 8:6a)

_____

We learned earlier in our Song that our maiden also was likened unto a fountain that was *sealed*. She was not a public drinking fountain to the passers by, nor did her water run freely in the streets. She was a private garden and a private fountain sealed and separated unto Him.

So, likewise, the Bridegroom addresses those newly born, birthed through His Bride into His Kingdom, to set Him as a seal upon their hearts (signifying their affections), and as a seal upon their arm (signfiying their strength). (Prov. 31:17; Gen. 49:24; Isa. 51:9) Set Me, He says, as a seal upon your affections; let them all be directed toward Me. Spend your strength and your energies only for Me and My Kingdom.

20. What did Jesus say the first and foremost commandment is? (Mark 12:29-30)

_____

_____

21. With what are we sealed? (Eph. 1:13)

_____

22. The Holy Spirit of promise is an engagement ring, given to us by God. What is it a pledge of? (Eph. 1:14)

_____

_____

To those who would be bridal souls He speaks, "let this Holy Spirit of Promise have preeminence over your affections and let it have first place in the use of your strength. Wear is as an engagement ring, as a seal, and know that it is a promise that I will return and completely redeem your spirit, soul and body from all the power of the enemy."

"You have begun as a loose group of undisciplined believers, but you will finish as the army of the Lord which will be revealed with Me at My appearing, bringing judgment and deliverance to the nations of the earth. When I am finished with My redemption plan, you will be one with Me, filled with My glory and I am finished with My redemption plan, you will be the Holy City, the Wife of the Lamb, the New Jerusalem. When I am finished, sin will be completely abolished from this earth and the curse will no longer be found in it. You will be my lovely Bride and we will rule for the ages to come."

23. How does Jesus describe His love for His blood-bought ones? (Song 8:6)
_____

Jesus speaks here of His own sacrificial death for the salvation of mankind.

24. What did Jesus say was the greatest display of love that one could demonstrate to another? (John 15:13)
_____

25. When Jesus took the last Passover with His disciples (of whose own death the Passover Supper prophesied), what did He say about the bread and the wine? (Matt. 26:26-28)
_____
_____

The scripture goes on to say that after supper they sang a hymn and went out to the Mount of Olives where He was to be delivered over to be crucified. The hymn that they sang was Psalm 118. Read this Psalm which was the last hymn Jesus sang before He gave His life for us.

26. This psalm is prophetic of Jesus' death, resurrection, His attitude, and the things His death would accomplish. Give four statements which reveal Jesus' attitude toward the cross that lay before Him. (Ps. 118:5-6, 19, 24, 27)
   a. _____
   b. _____
   _____
   c. _____
   _____
   d. _____

Jesus was completely willing to surrender to the cross. As He Himself said, "No man takes My life, I give it."

27. We find in this psalm what the writer of Hebrews spoke about when he wrote "for the joy that was set before Him he endured the cross." What was that joy? (Ps. 118:10-14, 15, 17)
   a. _____
   b. _____
   c. _____

28. How does Jesus describe His jealousy toward His blood-bought ones? (Song 8:6b)
_____
_____

29. What does the Lord jealousy desire? (James 4:4-5)
_____

30. What did Paul say about that jealousy? (II Cor. 11:2)
_____
_____

31. What does the Lord say about His desire for Jerusalem and Zion? (Zech. 1:14)
_____

It was that jealous love for a pure and a chaste Bride—for a Holy people devoted to Himself—that caused Jesus to go to the cross and into death and the very depths of hell to accomplish their redemption. His jealousy is like flashes of fire, burning up whatever is impure and unclean, that He might purify and purge and make holy His Bride in order to present it to Himself without spot or blemish or any such thing.

The Lord speaks to those who would be bridal souls of His intolerable jealousy toward any other lovers, idols, or things of this earth that would come between Him and those who are called to make up His Bride. He speaks to them of the purging fire with which they shall be purified, for they must be as pure as gold and as transparent as glass in the day when they are presented as the sharer of His throne. He sets before them the vision, the commitment which it will take, and the path which they must walk.

32. What does He say concerning the trials and testings which those who desire bridal affection must endure? (Song 8:7a)

_____

As the maiden can testify, the many waters of trials and testings have not quenched her love for Him. They have only caused her roots to sink deeper in Him, her love to grow stronger, her character to grow purer. They too will learn that nothing can separate them from the love of God. They will choose not, as some did, to forsake him, but rather they will follow Him all the way, knowing that no river or any persecution that the enemy can throw at them will overflow their commitment to Him.

33. What was the extent of Jesus' love toward us? (Song 8:7b)

_____

34. In Isaiah we find a prophecy of Jesus' death upon the cross. What does it say concerning this rejection that He failed? (Isa. 53:3)

_____

Jesus went into this great extent of shame and rejection to show His love toward the world. All the martyrs who have followed after Him have also displayed this self sacrificing love as they too have cried out with Him, "Father forgive them for they know not what they do."

35. John also speaks of this great and infinite love. What does John say of Him? (John 1:10-11)

_____

_____

36. But to as many as received Him what privilege did they receive? (John 1:12)

_____

Having spoken with the Living Word before whose eyes nothing can be hidden, their hearts are laid bare and their need is brought to light. Those souls to whom He is speaking are cut to the quick, their heart is pierced by the strength of His love, as they realize their own need for spiritual growth, maturity and ability to walk in this same sacrificial love.

37. Who do they inquire about and what question do they ask concerning her? (Song 8:8)

_____

In asking about their little sister, they are in essence asking about themselves: Lord, what must _we_ do; we are spiritually immature and have not grown in faith and love; we have no capacity for feeding others nor mature affections to satisfy Your heart. They ask: what can be done that we might be mature when You come for Your Bride. The answer to this question we will take up in a later study.

PERFECT LOVE

The Lord has chosen Zion;
He has desired it for His habitation.
This is my resting place forever;
Here I will dwell,
For I have desired it. —
Ps. 132:13-14

1. What statement of relationship does the Shulamite make? (Song 7:10)

_____

Here is the testimony of one who has found that *perfect love* toward the Lord where no fear reigns. This is the testimony of one who has assurance of heart and great confidence before Him — so much so that she is able to say, "His desire is for me."

2. We find that the Apostle John had a similar testimony. What did he call himself? (John 20:2; John 13:23; John 19:26; John 21:7, 20-21)

_____

Both John and those whom this maiden represents have entered into a place of relationship and union with the Lord where they are completely His. Their entire mental and spiritual vision is wholly set upon Him. Any concerns about self are totally out of their consciousness. They are consumed with Him — that He might have His way, that His heart's desire may be fulfilled, that His will might be accomplished, that His Kingdom may have come on earth as it is in heaven, that they might be everything He wants them to be. Therefore, they know that He is moved for them, that His heart strongly supports them, that His desire is toward them, for they are full of Bridal affections for their Beloved. They are one spirit with Him and their hearts have been knit together in love.

As we search the scriptures we discover that there are several things that cause the Lord's heart to be moved with great desire toward those who are His. Let us see what these things are in particular.

3. What does God not desire? (Ps. 40:6-8)

_____

Notice in this passage it is written, "My ears thou hast opened" (or "pierced" — see marginal reference), and, "I delight to do thy will O my God." In the same passage that tells us what God does *not* desire, it reveals to us what He *really wants* — one who *delights* to do His will.

4. "My ears Thou hast opened, or pierced", is a direct reference to a passage and a custom given in Exodus. What was that custom? (Ex. 21:2, 5-6)

_____
_____
_____
_____

This custom was allowed because love and the allegiance of love was prized more highly than personal freedom. This man was then called a bond-servant or a love-slave. This custom was what Paul was referring to when he called himself a bond-servant of Jesus Christ. The psalmist also employs this custom in expressing his commitment to the Lord, saying, "My ear Thou hast opened, or pierced": I do not desire to be my own free man. I love my God and I want to serve Him permanently. I do not desire to do merely what the law requires in sacrifice and offerings. For Thy law is within my heart, I delight to do Thy will O my God.

In saying these things, the Holy Spirit signifies that the Lord does not desire a people who serve Him or are committed to Him out of law — fulfilling only that which the law requires because the law requires it.

Rather He desires one who serves Him as an expression of love. He desires one who serves Him not out of duty, but from the sheer joy of serving the Lord; not out of fear, but from sincere appreciation.

5.   We see this relationship demonstrated in the marriage of Jacob to Leah and Rachel. What was Jacob's attitude toward each? (Gen. 29:18-30)

_____

Now *Leah* represents the *law*, for the relationship was born out of legalism. *Rachel* represents those with *bridal love* and affection, for the relationship was born out of true love and affection of heart.

Again we see that God does not desire for people to fulfill laws to try to gain His favor, but rather that it be a relationship of heartfelt commitment. He does not desire for us to have a deep and earnest desire to gain His approval because of fear of judgment, but rather a burning passion and delight to do His will.

6.   Secondly, what does the Lord desire? (Ps. 51:6)

_____

God desires those who not only delight to do His will and who want to serve him because of their great love for Him, but also those who are full of truth. He desires those who do not lie, who are honest, and do not let wickedness lurk in their hearts. Such a one is this Shulamite whom God desires.

7.   What is the heart cry of this maiden? (Ps. 43:3-4)

_____

_____

8.   Having found truth, what is her attitude toward it? (Prov. 23:23)

_____

9.   Having become one who is desirous of truth of God, having bound it around her neck (her will) and written it upon her heart, what has she found? (Prov. 3:3-4)

_____

Therefore, she can cry out,"I am my Beloved's and His desire is for me!"

10.   Along with truth, what quality does the Lord desire to see in those who love Him? (Matt. 9:10-13; Matt. 12:1-7)

_____

Our maiden is one with compassion and mercy whose heart is turned toward the spiritually hungry of the world. She is not one who is bound up with hypocrisy and religiosity. She is not as the Pharisees who cast away, scorned, and looked down on the sinner with a holier-than-thou attitude. With compassion and love she looks upon the lost in this world and extends to them that heart and hand of compassion and lovingkindness that has characterized the life of her Master. She is not one who is bound up in legalism, trying to keep every jot and title of the law or legalistically enforcing it upon others. She has found hidden in the law of God, not a lot of rules, but the Lawgiver Himself. His love has overwhelmed her. Through His Spirit that dwells within her she is able to interpret that law, in the same spirit of her Master. She has recognized that He is greater than the law. Therefore she judges righteously and perceives situations as the Lord Himself does. She is full of His compassion and mercy, therefore she is wholly desirable unto Him.

11.   What else does the Lord desire from those who love Him? (Ps. 45:10-11)

_____

We find that this was one of the first requirements that God also made of Abraham:

12.   What did the Lord ask Abraham to do? (Gen. 12:1)

_____

_____

13. We see this attitude displayed in Ruth's commitment to Naomi. What was that commitment? (Ruth 1:14-16)

_____

_____

_____

Naomi represents the Spirit of God, and Ruth represents those who have given themselves in complete abandonment to follow the Lamb wheresoever He goeth.

14. Jesus expressed this attitude also. When His mother and brothers came seeking Him, what did He say? (Matt. 12:46-50)

_____

_____

Jesus was saying, "Natural sentiments and ties do not move me, for I must do God's will."

Paul tells us that the relationship between a man and his wife demonstrates the relationship between Christ and His Church.

15. What is that relationship to be? (Eph. 5:31-32)

_____

_____

It is this leaving of one's natural parents and cleaving unto the Lord in all affection and love that our God desires. He desires for us to go wherever He goes, to lodge wherever He lodges, to be one Spirit with Him.

16. Again we see this lesson demonstrated in a teaching of Paul's on marriage. What did he say those who had wives should be as? (I Cor. 7:29)

_____

17. What did he say the unmarried man and woman cared about? (I Cor. 7:32-34)

_____

_____

18. What did he say the married man and woman cared about? (I Cor. 7:33-34)

_____

Paul goes on to say that the unmarried are concerned about the things of the Lord and how they may please the Lord, but the married have divided interests or two masters: Jesus and each other. Now Jesus himself said no man can serve two masters. Paul said also, "These things should not be."

19. Is it better then for Christians not to marry? What should each man and woman do? (I Cor. 7:35)

_____

_____

_____

We find Paul hitting at the core of human affection. His desire was not that people restrain from marriage, but rather that they not have divided interests. He is teaching here that men and women should not set their affections on the things of this world and how they may please one another, but rather that they set their affections on things above on how they may please the Lord and be holy in body and Spirit. Paul desires that they might, although married, retain the attitude of undistracted devotion to the Lord.

It is this undistracted devotion to the Lord, this cleaving unto Him, this wreckless abandonment unto Him that says, "Wherever you go, I will go, wherever you lodge, I will lodge, your people will be my people." It is this same attitude that says, "Who is my mother, my brother, my sister? Those who do the will of my Father."

As she refuses to allow natural affection to exalt itself above her love and commitment to her God, the King becomes greatly desirous of her beauty.

21. Who does Zion represent? (Ps. 125:1-2)

    _____

22. How does the Lord feel about those who trust Him? (Ps. 87:1)

    _____

23. What quality characterizes the people of Zion? (Ps. 68:16-17)

    _____

24. What befits God's house, whose house we are? (Ps. 93:5)

    _____

We have seen our maiden as one whose heart is completely the Lord's. We have seen that the maiden has chosen the Lord, deciding to follow on to know Him, not out of law, but out of heartfelt love and desire for her Master. She has forsaken all to follow Him. She has dedicated herself as a holy and separate vessel unto Him. As she trusts wholly in Him, she can say with great confidence, "I am the disciple that Jesus loves. I am one of those who was born in *Zion*. The Lord desires me for his habitation and for His dwelling place forever."

NOTES

STUDY 32

GOD'S FELLOW WORKER

*And it will come about in that day that I will
respond, declares the Lord.
I will respond to the heavens, and they will
respond to the earth,
And the earth, will respond to the grain, to the
new vine, and to the oil
and they will respond to Jezreel (God sows)
And I will sow her for myself in the land.
I will have compassion on her who had not
obtained compassion,
and I will say to those who were not my people,
'You are My people!' And they will say,
'Thou are my God!'
Hosea 2:21-23*

1. In her oneness of life and desire with her Master, what activity does her heart purpose to her King?
    (Song 7:11)

    _____

    _____

Notice in the marginal reference that the word for *country* literally means *field*.

2. What does the *field* represent? (Matt. 13:38)

    _____

The world lies before her. She is no longer interested only in her own little corner of God's work, but in the vast field of all His interests in the world, no matter what the spiritual level. She possesses a vision which transcends everything that pertains to this world. She views history as His story of His work in the earth. She feels a unity with the saints of years gone by who are watching from the other side of the veil. She feels a unity as well with those who perhaps have not reached the same understanding and maturity to which she has attained. She has become interested in the Lord's whole scope of operation and she is the one with Him in all of it.

3. As she says, "Let us spend the night in the villages," what is she confessing that Abraham too was able to confess? (Heb. 11:8-10, 13-16)

    _____

We see in our maiden the nature and character of a pilgrim in this world. She is not seeking a permanent home of her own, but rather is content to follow Him from village to village seeking those sheep who are lost and torn and in need of a shepherd. She is content to be a stranger and exile in this world, sojourning in this *land of promise* — which land she will inherit when she will reign with Him upon this earth. She has become free in spirit and in heart through His many dealings in her life and is now content to move about quickly with Him, saying as Ruth, "Wherever you go, I will go, and wherever you lodge, I will lodge. Your people are my people."

4. What other activity does she purpose to her Beloved? (Song 7:12a)

    _____

In the beginning of our Song, in her need for maturity of relationship with the Living God, she cried out, "They have made me the keeper of the vineyards, but mine own vineyard I have not kept." Having now grown in knowledge and relationship with the Lord, and having reached maturity, she is able to look after many vineyards.

5. What has she become and what has God prepared her for? (Eph. 2:10)

_____

There is a working which is soulish and there is a passivity that is another name for slothfulness. As the Lord has stilled the soulish activity in her life and brought her into restful co-operation with Him, she has become a mighty instrument for His work. In this going forth to the work, she is not busying herself doing works for God but through inspiration and motivation of His Spirit within her, she and her Lord move together into the field.

There is no room for slothfulness in the realm of obedience. *Let us get up early* indicates her industrious character. The difference between spiritual industriousness and slothfulness lies in the *use of time*.

6. Having grown in wisdom, what is she able to do? (Eph. 5:16)

_____

7. What does she desire to examine in the vineyards? (Song 7:12)
   a. _____
   b. _____
   c. _____

In union with Him, she goes forth into the vineyard searching for signs of life. The *vine* represents *the Church*, the *buds* represents *the newborn believers*, the *blossoms* represent *those whose lives are becoming a fragrance of Christ unto God*. She looks to discern the first tokens of fruit with a desire to bring Christ to His people. Of special joy and delight is to find the *blood-red flower of the pomegranate*, for it indicates the hidden beauty of *the bridal souls* who will satisfy and capitivate His heart.

8. What did the maiden say she was doing as she labored in His vineyard? (Song 7:12b)

_____

9. What did Jesus tell Peter to do as the evidence of great love for the Master? (John 21:15)

_____

Those who fervently love the Lord their God go farther than just their own personal relationship and concept of *me and mine*. As they are drawn ever closer to their Master in love, His compassion and love for humanity begins to pervade their soul as they become His hand extended to a lost and dying world.

The Shulamite is now able to demonstrate her love toward Him by laying down her life for His sheep and for His work in the earth. During her immature years, work appeared as a distraction from her communion with Him. She saw service as a hindrance. Service drew Martha away also whereas Mary enjoyed fellowship at Jesus' feet. But now as the Shulamite has entered into that complete union with Him, she has come to realize that in Him she lives, moves, and has her being. She sees that His Spirit prevades every particle of the atmosphere, and as she has become completely a vessel possessed by His life, she is able to see that, whether alone with Him or pouring her life out to the distressed, nothing can separate her from His presence.

In essence, she is an extention of His life in the earth, a vessel through which He can speak to the lost, comfort the mourning, heal the sick, and continue His work in the world. She sees herself not as an employee, but as a co-worker, a co-laborer with Him as she discerns their togetherness in their labor and toil.

10. In her willingness to lay down her life for others, what was she expressing toward the Lord? (John 15:13)

_____

11. Just as her Master, what has become the motivation of her heart? (Matt. 20:28)

_____

It is in being that chariot of God, that vehicle for His movement in the earth, that His Bride is able to give her Lord and Savior her love. The maiden demonstrates her mature and bridal love for Him as she gives herself in the field of the world. Holding forth the Word of Life, she seeks with Him for the lost, the torn and the maimed sheep of His pasture, desiring to bind up their wounds, heal their broken hearts, and to proclaim to them the glad tidings of salvation.

12. In showing these acts of love and mercy toward even the very least, who has she done this unto? (Matt. 25:40)

_____

13. What did the Shulamite say had given forth their fragrance and what time of year does their growth indicate? (Song 7:13; Gen. 30:14)

_____

14. Concerning this harvest season, Jesus Himself made reference. What did He say concerning it? (John 4:35; Luke 10:2)

_____

_____

15. Jesus said that the reason for lack of fruit was not because the harvest was not ripe. What reason then did He give for the lack of fruit? (Luke 10:2)

_____

The Shulamite is one of those whom the Lord of the harvest has raised up to labor in His fields. She has gone forth into the harvest and has not come back empty-handed.

16. What has she stored up for her Lord? (Song 7:13)

_____

17. What is her attitude, as was Paul's attitude, toward the fruit that she has gathered in for the Lord? (I Thes. 2:19-20)

_____

_____

18. As she has hungered after righteousness, what has God done for her? (Ps. 107:36-38a)

_____

_____

19. As she has become the branch of His planting, the work of His hands, what has she brought forth? (Isa. 4:2)

_____

20. As a righteous one, firmly planted by streams of water, what does she never cease from yielding? (Jer. 17:7-8)

_____

21. Where did she lay up this fruit? (Song 7:13)

_____

22. What is this a reference to? (Ex. 12:7, 21-23)

_____

_____

23. Thus what is the Holy Spirit signifying? (Acts 20:28)

_____

_____

As she has placed the fruit over the door, the fruit is as a wave offering to the Lord, as were the first fruits of the harvest season. The wave offering was offered unto God in faith of the greater and fuller harvest that was to come in. So, also, as this maiden offers back to the Lord the fruit of His harvest, she looks forward to that even greater harvest that the Lord spoke of by the mouth of His holy prophets when peoples and many nations will stream into God's Kingdom.

24. Now the fruits are said to be *new and old*. This speaks to us of the blessing of the Lord in harvest. What promise did the Lord give to Israel if they would love Him and serve Him only? (Lev. 26:4-5, 10)

_____

_____

_____

This speaks to us of the blessing of *continuous* harvest. One crop will not be completely eaten before the new crop is coming in. So it is with this maiden, for she has stored up fruits both new and old. While she is still ministering to and caring for *old* fruit that the Lord brought in during the first harvest — before they can get completely raised up to maturity and be sent forth themselves — the new fruit is coming in. The harvest is continuous and plentiful as she is a co-laborer with the Lord of the harvest.

NOTES

STUDY 33

HIS REDEMPTION PLAN

You who remind the Lord,
take no rest for yourselves;
And give Him no rest until He
establishes
And makes Jerusalem a praise
in the earth. —
Isa. 62:6b-7

In an earlier study (Study 30), those desiring spiritual growth and maturity asked what could be done for the little sister who had not matured. "What shall we do for her on the day that she is spoken for?"

1. What is His answer? (Song 8:9)

   _____

   _____

2. What are the qualifications for being a wall? (Jer. 15:19-21)
   a. _____
   b. _____

"If indeed she is totally committed unto Me and separated unto Me, if she is committed to a life of holiness and purity, to extracting the precious from the worthless, then there is ground upon which can be built a battlement or palace of silver. (Silver represents *redemption*.) Therefore, total redemption is available to her."

3. In what manner will she be built? (Isa. 54:11b-12)
   a. _____
   b. _____
   c. _____
   d. _____

"This description is like unto the description in Revelation 21 of the Holy City. If this little sister is totally committed and separated unto Me, perfecting holiness in the fear of God, then she can grow up in maturity and be one of mature bridal affection."

"We will lay her foundations with the presence of the revealed God and His anointing (the sapphire — a blue stone). We will make her battlements, her place of defense against the enemy, the precious blood of My passion (rubies). We will make her mind (gates) clear and pure as crystal, washed and renewed through the Word of God. Her entire wall, her life which she separated unto Me will be built with the wisdom and knowledge of God (precious stones)."

4. What else does God promise the little sister who is totally committed and separated unto Him in holiness? (Isa. 54:13-14, 17)
   a. _____
   b. _____
   c. _____
   d. _____
   e. _____

   _____

"But, if the little sister is a door, if indeed she is such a witness for Me that others may enter by her into the true knowledge of God, then we will baracade or enclose her with planks of cedar."

5. What did King Solomon build with cedar planks? (I Kings 6:15-18)

_____

Thus, the Lord says, we will build her into a Holy Temple for the Living God.

6. What was the cedar overlaid with? (I Kings 6:20-22)

_____

Gold represents *the divine nature*. If indeed she is a door of life that others may enter in to find the rest of God, then she will be built into a temple for the living God and will be overlaid with pure gold. The Lord will completely transform her appearance into that of the divine nature, for she will bear His likeness and His image before the world.

7. What will the Lord do for her? (II Cor. 3:18)

_____

8. As the Bride, the maiden of our Song, speaks what did she say about herself? (Song 8:10)

_____

_____

She views herself as one who is totally separated unto Him, as one who extracts the precious from the vile, and as one who is totally committed to holiness. For indeed her Master has said, "Be ye holy for I am holy."

Her testimony concerning her breasts was that she was one who had grown to full maturity, able to satisfy the Lord's heart with full bridal affections, and able to feed others spiritually. Her faith and love, righteousness and judgment had grown to maturity, thus causing her to move in the revelations and perfections of her master. Her breasts had become like towers, and were a place of refuge and strength against the enemy. The Lord had built up these virtues and strongly established her. Thus she had become as one who had found favor in His eyes and had entered into a walk of peace that comes from having that perfect love toward God.

9. As she has become a lover of the Word of God, what fruit has she reaped from it? (Ps. 119:165)

_____

10. As she has matured in righteousness (knowing that she is in right standing with God, as indicated by her breasts), what work has been accomplished in her life and consequently where does she dwell? (Isa. 32:17-18)

_____

_____

11. Solomon had a vineyard which he entrusted to caretakers. What was he supposed to receive for its fruit? (Song 8:11)

_____

The number 1,000 is 10 x 10 x 10

10 = fulness of testing

3 = completion of God

Silver = redemption

Therefore, through the fulness of testing, God will complete His redemption plan. The caretakers of His vineyard will pay Him the fruit that is produced from a mature life. As they labor together with Him, they will perfect the saints for the work of the ministry until they grow up into the knowledge of the Son of God, the unity of the faith, unto that perfect man, unto the measure of the stature of the fulness of Christ. The Lord, the husband-man, waits patiently for the precious fruit of the earth to be gathered in and to come to maturity. Blessed is that slave whom the Master finds so doing when He comes.

Solomon's vineyard was at Baalhamon. The name means *Lord of a multitude* and represents a type of Jesus who is the Lord of many servants. The fruit of the vineyard represents increase from the Lord. Some sow, some water, but it is God who gives the increase. As we are faithful to labor in the vineyard, it will yield the increase of the fruits. What is done for Him is never in vain. Even the giving of a cup of cold water shall have its reward. The 1,000 pieces of silver represent the bringing of those whom the caretakers labor among to full maturity. This is the payment that is due the Lord. It is the minimum requirement.

12. The Bridal soul is now singled out of the company of many, having her own vineyard which is at her disposal to labor in as she pleases. What was she able to produce as she labored together with Him? (Song 8:12)

    a. _____

    b. _____

We find from this that the maiden's labor not only yields fruit unto Jesus her King, but also blesses and prospers those who surround her. Her labor is not unto herself and her Lord alone, but as it is written by the prophet Isaiah, "I and the children you have given me are for signs and wonders in the earth" (Isa. 8:18). So it is with our maiden and the children that the Lord has given her.

In the beginning of our Song, our maiden was told that, if she desired to enter into a life of mature bridal affection, she should "go forth in the trail of the flock, and pasture your young goats by the tents of the shepherds." (Song 1:8) As she has gone forth into maturity of love and affection toward the Lord, walking in the footsteps of His righteous ones, she has not walked alone. She has brought with her the young goats and kids, the spiritual children which the Lord has given her.

We find the maiden and her kids at the end of the Song laboring together with the Lord in His vineyard. She has taken what the Lord has given her, imparted it to them, and raised them up also as a mature one who was capable of full bridal affections, able to satisfy the Lord's heart, and able to take care of God's vineyards themselves.

Therefore, she can say to Him, "See Solomon, my King of Peace, here is your 1,000 shekels of silver; here are mature ones in your image that I have produced for you as I have been a vessel for your divine life to flow through. And for my kids who are with me, I have given them 200."

The number 200 = 5 x 40

5 = number of grace

40 = number of deliverance, rest and enlarged dominion (Judges 3:11; Judges 8:28; II Sam. 5:4; I Kings 11:42)

She is saying, "By your grace, my King, I have brought the children which you have given me into a place of great deliverance, rest, and enlarged dominion."

13. As our maiden has hungered and thirsted after righteousness, what has God done for her? (Isa. 44:3-5)

    _____
    _____

14. The Bridegroom now speaks to all those who are Bridal souls. What does He say to them? (Song 8:13)

    _____
    _____

15. We see a picture of this in the story of Peter and Cornelius the Gentile. Why did God send Peter to the house of Cornelius? (Acts 10:30-33)

    _____

Cornelius had a heart cry to know God. When Peter arrived at his house, Cornelius had many Gentiles assembled to hear everything that God had commanded Peter to speak. "My companions are listening, waiting and watching to hear your voice, and to give them the words of this life. Go forth says the Bridegroom, "Open your mouth and I will fill it, for I have reserved for Myself 7,000 men who have not bowed their knee to Baal. I have many Cornelius' of this world who fear Me, who are My companions, who are waiting to hear the words of God more perfectly. My companions are listening, waiting for your voice. Let Me hear it!"

Rise up, O men of God!
Have done with lesser things;
Give heart and mind and soul and strength
To serve the King of Kings.

Rise up, O men of God!
His Kingdom tarries long;
Bring in the day of brotherhood
And end the night of wrong.

Rise up, O men of God!
The Church for you doth wait,
Her strength unequal to her task;
Rise up, and make her great! —

William Merrill, 1867-1954

NOTES

STUDY 34

HIS BRIDE HAS MADE
HERSELF READY

*Let us rejoice and be glad and give glory
to Him, for the marriage of the Lamb has come
and His bride has made herself ready! —
Rev. 19:7*

1. As our Song closes, our Bride speaks her heart's desire to her Bridegroom. What is her heart cry? (Song 8:14)

   _____

   _____

   In the young stag or gazelle, we again see Jesus in the power of His resurrection life. Her heart cry joins the cry of all the redeemed of the ages: "Come Lord Jesus, that the kingdoms of the world may become the kingdoms of our God and of His anointed Christ." (Mountains of spices)

2. We find this cry going forth from the book of Job which is the oldest book of the Bible. What is Job's heart cry? (Job 19:25-27)

   _____

   _____

   _____

3. What was the cry of Moses? (Ex. 33:18)

   _____

4. What is David's heart cry? (Ps. 42:1-2)

   _____

   _____

5. What did Enoch, the seventh generation from Adam, prophesy? (Jude 14)

   _____

6. What did Daniel see? (Dan. 7:13-14, 27)

   _____

   _____

   The heavens do not remain silent in regards to His coming and of this great union of Christ and His Bride. For as we have discussed earlier, they too are telling of the glory of God.

7. We find a glorious picture of the sun of righteousness who comes forth as that glorious Bridegroom. Give that description. (Ps. 19:1-6)

   _____

   _____

This is a magnificent picture of the heavenly Bridegroom, glowing under His wedding canopy, as the illustrious and glorious Son of God ready for His revelation. In the brightness of His appearing He shall go forth as a strong man in invincible energy to search and try the earth, revealing everything, testing everything, burning up everything which will exalt itself against Him who is *the King of Kings and Lord of Lords.*

Of His union with His Bride, we find this great event foretold in a beautiful star picture of the constellation Gemini.

Gemini is a picture of two young and beautiful figures sitting peacefully together. The one is a male figure with a club in his right hand while his left hand is clasped around the body of his companion. The female figure holds a harp in one hand and a bow and arrow in the other. Their heads lean against each other in a loving attitude and appear to be in joyful repose after a great victory has been gained. The word *Gemini* in the original Hebrew, Arabic, and Syriac gives the idea of *something completed*, as a year comes to completion or as a long bethrothal brought to its consummation in perfected marriage. The old Coptic name of this sign signifies *the united, the completely joined*.

In the left foot of the male figure shines a star named *Al Henah*, meaning *the hurt* or *the wounded*. This refers to him whose heel was bruised by the serpent. The principal star in his head is called *Pollux*, meaning *the ruler*, or *the judge*. The figure holds in his right hand the great club of power, as the One who bruises the serpent's head and shatters all the power of evil. The Egyptians call him *Hor* or *the Coming One: the One who slays the serpent and recovers the dominion*.

In the head of the female figure which he is embracing is a star called *Castor* and *Appollo*, meaning *the coming ruler or judge — born of the light*. It is she who destroys the wicked, who repels evil and who has the Spirit of prophecy and sacred song, which is indicated by the harp. She is said to be the one who protects and keeps the flocks, and the one who delights in establishing cities, kingdoms, and seated rule and order among men.

The two figures of this constellation are joined together in oneness. They are two and yet they are one. They are as *twins*, which the constellation is sometimes called, in the fact that they are born of one Father and bear the very same image and likeness. It is not the one by Himself in either case, but it is Christ with His Church, His Bride — who will sit together as that *one-ruling manchild* under whom the whole earth shall be delivered from the oppression and evil of that wicked one. It is under their rule that the eternal Kingdom will come and the entire world will enjoy its unending Sabbath.

We will look at one more star picture. This is one which pictures the Bride of Christ enthroned and is called *Cassiopeia*. The figure is that of a queenly woman, matchless in beauty and exalted dignity. In one hand she holds aloft the branch of victory and triumph and at the same time spreads and arranges her hair. With the other hand she arranges her garments as if for some great public appearance. Her name means *the beautiful*, or *the glorified woman*. The star that appears in her left breast, over her heart is called *Shedar*, which means *the freed*. The next star which appears in the top of her chair bears the Hebrew name *Caph*, which means *the branch*, corresponding with Isaiah's prophecy; "In that day the branch of the Lord will be beautiful and glorious." (Isa. 4:2) As she arranges her hair and her garments she is making herself ready for her glorious appearing as the Bride, the Wife of the Lamb. (For more information of these and other star pictures we would refer you to *The Gospel in the Stars* by Joseph A. Seiss, Kregel Publications.)

8. What did John see? (Rev. 19:6-8)

_____

9. What had the Bride done? (Rev. 19:7)

_____

Clothed in fine linen, bright and clean — without spot or wrinkle — the Bride, the Wife of the Lamb, had made herself ready. She had extracted the precious from the vile and submitted every spot in her life to the washing of the water of the Word. She had diligently given her mind to meditating on the Word day and night. She had kept it from everything that would defile it, therefore, she had become as clear as crystal and as transparent as glass.

She had kept herself with undistracted devotion to the Lord so that she might be holy and chaste in body and spirit for her heavenly Bridegroom. All her strength and energies had been spent for Him and for His Kingdom. For she knew her destiny: to become His wife, bone of His bone and flesh of His flesh. She knew she was to be the tabernacle of God, that He might dwell through her among men. She knew that all nations would walk in the light given through that Bride city and through that city partake of the Tree of Life whose leaves will bring healing for the nations.

She had given her life to Him as a living and holy sacrifice. She had denied herself, she had given her all. Yet, as Paul, she counted all things lost as dung for the great privilege of knowing and loving Him.

Because her heart was solely anchored in Him there her treasure was also. Therefore, she can be satisfied with nothing else than to be one with Him throughout eternity. On that great day when her Lord and Savior descends from heaven with a shout, with the voice of the archangel and the trumpet of God, when those who have gone before her and have attained to the resurrection of the dead arise to new life, she who has *prepared* herself will go out to greet them, receiving as her prize her resurrection body. She will reach out with the Bridal souls of all ages and take the hand of the One Who Inhabits Eternity, as His lovely Bride, the Wife of the Lamb. Her joy will know no bounds and His heart will be satisfied. Through endless ages they will grow together in that oneness and union as the two become one flesh. The mystical union of Christ and His Bride will be finished, for it will forever after be openly, formally, and most gloriously shown and exhibited throughout eternity before the eyes of all living. Thrones will be set up and she will reign with her glorious King upon the earth and in His Kingdom forever.

The Spirit and the Bride say, "Come."
He who testifies to these things says,
"Yes, I am coming quickly."
Even so, come Lord Jesus. —
Rev. 22:17, 20

The Church's one foundation is
Jesus Christ her Lord;
She is His New Creation,
By water and the Word;
From heaven He came and sought her
to be His Holy Bride;
With His own blood He bought her,
And for her life He died.

Elect from every nation,
Yet one o'er all the earth,
Her charter of salvation,
One Lord, one faith, one birth;
One Holy Name she blesses,
Partakes one holy food,
And to one goal she presses,
With every grace endued.

'Mid toil and tribulation
tumult of her war,
She waits the consummation,
of glorious peace forevermore;
Till with the vision glorious
Her longing eyes are blest,
And the great Church victorious
Will be the Church at rest.

Yet she on earth hath union
with God the Three in One,
And mystic sweet communion with
those whose rest is won:
O happy ones and holy!
Lord, give us grace that we,
Like them the meek and lowly,
On high may dwell with Thee.

— Samuel J. Stone
(1839-1900)

179.

ANSWERS

"Who is like the wise man and who
knows the interpretation of a matter?
A man's wisdom illumines him and
causes his stern face to beam."

(Ecclesiates 8:1)

STUDY 1

A SONG OF LOVE—
A SONG OF DESIRE

Correct Answers

1. The Song of Songs.
2. The 144,000 (those who overcome).
3. a. They have not been defiled with women, for they are celibates (separated from the harlot system).
   b. They follow the Lamb wherever He goes.
   c. They are first fruits to God and to the Lamb.
   d. No lie was found in their mouth.
   e. They are blameless.
4. He takes the poor and needy, lifts them from the dust and ash heaps, and makes them sit with nobles and inherit the throne.
5. May he kiss me with the kisses of his mouth—a desire for personal affection from the Lord.
6. a. Pray that the Father will give you a spirit of wisdom and of revelation in the knowledge of Him.
   b. Pray that the eyes of your heart would be enlightened to know the hope of His calling.
   c. Pray to know the riches of the glory of His inheritance in the saints.
   d. Pray to know the surpassing greatness of His power toward us who believe.
7. It is better than wine.
8. a. Your oils have a pleasing fragrance.
   b. Your name is like purified oil.
9. a. He emptied Himself.
   b. He humbled Himself by becoming obedient to the point of death.
   c. God highly exalted Him, and bestowed on Him the name above every name.
   d. At that name every knee shall bow, and every tongue confess that Jesus is Lord.
10. Draw me after you.
11. a. He draws us with love.
    b. He lifts the yoke of bondage from us.
    c. He feeds us (personally).
12. He brings her into His chambers.
13. King.
14. They rejoiced and were glad.
15. Rightly—because of who He is.
16. a. Love from a pure heart.
    b. A good conscience.
    c. A sincere faith.

STUDY 2

THE REVELATIONS IN THE
KING'S CHAMBERS

Correct Answers

1. I am black.
2. a. I retract, and repent in dust and ashes.
   b. Woe is me, for I am ruined!
3. She is lovely.
4. a. He counted all things (in his soul life) to be rubbish.
   b. He experienced the righteousness of God.
5. a. Through the obedience of Jesus.
   b. To the extent that the sin nature has reigned in man, God's nature will reign.
6. a. Like the tents of Kedar.
   b. Like the curtains of Solomon.
7. The righteous acts of the saints.
8. By faith.
9. The light of the moon will be as the light of the sun.
10. Do not stare at me for the sun has burned me.
11. In order to be Jesus' disciple we must hate our soul life.
12. a. Caught up in works (caretaker of the vineyards).
    b. Neglected her own personal relationship with the Lord.
13. a. Mary sat at Jesus' feet listening to His Word.
    b. Martha was distracted with much service.
14. Only a few things are necessary, really only one.
15. These things you should have done without neglecting the others.
16. Those who are born again.
17. They were walking according to the flesh.
18. Where do you pasture your flock, where do you make it lie down at noon?
19. Like the light of dawn that shines brighter and brighter until the full day.
20. Total victory—brighter than noonday.
21. Fellowship with His Son.
22. They were rebuked for following after men.
23. She did not want the hardness of mind or heart, but an openness to receive revelation.
24. a. Go forth on the trail of the flock.
    b. Pasture your young goats by the tents of the shepherds.
25. a. Imitate those who through faith and patience inherit the promises.
    b. Imitate the faith of those who led you and spoke the Word of God to you.
    c. Follow in Christ's steps.
26. The five-fold ministry.
27. a. Those for whom you are responsible.
    b. Feed them and bring them by the shepherd's tents.
28. Most beautiful among women.
29. One that worships Him in spirit and truth.
30. He will love her and disclose Himself to her.

STUDY 3

THE BANQUETING HOUSE

Correct Answers

1. Like his mare among the chariots of Pharoah.
2. We are to seize the Kingdom by force, as a precious prize, with most ardent zeal and intense exertion.
3. a. Warhorse, full of the strength of the Lord.
   b. He laughs at fear.
   c. He does not turn back from the sword.
   d. He does not stand still at the voice of the trumpet.
   e. He scents (discerns) the battle and knows the war cry.
4. Chariots of Pharaoh, ornaments, strings of beads.
5. Ornaments of gold and beads of silver.
6. God will perform His Word.
7. The King at His table.
8. An openness.
9. Much bread and strong meat.
10. a. Accustomed to the word of righteousness.
    b. Not a babe.
    c. Mature.
    d. Has senses trained to discern good and evil because of practice.
11. Her perfume gave forth its fragrance.
12. Mary anointed Jesus with spikenard.
13. They become the joy and delight of your heart.
14. a. Shouting for joy.
    b. Radiant.
    c. Their life will be like a watered garden.
    d. Rejoice in the dance.
    e. Soul will be filled with abundance.
15. He is to her a pouch of myrrh.
16. 1. Total death to self.
    2. Divine promises, escaping the corruption in the world.
    3. Washing of the water of the Word.
    4. The yoke will be broken by the anointing.
    5. The Word brings health.
    6. Manifests a sweet aroma of the knowledge of Him.

STUDY 4

JESUS, LOVER OF MY SOUL

Correct Answers

1. A cluster of henna blossoms in the vineyards of Engedi.
2. How beautiful you are! Your eyes are like dove s.
3.   a. When your eye is clear (single) your whole body is full of light.
     b. Watch out that the light in you may not be darkness.
     c. You shall be wholly illumined.
4. We shall have the light of life.
5. How handsome you are, and so pleasant.
6. It is green and leafy (fresh, full of vigor and prosperity, and flourishing).
7.   a. The righteous will flourish like the green leaf.
     b. Like a tree whose leaves are green.
8. Makes them lie down in green pastures.
9. The beams are cedars, the rafters cypresses.
10.   1. The saints will dwell in high spiritual places. They will see the King and behold things afar off.
     2. The saints will take root and grow.
     3. The saints are going from strength to strength.
     4. The saints will be full of sap (life) and yield fruit. Nations shall be governed by the saints.
     5. We are being built together into a dwelling of God.
11. I am crucified with Christ; the life I now live, I live by faith in the Son of God.
12. The members of the Body of Christ fitly joined together.

THE OVERPOWERING LOVE OF GOD

Correct Answers

1. I am the rose of Sharon, the lily of the valleys.
2. She is a lily among thorns.
3. The cursed earth.
4. 1. We are a sweet aroma of Christ in every place.
   2. Righteousness and purity of the saints.
   3. The whole earth will be filled with fruit—His glory, knowledge and kingdom.
   4. The Kingdom of God will be exalted above all.
   5. The King's daughter is all glorious within.
5. Like an apple tree among the trees of the forest.
6. a. You will pray to Him, and He will hear you.
   b. You will decree a thing and it will be established.
   c. Light will shine on your ways.
   d. When you are cast down, you will speak with confidence.
7. Like a word spoken in right circumstances.
8. We will be able to sustain a weary one with a word.
9. a. Protection from natural circumstances.
   b. Protection from all evil.
   c. He will keep your soul.
   d. He will guard your going out and your coming in.
10. A revelation of His love.
11. The friendship of God.
12. To be strengthened.
13. He fell at His feet as a dead man.
14. We cannot bear them now.
15. Let His left hand be under my head and His right hand embrace me.
16. The will of God in action, in judgment against the devil, his angels, and the wicked.
17. All principalities and powers.
18. It signifies the will of God in action, in exaltation and favor. The right hand of God, the right hand of the throne, etc., speaks of the seat of honor in the Messianic Kingdom.
19. His one desire was to behold the Lord. His soul thirsted for God, even the depths of his soul. He longed for God's presence above all else.
20. Rest.

STUDY 6

THE CALL TO ESCAPE FROM SELF
AND ENTER INTO THE
RESURRECTION POWER OF THE LAMB

Correct Answers

1. Like a gazelle or a young stag.
2. Climbing on the mountains, leaping on the hills.
3. Your God reigns.
4. Arise and come along.
5. a. Set her on high places.
   b. Train her hands for battle.
   c. Give her the shield of Thy salvation.
   d. Enlarge her steps.
   e. Cause her to pursue and destroy the enemy.
6. She will see great miracles and deliverances. There will be liberty and victory all about.
7. A wall.
8. The groaning of the prisoner, those who were doomed to death.
9. At the last, the Redeemer will take His stand on the earth, and we shall see Him.
10. They will be the deliverers to set the creation free.
11. a. Look out for the interests of others, and not merely your own personal interests.
    b. Have the attitude that was in Christ Jesus who emptied Himself.
    c. Do not expect to be served, but serve, and give your life a ransom for many.
12. By Him we can leap over a wall.
13. He wants to teach her to be a fisher of men. She should immediately follow.
14. His presence is always with us.
15. Winter.
16. She has been rooted and grounded in His love.
17. Spring, it is fruitful.
18. Not seeking your own ways, but doing the will of God.
19. Making a lot of plans.
20. a. Trained for war.
    b. Could handle shield and spear.
    c. Faces like the faces of lions.
    d. As swift as the gazelles on the mountains.
21. There is a time for everything.

JESUS, THE ROCK OF MY SALVATION

Correct Answers

1. The shortness of man's life.
2. It speaks of tests and trials that must be endured in order to bring forth more fruit.
3. a. When the fig tree puts forth its leaves, summer (the end) is near.
   b. All things must be restored which were spoken of by the prophets.
4. No.
5. Dove.
6. God calls into being that which doesn't exist. He sees us through eyes of faith, seeing what we will become.
7. In the clefts of the rock.
8. Jesus.
9. The crucifixion of Jesus.
10. Being conformed to His death.
11. 1. Nothing can shake those who have been built on the rock.
    2. God is our dwelling place as we abide in love.
    3. We are seated with Christ in heavenly places and are to seek the things above.
    4. Spiritual vision.
    5. A refuge and defense.
    6. Jesus is the same yesterday, today and forever.
    7. The Word.
    8. In Christ are hidden all the treasures of wisdom and knowledge.
    9. The oil of the Spirit.
    10. The river of the water of life.
    11. We must allow God to break us, or else we will be crushed.

STUDY 8

THE CALL TO INTIMATE FELLOWSHIP

Correct Answers

1. In the secret place of the steep pathway.
2. On a great and high mountain.
3. We see the Lord standing at the top of the ladder with the promise of inheritance.
4. We see a picture here of the mind of man facing the mind of Christ. There must be an ascending of the stairs before the mind (gate) can be measured by the measurement of God and be found in His image.
5. a. Fear God.
   b. Through wisdom and balance (two sides).
   c. Understanding parables.
   d. Revelation knowledge.
6. The little foxes that are ruining the vineyards.
7. Foolishness, pride, spreading strife and slander, or backbiting, anger, laziness, and answering too quickly.
8. Listen to counsel and accept discipline and rebuke.
9. She sees God primarily as belonging to her, rather than her being possessed by Him.
10. Among the lilies.
11. She wants to remain separate.
12. Because of disobedience He does not communicate with her.
13. Seeking the Lord.
14. a. As you give yourself to others, your light will rise in darkness.
    b. The Lord will continually guide you.
    c. You will be like a watered garden.
15. She is being tried.
16. Arise and go.
17. The watchmen.
18. To warn the people; to hear the message of the Lord and give it.
19. Obey the watchmen.
20. She finds Him.
21. She has gone through discipline and testing, which produced endurance.
22. The crown of life.

STUDY 9

TRANSFIGURATION, A LIFE OF INTIMATE UNION

Correct Answers

1. A renewed hope and joy.
2. Husband instead of a master.
3. From the wilderness.
4. He came out in the power of the Spirit.
5. They were destoyed.
6. No. Their children did.
7. Columns of smoke.
8. a. God's presence was manifested in a pillar of cloud.
   b. The outpouring of the Spirit.
   c. All scented powders of the merchant.
9. a. Myrrh.
   b. Frankincense.
   c. All scented powders of the merchant.
10. The intercessory prayer life of the priest.
11. Selling all for the Kingdom of God.
12. The traveling couch of Solomon.
13. The Son of Man has nowhere to lay His head.
14. Sixty.
15. a. Mighty men of Israel.
    b. Wielders of the sword.
    c. Expert in war.
16. a. From the timber of Lebanon.
    b. Posts of silver.
    c. Back (support) of gold.
    d. Seat of purple fabric.
    e. Interior lovingly fitted out by the daughters of Jerusalem.
17. The Body being fitly joined together.
18. Wedding day, the day of His gladness of heart.
19. Divine union with the King.

STUDY 10

BEAUTY OF THE NEW CREATION

Correct Answers

I. THE EYES

1. Your eyes are like doves behind your veil.
2. a. That God may give you a spirit of wisdom and revelation in the knowledge of Him.
   b. That the eyes of your heart may be enlightened to know the hope of His calling, the riches of the glory of His inheritance and the greatness of His power toward us.
3. He has blinded the minds of the unbelieving that they may not see the light of the gospel of the glory of God.
4. Leah's eyes were weak.
5. She was beautiful of form and face. Jacob loved her more than Leah.
6. By being accustomed to the word of righteousness, and practicing it, partaking of the *solid food* or *strong meat* of the Word.
7. A plumb line.
8. A plumb line with seven eyes on the plummet stone which are the seven eyes of the Lord that run to and fro across the earth.
9. 1. Spirit of wisdom.
   2. Spirit of understanding.
   3. Spirit of counsel.
   4. Spirit of strength.
   5. Spirit of knowledge.
   6. The fear of the Lord.
   7. Quick understanding.
10. They were full of eyes.

II. THE HAIR

1. Your hair is like a flock of goats that have descended from Mount Gilead.
2. The hair signifies separation unto God.
3. His strength left him and he became like any other man.
4. a. Burnt offerings.
   b. Peace offerings.
5. The eyes of the Lord run to and fro throughout the earth that He may strongly support those whose heart is completely His.
6. For the curtains for the tent over the tabernacle.
7. "Behold, the tabernacle of God is among men."

III. THE TEETH

1. Like a flock of newly shorn ewes which have come up from the washing, all of which bear twins.
2. Those who are accustomed to the word of righteousness, those who are mature, and those who, because of practice, have their senses trained to discern good and evil.
3. The washing of the water of the Word.
4. These *ewes* have been newly shorn of their wool.
5. Wool suggests the earthly life that the Lord has cursed.
6. The *twins* represent *balance*, for sound wisdom has two sides.
7. She received wisdom, very great discernment and breadth of mind like the sand that is on the seashore.

IV. THE LIPS

1. The lips are like a scarlet thread and the mouth is lovely.
2. We find the scarlet thread mentioned in the story of Rahab. The thread brought redemption to Rahab and her household.
3. a. Preaching the gospel.
   b. Announcing salvation and peace.
   c. Saying to Zion, "Your God reigns."
   d. Shouting joyfully.

4. They have flattering lips and a tongue speaking great things. Their lips are their own and they do not submit to the Lordship of Jesus.
5. She speaks the Words of the Lord. They are pure Words as silver tried in a furnace on the earth, refined seven times.
6. No lie was found in their mouth; they are blameless.
7. If any man does not stumble in what he says, he is a perfect man and able to bridle the whole body.

V. THE TEMPLES
1. Your temples are like a slice of a pomegranate behind your veil.
2. He desires the meditation of his heart to be acceptable in God's sight. He desires that God would search his heart and try his thoughts to reveal any hurtful thing.
3. Pomegranates.
4. A pillar in the temple of God.
5. The weapons of her warfare are not of the flesh but divinely powerful for the destruction of fortresses.
   a. Destroying speculations.
   b. Destroying every lofty thing raised up against the knowledge of God.
   c. Taking every thought captive to the obedience of Christ.

VI. THE NECK
1. The neck is like the tower of David built with rows of stones, on which are hung a thousand shields — all the round shields of the mighty men.
3. They are obstinate and their neck is an iron sinew.
2. It suggests strength against the enemy.
4. David was a man after God's own heart whose will was to do *all* God's will.
5. The former dominion (which Adam lost) will come to you, O tower of the flock.
6. Shields.
7. The shield of faith, which is able to extinguish all the flaming missiles of the evil one.
8. a. Mighty men of valor.
   b. Trained for war.
   c. Who could handle shield and spear.
   d. Whose faces were like the faces of lions.
   e. Who were as swift as the gazelles on the mountains.
9. a. By faith they conquered kingdoms.
   b. Performed acts of righteousness.
   c. Obtained promises.
   d. Shut the mouths of lions.
   e. Quenched the power of fire.
   f. Escaped the edge of the sword.
   g. From weakness were made strong.
   h. Became mighty in war.
   i. Put foreign armies to flight.
   j. Were persecuted, tortured and martyred.
   k. Men of whom the world was not worthy.
10. Be not sluggish, but imitators of those who through faith and patience inherit the promises.

VII. THE BREASTS
1. Your two breasts are like two fawns, twins of a gazelle, which feed among the lilies.
2. The breastplate of faith and love.
3. The breastplate of righteousness and judgment.
4. A skillful workman.
5. We must be exercised in the word of righteousness, having our senses trained to discern good and evil.
6. The Urim and the Thummim were used to judge the sons of Israel and to inquire before the Lord.
7. a. That you may receive a spirit of wisdom and revelation in the knowledge of Him.
   b. That the eyes of your heart may be enlightened.
8. That you may know:
   a. What is the hope of His calling.
   b. What are the riches of the glory of His inheritance in the saints.
   c. What is the surpassing greatness of His power toward us who believe.

9. Order on order, order on order, line on line, line on line, a little here—a little there.
10. A mature or perfect man; the measure of the stature which belongs to the fulness of Christ.
11. It is through the washing of the water of the Word (revelation knowledge) that we are perfected. The Word of God divides our soul and spirit and judges the thoughts and intents of our heart.
12. a. They were tried and refined, went through fire and water, were oppressed, purified as gold and silver.

    b. They were brought out into a place of abundance and were tried so that they might offer to God offerings of righteousness.
13. You are to be perfect as your Father in heaven is perfect.
14. They are feeding among the lilies.
15. They are being fed by the apostles, prophets, evangelists, pastors and teachers and are being built together with the rest of the joints (members of the body), being built into maturity.

STUDY 11

THE DESIRE OF THE KING

Correct Answers

1. To the mountain of myrrh, and to the hill of frankincense.
2. She must always carry about in her body the dying of Jesus, that His life might be manifested.
3. a. The power of His resurrection.
   b. The fellowship of His sufferings.
   c. Being conformed to His death.
4. Are you able to drink the cup that I drink, or to be baptized with the baptism with which I am baptized?
5. To come with Him to the mountains.
6. The dens of lions and the mountains of leopards.
7. Our struggle is against the rulers, the powers, the world forces of this darkness, against the spiritua forces of wickedness in the heavenly places.
8. Position: In the high places.
   Preparation:
   a. He trains my hands for battle.
   b. Gives me the shield of salvation.
   c. Upholds me with His right hand.
   d. His gentleness makes me great.
   e. He enlarges my steps.
   Source of strength: The Lord girds me with strength.
   Purpose and result:
   a. The enemy is subdued.
   b. The enemy is turned back and destroyed.
9. My bride.
10. He is one spirit with Him.
11. a. I have many more things to say to you, but you cannot bear them now.
    b. You were not able to receive solid food because you were fleshly, babes in Christ.
12. My sister.
13. Both He who sanctifies and those who are sanctified are all from one Father.
14. Made it beat faster.
15. a. A single glance of her eyes.
    b. A single strand of her necklace.
16. He went outside and wept bitterly.
17. When your eye is clear, your whole body also is full of light.
18. Through meditating on the Word.
19. Keeping the Word of God.
20. It is better than wine.
21. The queen in gold from Ophir.
22. a. She has forgotten her people.
    b. She has forgotten her father's house.
23. The fragrance of her oils is better than all kinds of spices.
24. Manifest the sweet aroma of Him in every place.
25. a. You will be a crown of beauty in the hand of the Lord.
    b. You will be a royal diadem in the hand of your God.
    c. The Lord delights in you.
    d. As the bridegroom rejoices over the bride, so your God will rejoice over you.
26. Your lips drip honey; honey and milk are under your tongue.
27. Wisdom.
28. She listened to His voice and walked in His ways.
29. Their fragrance is like the fragrance of Lebanon.
30. The believer has grown and flourished, bearing fruit.

STUDY 12

THE GARDEN OF THE LORD

Correct Answers

1. A rock garden locked, a spring sealed up.
2. He has comforted her waste places, making her wilderness like Eden, her desert like the garden of the Lord.
3. Every open vessel which has no covering tied down upon it shall be unclean.
4. She has kept herself from worldliness. God jealously desires the Spirit which He has made to dwell in us; He jealously desires her for Himself.
5. A *stone heap* signifies an altar on which sacrifice is made to God.
6. Burnt offerings and peace offerings were offered on it.
7. He walked in the garden and called to Adam, desiring his fellowship.
8. a. An orchard of pomegranates.
    b. Choice fruits.
    c. Henna with nard plants.
    d. Nard and saffron.
    e. Calamus and cinnamon.
    f. All the trees of frankincense.
    g. Myrrh and aloes.
    h. All the finest spices.
9. By dwelling upon God's Word day and night, keeping and speaking His Word.
10. a. Wiser than her enemies.
    b. More insight than all her teachers.
    c. More understanding than the aged.
11. This is a reference to the fruit of the Spirit and being fruitful unto every good work.
12. She used the expression to describe the King.
13. Beholding the glory of the Lord, she is being transformed into the same image.
14. While the King was at His table her perfume, or nard, gave forth its fragrance.
15. She anointed Jesus' feet with spikenard ointment and wiped His feet with her hair.
16. Cinnamon and the finest spices were components of the holy anointing oil.
17. The holy anointing oil was used to anoint the place where God would meet with man and make it holy, and to anoint Aaron and his sons that they might minister unto the Lord.
18. Frankincense was used to make the *priestly incense.*
19. It was offered with the prayers of the saints.
20. Frankincense represents praise and thanksgiving.
21. It was placed on the grain offering.
22. A life of praise and thanksgiving pouring out from the sons of the kingdom unto the Lord of hosts.
23. a. A new song.
    b. Rejoicing and being glad in Him.
    c. Dancing.
    d. Playing of the timbrel and lyre.
    e. Singing for joy on your bed.
    f. High praises.
24. The King's garments smell of myrrh and aloes.
25. He was anointed with *myrrh and aloes.*
26. Jesus' death was an external manifestation of His love.
27. By enduring trials and persecutions for being a Christian, being reviled for His name and rejoicing with exultation.
28. They were flogged for their testimony, persecuted, slandered, were considered the scum of the earth, yet went away rejoicing that they had been considered worthy to suffer shame for His name.
29. Love is as strong as death, many waters cannot quench love nor will rivers overflow it. If a man were to give all the riches of his house for love, he would be utterly despised.
30. The garden spring, the well of fresh water and streams flowing from Lebanon.
31. Rivers of living water are flowing from her inner most being, for the water that the Lord has given has become a well of fresh water which springs up to eternal life.

32. a. That the north and south wind might blow upon her garden that the fragrance may go out.
    b. That the Lord may come into His garden and eat its choice fruits.
33. The Spirit of God.
34. The negative and positive circumstances that the Spirit of God brings into your life.
35. Christ is exalted in your body.
36. The house was filled with the fragrance of the ointment.
37. Jesus.
38. "She has done a good deed to Me; for the poor you always have with you, but you do not always have Me."
39. Torches.
40. They blew the trumpets and broke the pitchers crying, "A sword for the Lord and for Gideon."
41. They came to life and stood on their feet, an exceedingly great army.
42. He will give life to our mortal bodies.
43. To have a life that is acceptable and well-pleasing unto the Lord.
44. He accepts.
45. That I might lay hold of that for which Christ has laid hold of me.
46. They must call.
47. We must call upon Him and come and pray to Him.
48. We must seek and search for Him with our whole heart.
49. He will be satisfied.
50. His friends, His lovers.
51. Those who have His commandments and keep them — those who do His will.
52. Giving His servants their rations or meat.
53. No.
54. A sealed spring.
55. It is sealed.
56. He rolled the stone from the mouth of the well and watered the flock of Labon, his mother's brother.
57. Those who do the will of God.
58. They shall be satisfied with God's goodness.
59. He desires to feed His sheep on good grazing ground and rich pasture, and to lead them to rest.
60. Feed His sheep.

STUDY 13

GETHSEMANE – THE FELLOWSHIP
OF HIS SUFFERINGS

Correct Answers

1. I was asleep but my heart was awake.
2. I am crucified with Christ, nevertheless I live. Yet not I, but Christ lives in me.
3. Her beloved.
4. a. My sheep hear My voice.
   b. I know them.
   c. They follow Me.
5. He asks her to open the door and let Him in.
6.

Title	Significance
a. My sister.	She did the will of God.
b. My darling.	She has become a letter of Christ in the earth – the very extension of His life.
c. My dove.	She was possessed by the Holy Spirit.
d. My perfect one.	She has been through the testing of her faith and has endured, inheriting God's promises.

7. My head is drenched with dew and my locks with the damp (drops) of the night.
8. Being in agony He was praying fervently and His sweat became like drops of blood, falling down upon the ground.
9. That this cup of suffering might pass from Him.
10. That not His will, but God's will be done.
11. Are you willing to drink the cup that I drink and to be baptized with the baptism I am to be baptized with?
12. We are – we will never forsake you.
13. They all left Him and fled.
14. Always carrying about in our body the dying of Jesus and constantly being delivered over to death, that the life of Jesus may be manifested in our mortal flesh.
15. a. I have taken off my dress, how can I put it on again?
    b. I have washed my feet, how can I dirty them again?
16. She has laid aside the old self and put on the new.
17. Complete cleansing.
18. Dominion.
19. Every place that the sole of your foot treads upon, I have given it to you.
20. a. For this purpose came I to this hour.
    b. Father, glorify Thy name.
21. She arose to open the door of her heart.
22. He cried out, "My Lord and my God."
23. He wept bitterly in repentance.
24. Liquid myrrh.
25. He has turned away.
26. The cup which the Father has given Me, shall I not drink it?
27. This hour and the power of darkness are yours; you would have no power over Me unless it was given to you from above.
28. They spat in His face, beat Him with their fists and slapped Him.

29. They struck her and wounded her.
30. Let him alone, if the Lord has allowed him to curse me, who am I to stop him?
31. The power of darkness.
32. Satan has demanded permission to sift you like wheat.
33. I have prayed for you, that your faith may not fail.
34. They would sit upon thrones in His kingdom judging the 12 tribes of Israel.
35. There is no one like him on the earth, a blameless and upright man, fearing God and turning away from evil.
36. If you take away everything that Job has, he will curse Thee to Thy face.
37. He gave Satan permission to take everything from Job, except for his life.
38. (v. 16) My soul is poured out within me and I am afflicted.
    (v. 18) The feeling of being bound or tied. It is difficult to accomplish much.
    (v. 20) Crying out to God for help, but there is no answer from Him.
    (v. 21) It is as if God has become cruel.
    (v. 24) The soul is in a heap of ruins.
    (v. 26) When I was expecting good, evil came, when I was expecting light, darkness came.
    (v. 27) Seething within, cannot relax.
    (v. 28) Mourning without comfort, crying out for help in the assembly.
    (v. 29) Dwelling in desert places (the habitation of jackals and ostriches).
    (v. 31) No ability to worship or commune with the Lord.
39. The dark is not dark to God, it only appears dark to us. Looking from God's perspective it is as bright as day, for there is nowhere that I can flee from His Spirit or His presence.
40. Whether I go forward or backward, I cannot perceive Him, to the right or the left, I cannot see Him. Yet, He knows the way I take, and when He has tried me. I shall come forth as gold.
41. My God, my God, why has thou forsaken me?
42. Perhaps the Lord will look upon my affliction and return good to me instead of His cursing this day.
43. a. There is no one I have or nothing I desire besides Thee.
    b. Though my flesh and my heart fail, God is the strength of my heart and my portion forever.
44. a. The Lord has given and the Lord has taken away, blessed be the name of the Lord.
    b. Through all of this Job did not sin nor did he blame God.
45. Who being reviled, did not revile in return.
46. We are to follow in His steps.
47. They took away her shawl or veil.
48. They stripped Him and mocked Him.
49. The Spirit of Glory and of God was resting upon her.
50. We are to have an unveiled face.
51. As the face of an angel.
52. They are a proof of our faith.
53. That we are to obtain an inheritance, which is to us a living hope.
54. The power of God through faith.
55. Tell my beloved that I am sick with love.

STUDY 14

THE KING OF GLORY

Correct Answers

1. a. Dazzling.
    b. Ruddy.
    c. Outstanding among ten thousand.
2. a. His face shone like the sun.
    b. His garments became as white as light.
3. A sun and shield.
4. Like the sunlight.
5. His face was like the sun shining in its strength.
6. Jesus.
7. The Ancient of Days.
8. a. Wonderful.
    b. Counselor.
    c. The Mighty God.
    d. The Eternal Father.
    e. The Prince of Peace.
9. a. To Him who loves Him and keeps His commandments.
    b. To those who diligently seek Him.
10. I am.
11. Before Abraham was born, I Am.
12. Face to face, as a man speaks to his friend.
13. He was faithful.
14. a. Like a jasper stone.
    b. Like a sardius stone.
15. The one who sits on the throne is the Alpha and the Omega, the first and the last.
16. a. The One who is.
    b. The One who was.
    c. The One who is to come.
    d. The Almighty.
17. a. The Living One.
    b. I was dead.
    c. I am alive forevermore.
    d. I have the keys of death and of Hades.

THE KING OF GLORY:
THE HEAD OF GOLD

Correct Answers

1. He is outstanding among 10,000.
2. As Moses lifted up the serpent in the wilderness, that whoever believes in Him may have eternal life.
3. The people were being bitten by firey serpents and were dying. He set a bronze serpent on a standard and whoever looked upon it lived according to the Word of the Lord.
4. Behold the Lord came with 10,000 of His Holy Ones.
5. a. (v. 12) His eyes are a flame of fire.
   b. (v. 12) Upon His head are many diadems.
   c. (v. 13) He is clothed with a robe dipped in blood.
   d. (v. 15) From His mouth came a sharp sword.
   e. (v. 16) On His robe and on His thigh is a name written "King of Kings and Lord of Lords."
6. The chariots of God.
7. a. As at Sinai.
   b. In holiness.
8. a. Thunder.
   b. Lightning flashes.
   c. A thick cloud.
   d. A very loud trumpet sound.
   e. Smoke of a furnace.
   f. Fire.
9. a. (v. 14) He was not living in sin and was not godless.
   b. (v. 15) He walked righteously.
   c. (v. 15) He spoke with sincerity.
   d. (v. 15) He rejected unjust gain.
   e. (v. 15) He would not take a bribe.
   f. (v. 15) He stopped his ears from hearing about bloodshed.
   g. (v. 15) He shut his eyes from looking upon evil.
10. a. (v. 16) He will dwell on the heights.
    b. (v. 16) His refuge will be the impregnable rock.
    c. (v. 16) His bread will be given to him.
    d. (v. 16) His water will be sure.
    e. (v. 17) His eyes will see the King in His beauty.
    f. (v. 17) He will be able to behold a far-distant land.
11. He head is like pure gold.
12. He is the image of God.
13. All the fulness of Diety dwells in Him in bodily form.
14. He is the head over all rule and authority.
15. He who has seen Me has seen the Father.
16. Many diadems.
17. a. A beautiful crown and a glorious diadem.
    b. A spirit of justice when sitting in judgment.
    c. A strength when repelling the onslaught at the gate.
18. That we will reign in life through Jesus.
19. Authority to tread on serpents and scorpions and over all the power of the enemy.
20. a. Christ's divine presence within preserves her from evil.
    b. The wicked one cannot touch her.
21. The sovereignty, the dominion, the greatness of all the kingdoms under the whole heaven.
22. By enduring with Jesus and standing by Him in His trials.
23. As sin has reigned in death, even so grace will reign through righteousness.
24. a. Not by what her eyes see.
    b. Not by what her ears hear.
    c. Judges with righteousness.
    d. Decides with fairness.

25. a. Wisdom.
    b. Discernment.
    c. Experience.
26. a. You must not show partiality in judgment.
    b. You must not fear man.
    c. The judgment is God's.
27. a. Loving God's law.
    b. Meditating on God's law all day.
    c. Observing God's precepts.
    d. Restraining your feet from every evil way.
    e. Hating every false way.
28. By practice.
29. He who rejects my sayings has one who judges him; the word I speak is what will judge him, for I did not speak on my own, but the Father has given me commandment what to say and what to speak.
30. Jesus Christ our Lord.
31. a. That the One with her is greater than he who is in the world.
    b. The Lord her God is with her to fight the battles.
32. a. Her light.
    b. Her salvation.
    c. The defense of her life.
33. a. My heart will not fear.
    b. In spite of this, I shall be confident.
34. He who is born of God.
35. Our faith.
36. Have faith in God, for whoever says to this mountain be taken up and cast into the sea and does not doubt in his heart but believes that what he says is going to happen, it shall be granted him.

STUDY 16

THE KING OF GLORY:
HIS HIDING PLACE, THE WATER OF LIFE,
HIS HUMILITY AND OBEDIENCE

Correct Answers

1. His locks are like clusters of dates and black as a raven.
2. Separation unto God.
3. a. Holy.
   b. Innocent.
   c. Undefiled.
   d. Separated from sinners.
   e. Exalted above the heavens.
4. He hides Himself.
5. So they would not perish.
6. Darkness, darkness of waters, thick clouds of the sky.
7. No man shall see the Lord.
8. That she might share His holiness.
9. The peaceful fruit of righteousness.
10. a. High.
    b. Holy.
    c. With the contrite.
    d. With the lowly of spirit.
11. a. Righteousness.
    b. The upright.
12. a. That he may not remain in darkness but have light.
    b. He will be given the treasures of darkness and the hidden wealth of secret places.
13. They are like doves beside streams of water, bathed in milk and reposed in their setting.
14. The righteous.
15. The majestic one, the Lord, has become for her a place of rivers and wide canals.
16. a. Water was trickling.
    b. Water reaching the ankles.
    c. Water reaching the knees.
    d. Water reaching the loins.
    e. Water enough to swim in, a river that could not be forded.
17. He who believes in Me, from his innermost being shall flow rivers of living water—this water will become a well of water springing up to eternal life.
18. a. They drink their fill of the abundance of thy house.
    b. They drink of the river of God's delight.
19. From the throne of God and of the Lamb.
20. They will be made glad.
21. She is a holy dwelling place of the most high. God is in the midst of her, she shall not be moved.
22. All thy breakers and thy waves have rolled over me.
23. His cheeks are like a bed of balsam and banks of sweet-scented herbs.
24. He gave His cheeks to those who pluck out the beard and did not cover His face from humiliation and spitting.
25. The Lord helps me therefore I am not disgraced and know that I shall not be ashamed.
26. He emptied Himself, took on the form of a bondservant and humbled Himself by becoming obedient to the point of death.
27. Arm yourselves with the same purpose.
28. a. He has ceased from sin.
    b. Living the rest of the time in the flesh not for the lusts of men but for the will of God.
29. a. He committed no sin.
    b. No deceit was found in His mouth.
    c. While being reviled, he did not revile in return.
    d. While suffering, he uttered no threats.
    e. He kept entrusting Himself to God who judges righteously.

STUDY 17

THE KING OF GLORY:
THE LIPS OF THE KING

Correct Answers

1. His lips are like lilies dripping with liquid myrrh.
2. a. Things which eye has not seen.
   b. Things which ear has not heard.
   c. Things which have not entered the heart of man.
3. God reveals them to us by His Spirit.
4. By combining spiritual thoughts with spiritual words.
5. a. It was not in the great strong wind which was rending the mountains and breaking the rock in pieces.
   b. It was not in the earthquake.
   c. It was not in the fire.
   d. It came to him as the sound of a gentle blowing.
6. Thy words were found and I did eat them and they were to me the joy and rejoicing of my heart.
7. He awakens my ear to listen as a disciple; He has opened my ear.
8. I was not disobedient nor did I turn back.
9. a. My heart stands in awe of Thy words.
   b. I rejoice at thy Word as one who finds great spoil.
10. a. He made him lie down in green pastures.
    b. He lead him beside quiet waters.
    c. He restored his soul.
    d. He guided him in paths of righteousness.
11. a. Powerful.
    b. Majestic.
    c. Breaks the cedars (breaks through the soul-life of His saints).
    d. Make Lebanon skip like a calf (causes one to rejoice in the dance).
    e. Hews out flames of fire (His word is like fire, purifying).
    f. It shakes the wilderness (shaking out everything from our lives that can be shaken).
    g. Makes the deer to calve (causes His people to reproduce spiritually).
    h. Strips the forest bare (lays bare the thoughts and intentions of the heart, stripping our souls of everything that is fleshly and worldly).
12. a. I have not departed from the command of His lips.
    b. I have treasured the words of His mouth more than my necessary food.
    c Habakkuk was listening, watching, as a watchman would guard a city at night, he was on the alert to see what God would speak to him.
13. A vision for the appointed time which he was to write down so that others would be instructed.
14. The capitals on top of the pillars were of lily work.
15. He that overcomes.
16. a. Five cubits.
    b. Molten bronze.
17. Wherever the Spirit was to go they went.
18. Those who are led by the Spirit of God.
19. The cast metal sea.
20. a. Ten cubits from brim to brim.
    b. Five cubits high.
    c. Thirty cubits in circumference.
21. It stood on twelve oxen, three facing north, three facing west, three facing south, three facing east with their rear parts turned inward.
22. The ministers of the gospel.
23. The preaching of the gospel to the ends of the earth.
24. He speaks the words of God and has the Spirit without measure.
25. Solomon in all his glory was not arrayed like one of these.
26. His wisdom.

27. a. Christ, Himself, in whom are hidden all the treasures of wisdom and knowledge.
   b. Potential to receive all the wealth that comes from the full assurance of understanding resulting in a true knowledge of God's mystery.

STUDY 18

THE KING OF GLORY:
HIS HANDS

Correct Answers

1. a. The unity of the faith.
    b. The knowledge of the son of God.
    c. A mature man.
    d. The measure of the stature which belongs to the fulness of Christ.
2. The fulness of Him who fills all in all.
3. His hands are rods of gold set with beryl.
4. He desires to rule from Zion in the midst of His enemies.
5. Those who trust in the Lord.
6. Their food is to do the will of Him who sent them and to accomplish His work.
7. They seek not their own will, but the will of Him who sent them.
8. Here is a man after My heart who will do all My will.
9. a. He has rays flashing from His hand.
    b. There is the hiding of His power.
10. a. They speak the words of God.
    b. He gives them His Spirit without measure.
11. Lightning.
12. It is like a fire and like a hammer which shatters the rock.
13. Burning coals of fire. The fire was bright and lightning was flashing from the fire.
14. They ran to and fro like lightning.
15. Thou dost open Thy hand and dost satisfy the desire of every living thing.
16. The creation itself will be set free from slavery to corruption into the freedom of the glory of the children or sons of God. For this is the desire of all creation; for this creation eagerly waits.
17. Beryl.
18. a. That I may know Him.
    b. That I may know the power of His resurrection.
    c. That I may know the fellowship of His sufferings.
    d. That I may be conformed to His death.
19. To be in the likeness of His resurrection.
20. Sparkling beryl.
21. The spirit of man.
22. The names of the sons of Israel.
23. Zebulun means dwelling or dweller. Leah named him this in hopes that her husband would honor her and dwell with her.
24. a. Sixty queens.
    b. Eighty concubines.
    c. Virgins without number.
    d. My dove, my undefiled one.
25. a. (v. 1) How lovely are thy dwelling places.
    b. (v. 2) My soul longs and yearns for the courts of the Lord.
    c. (v. 10) A day in thy courts is better than a thousand outside.
    d. (v. 10) I would rather stand at the threshold of the house of my God than to dwell in the tents of wickedness.
26. That I may dwell in the house of the Lord all the days of my life, to behold the beauty of the Lord and to meditate in His temple.
27. a. (v. 16) God has desired them for His abode.
    b. (v. 16) He will dwell there forever.
    c. (v. 1-3) The Lord loves the gates of Zion more than all the other dwelling places of Jacob.
28. a. I will abundantly bless her provision.
    b. I will satisfy her needy with bread.
    c. I will clothe her priests with salvation.
    d. They will sing aloud for joy.

e. I will cause the horn of David to spring forth there.

f. I have prepared a lamp for Him.

g. His crown shall shine upon Him.

29. a. (v. 12) Rebuild the ancient ruins.

b. (v. 12) Raise up the age old foundations.

c. (v. 12) Repair the breach.

d. (v. 12) Restore paths in which to dwell.

e. (v. 7 of Hosea) Those who live in His shadow will again raise grain and blossom like the vine.

THE KING OF GLORY:
HIS THRONE, HIS LORDSHIP

Correct Answers

1. His abdomen is carved ivory inlaid with sapphires.
2. His throne.
3. Rivers of living water.
4. The throne was made of ivory and overlaid with refined gold. There were six steps to the throne and a round top to the throne at its rear. There were arms on each side of the seat with two lions standing beside the arms, one on each side. Twelve lions were standing there on the six steps, six on one side and six on the other.
5. a. The righteous are as bold as a lion. They are fearless in the face of their enemies.
   b. We are more than conquerors through Christ.
   c. Men fear righteous and holy men.
   d. The righteous are strong in the Lord and the power of His might.
      1. The fear of the Lord.
      2. They have and use His precious name.
      3. Wisdom, knowledge, receive counsel (don't have an independent spirit).
      4. They know their God.
      5. From their weakness they were made stronger than their enemies.
      6. God is their refuge, He is a tower of strength against the enemy.
   e. The godly shall, in the latter days, make a prey of their adversaries. They shall trample down their enemies and there shall be none to rescue.
6. There were two lions standing beside the arms and there were twelve lions standing on the six steps, half on one side and half on the other.
7. The Word of the Lord and the Spirit.
8. It is inlaid with sapphires.
9. a. When the elders saw the God of Israel, under His feet appeared a pavement of sapphire.
   b. When Ezekiel saw his vision the throne of God appeared like lapis lazuli or sapphire.
10. It is the fifth stone in the breastplate and the second stone in the foundation of the New Jerusalem.
11. It was ablaze with flames, its wheels were a burning fire, a river of fire was flowing out from before Him.
12. He is a consuming fire.
13. a. He who walks righteously.
    b. He who speaks with sincerity.
    c. He who refuses to accept a bribe.
    d. He who refuses to hear about bloodshed.
    e. He who shuts His eyes from looking upon evil.
14. The Word of God.

THE KING OF GLORY:
THE REVEALED WORD

Corrrect Answers

1. His legs are pillars of alabaster set on pedestals of pure gold.
2. a. The counsel of the Lord.
   b. The plans of the Lord.
   c. The Word of the Lord.
3. They were not broken.
4. I will not violate My covenant nor alter the utterance of My lips.
5. a. His friends.
   b. His servants the prophets.
6. By doing what He commands them to do.
7. The pillar of stone or cloud marked the place where God spoke with man face to face as with a friend, revealing His plans and purposes.
8. Oil.
9. She fell at His feet and began to wet His feet with her tears and kept wiping them with her hair; kissing them, she anointed them with oil.
10. If this man were a prophet he would know what sort of person this woman is, that she is a sinner (or immoral woman).
11. Her sins which are many have been forgiven, for she loved much; but he who is forgiven of little loves little.
12. She poured oil on His head.
13. They were indignant and felt it was a waste of money and should have been given to the poor.
14. The poor you always have with you, but you do not always have Me. The woman has anointed Me for My burial.
15. On pedestals of pure gold.
16. The Lord Himself is watching over His Word to perform it. It is He who will accomplish all things that He has spoken.
17. a. A promise.
    b. An oath.
18. Those who believe that there will be a fulfilment of what has been spoken to them by the Lord.
19. His appearance is like Lebanon, choice as the cedars.
20. The righteous man.
21. a. He is the first born among many brethren.
    b. He is the last Adam from which springs forth the new race, the new creation.
22. 1. Grace will reign through righteousness to eternal life through Jesus Christ our Lord.
    2. The free gift arose from many transgressions resulting in justification.
    3. Those who receive grace and the gift of righteousness will reign in life through Jesus.
    4. Through one act of righteousness there resulted justification to all men.
    5. Through the obedience of the One the many will be made righteous.
23. We must bear the image of the heavenly and be conformed into the image of the Son.

STUDY 21

THE KING OF GLORY:
HE IS THE DESIRE OF ALL NATIONS

Correct Answers

1. Thy mouth is full of sweetness.
2. How sweet are Thy words to my taste, sweeter than honey to my mouth.
3. In the carcass of the lion was found honey. Out of the strong came something sweet. The death of Jesus, the Lion of Judah, made it possible for man to experience the sweetness of fellowship and communion with the living God.
4. Wisdom.
5. a. There will be a future.
   b. Your hope will not be cut off.
6. a. The hope of His calling.
   b. The riches of the glory of His inheritance in the saints.
   c. The surpassing greatness of His power toward us who believe.
7. He is wholly desirable.
8. a. Telling of the glory of God.
   b. Declaring the work of His hands.
   c. Revealing knowledge.
9. a. To separate the day from night.
   b. For signs.
   c. For seasons.
   d. For days.
   e. For years.
   f. To separate the light from the darkness.
10. The Lord, the Holy One.
11. Pleiades, Orion, the Bear.
12. Where is He who has been born King of the Jews? For we saw His star in the East and have come to worship Him.
13. Whom have I in heaven but Thee? Besides Thee, I desire nothing on earth.
14. His name, even His memory.
15. Her soul longs for Him, her spirit within her seeks Him diligently.
16. That she might dwell in the house of the Lord all her life; that she might behold His beauty and meditate in His temple.
17. As the deer pants for the waterbrooks so my soul pants for Thee O God. My soul thirsts for the living God.
18. Blessed are those who hunger and thirst after righteousness, for they shall be filled.
19. This is my Beloved, and this is my friend.
20. Where has your beloved gone that we may seek Him with you?
21. She has let her light shine before men so that they could see her good works and glorify the Father who is in heaven.
22. a. The light of the world.
    b. A city set on a hill which cannot be hidden.
23. She has given light to all who are in the house.
24. He was pleased to reveal His Son in her that she might preach Him.
25. Incline your ear, come to Me; listen that you may live and I will make an everlasting covenant with you. Seek the Lord while He may be found; call upon Him while He is near.
26. The daughters were drawn to Him.
27. I have loved you with an everlasting love; therefore, I have drawn you with lovingkindness.
28. The ministry of reconciliation.

STUDY 22

FAITH AT ITS BEST

Correct Answers

1. She was to trust in the name of the Lord and rely on her God.
2. He had gone down into his garden to the bed of balsam.
3. a. Trust in the Lord with all your heart.
   b. Do not lean on your own understanding.
   c. In all your ways acknowledge Him.
   d. And He will direct your paths.
4. a. She gave herself to the hungry and satisfied the desire of the afflicted.
   b. Light began to arise out of darkness and her gloom became like midday.
5. a. The Lord was her guide continually.
   b. He satisfied her desire in scorched places.
   c. He gave strength to her bones.
   d. She became like a watered garden.
   e. She became like a spring of water whose waters do not fail.
6. He went to the bed of balsam.
7. The cheeks of the Lord are described as a bed of balsam.
8. He is pasturing His flocks and gathering lilies.
9. Where do you pasture your flock? Where do you make them lie down at noon?
10. Gathering lilies.
11. His lips.
12. I am my beloved's and my beloved is mine.
13. She has become convinced that there is nothing that can separate her from the love of God which is in Christ Jesus our Lord.
14. That there is no where she can go to escape the presence of His Spirit and that in Him she lives, moves, and has her being.
15. a. To hold fast the confession of her hope without wavering.
    b. He is faithful.
16. a. She has become careful not to throw away her confidence.
    b. The quality of endurance.
17. a. That we show the same diligence.
    b. That we might realize the full assurance of hope.
18. Those who through faith and patience inherit the promises.
19. a. He did not waver in unbelief.
    b. He grew strong in faith.
    c. He gave glory to God.
    d. He was fully assured that what he had promised He was also able to perform.
20. Righteousness.

STUDY 23

THE HIDDEN LIFE WITHIN THE VEIL

Correct Answers

1. a. You are as beautiful as Tirzah.
    b. As lovely as Jerusalem.
    c. As awesome as an army with banners.
2. She walks before Him blameless.
3. Holiness.
4. On a high and holy place with the contrite and lowly of spirit.
5. Jesus Himself has established her heart unblameable in holiness.
6. Within the veil, where Jesus is.
7. The hope that is set before her that when He appears we shall be like Him — Christ in you, the hope of realizing that glory.
8. He sees her as His Holy Bride.
9. She is an overcomer and has been made a pillar in the temple of God.
10. When Christ who is her life is revealed, then she also will appear with Him in glory.
11. Victory.
12. Truth.
13. God's Word.
14. It will set you free.
15. Ignorance of the Word.
16. With the breath of His mouth.
17. Their minds are blinded that they might not see the light of the gospel.
18. By the renewing of your mind.
19. Buy the truth and sell it not.
20. a. As a covenant to the people.
    b. As a light to the nations.
    c. To open blind eyes.
    d. To bring out prisoners from the dungeon.
    e. To bring out those who dwell in darkness from the prison.
21. a. The Lord will go forth like a warrior.
    b. He will arouse His zeal like a man of war.
    c. He will utter a shout and raise a war cry.
    d. He will prevail against His enemies.

STUDY 24

THE EYES OF LOVE

Correct Answers

1. Your eyes are like doves.
2. Turn away your eyes for they have confused me or overcome me.
3. a. Moses' intercession for Israel.
   b. Jacob's wrestling with God.
   c. The death of Lazarus.
4. The Lord changed His mind about the harm which He said He would do to His people.
5. You have striven with God and with men and have prevailed.
6. Do not give what is holy to the dogs or cast your pearls before swine lest they trample them under their feet and turn and tear you to pieces. The Lord rewards those who diligently seek Him and will let them find Him.
7. That God would bless him.
8. The Lord said "Why do you ask Me My name?" Jacob did not respond or seek Him any further.
9. He desired to know God and His ways so that he might find favor in God's sight, desiring to please God from a heart of love.
10. My presence shall go with you and I will give you rest.
11. If Thy presence does not go with us, do not lead us up from here.
12. Yes.
13. He desired to see God's glory.
14. The Lord showed Him His glory.
15. Because Jacob was half-hearted in his search for God and was concerned more with the Lord's blessings than with knowing the Lord.
16. He loved them very much.
17. If you had been here my brother would not have died. Even now I know that God will give you whatever you ask.
18. I am the resurrection and the life, he who believes in Me shall live even if he dies and everyone who lives and believes in Me shall never die. Do you believe this?
19. Yes Lord; I have believed that you are the Christ, the Son of God, even He who comes into the world.
20. She fell at His feet weeping, saying, "Lord if you had been here my brother would not have died."
21. He was deeply moved in His Spirit and troubled.
22. At the foot of the cross.
23. At the tomb.
24. She remained there weeping, still seeking His body.
25. She beheld and talked to the resurrected Son of God.
26. Three of the thirty chief men.
27. At harvest time.
28. The troop of Philistines were camping in the valley of Rephaim and the garrison of the Philistines was in Bethlehem.
29. They broke through the camp of the enemy and drew water from the well of Bethlehem and brought it to David.
30. David would not drink it, but poured it out on the ground to the Lord saying, "Shall I drink the blood of these men who went in jeopardy of their lives?"

STUDY 25

THE WIFE OF THE KING OF LIGHT

Correct Answers

1. As a flock of goats.
2. Separation unto God.
3. As a flock of ewes which have come up from their washing, all of which bear twins and not one among them has lost her young.
4. Newly shorn.
5. She is filled with the knowledge of His will in all spiritual wisdom and understanding.
6. a. She walks in a manner worthy of the Lord.
   b. Pleasing Him in all respects.
   c. Bearing fruit in every good work.
   d. Increasing in the knowledge of God.
7. They are like a slice of pomegranate behind her veil.
8. When Christ who is her life is revealed, she also will be revealed with Him in glory.
9. Jesus knew that the Father had given all things into His hands and that He had come forth from God and was given back to God. Yet, He was able to wash the disciples' feet.
10. a. Sixty queens.
    b. Eighty concubines.
    c. Maidens or virgins without number.
    d. My dove, my perfect one.
11. a. A dove.
    b. A perfect one.
    c. Unique, her mother's only daughter.
    d. The pure child of the one who bore her.
12. That they may all be one as Jesus and the Father are one; that they may be perfected in unity; that the world might know that you sent Me.
13. It was not able to perfect those who drew near.
14. It was able to perfect forever those who are sanctified.
15. It is not able to take away sins.
16. Behold the Lamb of God who takes away the sin of the world.
17. a. The Church in all her glory.
    b. Having no spot or wrinkle.
    c. Holy and blameless.
18. By the washing of the water of the Word.
19. a. The blood of the Lamb.
    b. The Word of their testimony.
    c. Loving not their lives even unto death.
20. a. Those who love Him.
    b. Those who eagerly await Him for salvation.
21. The five wise virgins.
22. a. Grows like the dawn.
    b. As beautiful as the full moon.
    c. As pure as the sun.
    d. As awesome as an army with banners.
23. They will be known and recognized as the seed which the Lord has blessed.
24. The skin of his face shone because of his speaking with God. Even more glory.
25. Glory.
26. a. It abounds in glory.
    b. The glory that accompanies the new covenant surpasses the glory which accompanied the old.
    c. The glory of the new covenant remains rather than fades away.
27. a. With unveiled face.
    b. Beholding as in a mirror the glory of the Lord.
    c. We are being transformed into the same image.
28. God reveals to her His wisdom and she becomes illumined; her stern face begins to beam.

29.   a. Those who have insight.

      b. Those who lead the many to righteousness.

30. It is like the light of dawn that shines brighter and brighter until the full day.

31.   a. The difference between the holy and the profane.

      b. Causes them to discern between the unclean and the clean.

32. She is able to stand and judge it according to God's ordinances.

33.   a. Her lips preserve knowledge.

      b. Men seek instruction from her mouth.

      c. She is a messenger of the Lord of hosts.

34. Like the rising of the sun in its might.

35. The Lord our God is a sun and shield.

36. His face shone like the sun in its strength and His garments become as white as light.

37. His face was like the sun shining in its strength.

38. A woman clothed with the sun and the moon under her feet. On her head was a crown of 12 stars.

39. They will shine forth as the sun in the Kingdom of their father.

40. As the dawn spread over the mountains.

41. It is like the garden of Eden.

42. The people are in anguish; all faces turn pale.

43.   a. They march in line.

      b. They do not deviate from their paths.

      c. They do not crowd each other.

      d. Every one marches in his own path.

      e. They do not break ranks.

      f. They do not burst through the defenses.

44.   a. I went down to the orchards of nut trees.

      b. To see the blossoms of the valley.

      c. To see whether the vine had budded.

      d. To see if the pomegranates had bloomed.

45. The disciples were trying to cast out a demon of epilepsy, there was a large crowd, and the scribes were standing around arguing with the disciples.

46. To shepherd His sheep.

47. They were discussing which of them were the greatest. Jesus desired for them to have pure and godly thoughts.

48. Her soul set her over the chariots of her noble people.

49. A people who will volunteer freely and who walk in holiness.

STUDY 26

THE TESTIMONY IN THE DANCE
OF VICTORY

Correct Answers

1. Return that we may gaze at you.
2. When Jacob met the angels of God along his way he named that place Mahanaim, saying this is God's camp.
3. Victory over the enemy.
4. How beautiful are your feet in sandals, O prince's daughter!
5. a. She has brought good news.
   b. She has announced peace.
   c. She brings good news of happiness.
   d. She announces salvation.
   e. She says to Zion, "your God reigns."
6. a. Their gladness increases.
   b. They are glad at thy presence, as the gladness of harvest.
   c. They are as glad as men who rejoice when they divide the spoil.
7. He will break the yoke of their burden, the staff on their shoulders and the rod of the oppressor.
8. He delivered them from the domain of darkness and transferred us to the Kingdom of His beloved Son.
9. a. How shall they call upon Him of whom they have not believed?
   b. How shall they believe in Him of whom they have not heard?
   c. How shall they hear without a preacher?
   d. How shall they preach unless they are sent?
10. To seek and save the lost.
11. Like jewels, the work of the hands of an artist.
12. The lips of knowledge and wisdom.
13. a. Wisdom.
    b. Understanding.
    c. Counsel.
    d. Strength.
    e. Knowledge.
    f. The fear of the Lord.
14. Your navel is like a round goblet, which never lacks mixed wine.
15. Being drunk with sweet wine.
16. Rivers of living water, thus signifying the Holy Spirit.
17. a. Everything will live wherever the river goes.
    b. There will be very many fish because these waters go there.
18. Your belly is like a heap of wheat fenced about with lilies.
19. Give life to the world.
20. I am the living bread that comes down out of heaven, if any one eats of this bread he shall live forever.
21. Lord you have the Words of eternal life.
22. To do the will of God and finish His work.
23. The hidden manna.
24. Your breasts are like two fawns, twins of a gazelle.
25. a. Be joyful with Jerusalem and rejoice for her all you who love her.
    b. Nurse and be satisfied with her comforting breasts.
    c. Suck and be delighted with her bountiful bosom.
26. a. They will be comforted.
    b. Their heart will be glad.
    c. Their bones shall flourish like the new grass.
    d. The hand of the Lord will be made known to them.

THE DANCE OF MAHANAIM:
THE SUBMISSIVE WILL, LIVING WATER
AND HER GREAT PEACE

Correct Answers

1. A tower of ivory.
2. She has come to do God's will.
3. I delight to do Thy will O my God; Thy law is written on my heart.
4. The former dominion.
5. Your eyes are like pools in Heshbon by the gate of Bath-rabbim.
6. They found in her a pool of water to quench their thirst after God.
7. The Lord Himself.
8. If you knew the gift of God and who it is who says to you, give me a drink, you would have asked Him and He would have given you living water.
9. Covenant of peace.
10. She has loved God's law and kept His commandments with her whole heart.
11. Announcing peace.
12. a. Wonderful Counselor.
    b. Mighty God.
    c. Eternal Father.
    d. Prince of Peace.
13. There would be no end to the increase of His government or of peace.
14. He will guide our feet into the way of peace.
15. I give you peace which the world does not understand or know.
16. a. Do not let your heart be troubled.
    b. Do not let your heart be afraid.
17. The chastisement of our peace was upon Him.
18. Peace be with you.
19. Her trust in the Lord her God has delivered her from all fear.
20. Perfect love.

STUDY 28

THE DANCE OF MAHANAIM:
HER STRONG DISCERNMENT, THE HIGHWAY OF HOLINESS,
AND THE CAPTIVATED HEART

Correct Answers

1. Your nose is like the tower of Lebanon which faces toward Damascus.
2. Discernment.
3. She has loved God's Word, meditated on it all the day, and kept its precepts.
4. a. She is wiser than her enemies.
   b. She has more insight than all her teachers.
   c. She understands more than the aged.
   d. By understanding she is able to hate every false way.
5. Not by what her eyes see or what her ears hear.
6. a. Judge righteously.
   b. Show no partiality in judgment.
   c. Do not fear man.
   d. The judgment is God's.
7. a. The word I spoke is what will judge him.
   b. For I did not speak on my own initiative.
   c. I speak only what the Father has told Me.
8. An understanding heart to judge Thy people, to discern between good and evil.
9. The King ordered that the child be divided in two, giving half to one mother and half to the other mother. As a result the real mother was willing to yield possession of the child in order to spare his life. The other mother insisted that he be divided in two and belong to neither one.
10. The glory of God.
11. The Highway of Holiness.
12. a. The unclean.
    b. The fool.
    c. The lion (Satan).
    d. The vicious beast (demonic hosts).
13. The redeemed and the ransomed of the Lord who walk in holiness.
14. To depart from evil.
15. To teach God's people the difference between the holy and the profane and cause them to discern between the unclean and the clean.
16. A voice calling in the wilderness, "Prepare ye the way of the Lord."
17. A glorious church without spot or wrinkle, holy and blameless.
18. It crowns you like Carmel.
19. Elijah acted for God. He battled there with all that was of Baal and demonstrated the victory of the Lord over everything false and evil.
20. Father, I thank you that you hear Me. I know that You hear Me always, but because of the people standing around I said it that they might believe.
21. a. She knows that whatever she asks the Father according to His will He hears.
    b. Because she knows that He hears her, she also knows that she has the requests which she asked of Him.
22. Her heart does not condemn her.
23. a. Because she keeps His commandments.
    b. She does the things that are pleasing in His sight.
24. If you ask anything in My name I will do it for you.
25. The flowing locks of your head are like purple threads; the King is captivated by your tresses.
26. The royal priesthood.
27. His desire was to see God's name glorified in the earth.
28. Moses was close to God's heart; therefore, Jesus shared with Moses His innermost feelings.
29. They shall reign with Him.
30. Take no rest for yourselves you who remind the Lord, give Him no rest until He establishes and makes Jerusalem a praise in the earth.

THE DANCE OF MANAHAIM:
THE FULNESS OF HIS STATURE, THE HEART OF A SHEPHERD,
AND THE WINE OF MILLENNIAL DELIGHT

Correct Answers

1. Your stature is like the palm tree.
2. The measure of the stature of the fulness of Christ.
3. The righteous man.
4. 1. She is seeking those things which are above; her mind and her spiritual affections are not set upon the things of the earth.

   2. Her hidden union with Jesus causes her to blossom and bear fruit without being affected by worldly influences. Her roots sink deep into Him and she draws from that river of living water that is within.

   3. Because she draws her life from the living water of God, she is always fresh, always full of life and even producing fruit. Her leaf is for the healing of the nations. She bears fruit continuously and even more so in old age for she is full of sap and whatever she does prospers.

   4. Through the relationships with the five-fold ministry, the Body of Christ (and individual members in particuar) has grown up into Him; having been strengthened by her brothers and sisters in the Lord. They are joined together into a unit of strength. They are fat and flourishing. In this story of Moses we see a beautiful picture of body ministry and the strength and victory which is available in unity.

   5. All trials and testings that have come upon the Shulamite have caused her to reach upward, challenging her to go up to a higher plane spiritually. As she persevered under trial, the Spirit of glory and of God rested upon her. She has received her crown of life.

   6. Having separated herself from all worldliness, the counsel of the ungodly, and the path of sinners and scoffers, she has become a holy vessel unto the Lord. She is planted, not in the dunghill of worldliness, but in the courts of her God.
5. As the cluster of the palm.
6. I will climb the palm tree, I will take hold of its fruit stalk.
7. Those whose heart is completely His.
8. a. The breasts which are likened to clusters of the vine.

   b. The fragrance of the breath, which is likened to apples.

   c. The mouth which is likened to the best wine.
9. Tending His lambs and shepherding His sheep.
10. As a shepherd He will tend His flocks, in His arm He will gather the lambs and carry them in His bosom, gently leading the nursing ewes.
11. a. She knows the sheep very intimately.

    b. She lays down her life for the sheep.
12. That which makes man a living being.
13. The best wine.
14. The good wine or best wine that Jesus made at the wedding feast.
15. The Marriage Supper of the Lamb celebrating the union of the Lamb and His Bride.
16. The third day.
17. I reach my God.
18. Those who do the will of God.
19. What do I have to do with you? My hour has not yet come.
20. Whatever He says to you, do it.
21. a. Six.

    b. For purification or washing.

    c. Twenty or thirty gallons.
22. a. For the revealing of the Sons of God.

    b. For the redemption of the Body.

    c. Eagerly await Him for salvation.
23. a. Conquered kingdoms.

    b. Performed acts of righteousness.

    c. Obtained promises.

     d. Shut the mouths of lions.

     e. Quenched the power of fire.

     f. Escaped the edge of the sword.

     g. From weakness were made strong.

     h. Became mighty in war.

     i. Put foreign armies to flight.

24. That apart from us they should not be made perfect.

25. The abundance of the heart, or that which fills the heart.

26. It goes down smoothly for my beloved, flowing gently through the lips of those who fall asleep.

27. At the resurrection of the dead.

28. a. Those who had been beheaded for their testimony and the Word of God.

     b. Those who had not worshipped the beast.

     c. Those who had not received His mark.

     d. Those who were holy.

29. a. Lay aside every encumbrance and the sin which so easily entangles us.

     b. Let us run with endurance the race that is set before us.

     c. Fixing our eyes on Jesus.

30. a. Consider Him who has endured such hostility by sinners.

     b. You have not yet resisted to the point of shedding blood in your striving against sin.

GOD'S DESIRE FOR MANY SONS
IN HIS IMAGE

Correct Answers

1. O that you were like a brother to me who nursed at my mother's breasts. If I found you outdoors I would kiss you.
2. His disciples, whoever shall do the will of My Father who is in heaven.
3. That she might come into that intimate fellowship and union with her fellow believers, whose heart cry is the same as her heart cry. She desires that unity of Spirit with her brother that Jesus cried out for in Gethsemane.
4. The unity of the faith.
5. a. Good.
    b. Pleasant.
    c. Like the anointing that flowed from the top of Aaron's head down the skirts of his garments.
    d. Like the dew of Hermon descending on Mount Zion.
    e. There the Lord commanded the blessing—life forever.
6. Special wine from the juice of her pomegranates.
7. Eat my food and the wine I have mixed. Forsake your folly and live and proceed in the way of understanding.
8. The eternal God who supports her with His everlasting arms.
9. Protecting His Bride from needless activity and anything that would disturb her rest.
10. Her Beloved.
11. a. She trusts in the Lord with all her heart.
    b. She does not lean on her own understanding.
    c. In all her ways she acknowledges Him.
12. He will make her paths straight.
13. The children of Israel moved only at the command of the Lord as they trusted their path to Him and did not lean to their own understanding.
14. I awakened you, there your mother was in labor with you and gave you birth.
15. Labor.
16. She brings forth her sons.
17. She was with child and cried out in pain to give birth.
18. She gave birth to a son, a male child, who is to rule all the nations with a rod of iron.
19. Put me like a seal over your heart. Like a seal on your arm.
20. You shall love the Lord your God with all your heart, with all your soul, with all your mind, with all your strength.
21 The Holy Spirit of Promise.
22. It is a pledge of our inheritance with a view to the redemption of God's own possession.
23. It is as strong as death.
24. To lay down his life for his friends.
25. This is My body, this is the blood of the covenant which is to be shed on behalf of many for forgiveness of sins.
26. a. The Lord is for me, I will not fear, for what can man do to me.
    b. Open to me the gates of righteousness. I shall enter through them and give thanks to the Lord.
    c. This is the day which the Lord has made, let us rejoice and be glad in it.
    d. Bind the festival sacrifice with cords to the horns of the altar.
27. a. Victory over Satan's power.
    b. Joyful shouting and salvation in the tents of the righteous.
    c. The resurrection.
28. Jealousy is severe as Sheol. Its flashes are flashes of fire, the very flame of the Lord.
29. His Spirit which he has made to dwell in us.
30. I am jealous over you with a godly jealousy that I might present you as a pure virgin unto Jesus.
31. I am exceedingly jealous for her.
32. Many waters cannot quench love, nor will rivers overflow it.
33. He gave all the riches of his house for love and it was utterly despised.

34. He was despised and forsaken of men, a man of sorrows and acquainted with grief. Men hid their face from Him. He was despised and we did not esteem Him.
35. The world was made by Him and they did not know Him. He came to His own and they did not receive Him.
36. The right to become children of God.
37. We have a little sister who has no breasts, what shall we do for her on the day when she is spoken for?

PERFECT LOVE

Correct Answers

1. I am my beloved's and His desire is for me.
2. The disciple whom Jesus loved.
3. He does not desire sacrifice or meal offering, burnt offering or sin offering.
4. A Hebrew slave was allowed to go out as a free man during the seventh year of servitude. If a slave plainly said "I do not want to be free, but I love my master and want to serve him," then the master takes Him before the elders or judge, brings him to the door and pierces his ear with an awl. He shall then serve the master permanently.
5. Jacob loved Rachel much more than Leah.
6. Truth in the inward parts.
7. Send out Thy light and Thy truth and let them lead me and bring me to Thy Holy Hill and Thy dwelling places.
8. Buy the truth and sell it not.
9. Favor and good repute in the sight of God and man.
10. Compassion or mercy.
11. Forget your people and your Father's house.
12. Leave your country, your father's house, your relatives, and go to the land which I show you.
13. Do not urge me to leave you or turn back from following you, for where you go, I will go, where you lodge, I will lodge. Your people shall be my people and your God, my God.
14. Those who do the will of God, the same is my brother, my sister, and my mother.
15. For this cause a man shall leave his father and mother and shall cleave to his wife and the two shall become one flesh.
16. As those who had none.
17. The things of the Lord, how they might please the Lord and be holy in body and spirit.
18. The things of the world, how they might please husband or wife.
19. Paul does not desire to put a restraint upon the people for marriage but that each husband and wife should not have divided interests, but should display undistracted devotion to the Lord.
20. Zion.
21. Those who trust in the Lord.
22. He loves them more than all the other dwelling places of Jacob.
23. Holiness.
24. Holiness.

STUDY 32

GOD'S FELLOW WORKER

Correct Answers

1. Let us go into the country and spend the night in the villages.
2. The world.
3. She is a stranger and a pilgrim on the earth.
4. Let us rise early and go to the vineyards.
5. His workmanship created and prepared for good works.
6. To make the most of her time.
7. a. To see if the vine has budded.
   b. To see if the blossoms have opened up.
   c. To see if the pomegranates have bloomed.
8. Giving Him her love.
9. Tend and shepherd His lambs and sheep.
10. The greater love which she has toward Him.
11. She seeks to serve and give her life a ransom for many.
12. Unto the Lord.
13. The mandrakes. Harvest time.
14. Do not say that the harvest is in the future, but the fields are ripe now for harvest.
15. Lack of laborers.
16. All choice fruits, new and old.
17. For who is my hope, my joy, my crown of exultation? It is you, you are my glory and my joy in the presence of His coming.
18. He has caused her to sow and plant vineyards, to gather a fruitful harvest. He has greatly multiplied her.
19. The fruit of the earth.
20. Fruit.
21. Over our doors.
22. The blood of the Passover Lamb which was applied above the door.
23. This is the fruit which He purchased with His own blood.
24. Your land will yield its produce, the threshing will last until grape gathering and the grapes will last until sowing time, you will eat the old supply and clear out the old because of the new.

HIS REDEMPTION PLAN

Correct Answers

1. If she is a wall, we shall build on her a battlement of silver. If she is a door we shall barricade her with planks of cedar.
2. a. Return to the Lord — total commitment.
   b. One who extracts the precious from the worthless (separated totally unto Him and committed to a life of holiness).
3. a. Your foundations I will lay in sapphires.
   b. I will make your battlements of rubies.
   c. Your gates crystal.
   d. Your entire wall of precious stones.
4. a. Your sons will be taught of the Lord.
   b. Their peace or well-being will be great.
   c. You will be established in righteousness.
   d. You will be far from oppression, terror and fear.
   e. No weapon that is formed against you shall prosper and every tongue that accuses you in judgment will be condemned.
5. The temple of the Lord.
6. Pure gold.
7. He will transform her into His image from glory to glory by the Lord.
8. I was a wall and my breasts were like towers, then I became in His eyes as one who finds peace.
9. Great peace.
10. Peace, quietness and confidence forever, thus she dwells in a peaceful habitation and in secure and undisturbed resting places.
11. One thousand shekels of silver.
12. a. One thousand shekels of silver for Solomon.
    b. Two hundred for those who take care of its fruit.
13. He has poured out water upon her, and poured out His Spirit upon her offspring and her descendants.
14. O you who sit in the gardens, my companions are listening for your voice. Let me hear it.
15. Cornelius had a heart cry to know God.

STUDY 34

HIS BRIDE HAS MADE
HERSELF READY

Correct Answers

1. Hurry my Beloved and be like a gazelle or a young stag on the mountains of spices.
2. I know that my Redeemer lives and at last He will take His stand upon the earth. I shall see God, whom I myself shall behold and whom My eyes shall see.
3. Lord, show me Your glory!
4. My soul thirsts for the living God, when shall I come and appear before God?
5. Behold the Lord came with many thousands of His holy ones.
6. All the kingdoms under heaven were given to the saints and all nations will serve and obey the Lord.
7. He is as the sun, coming out from His chamber. His rising is from one end of the heavens to the other. There is nothing hidden from its heat.
8. The marriage of the Lamb.
9. She had made herself ready.

WORD STUDY

"Lightning"

Note: The things given in parenthesis are notes made from the context of the passage in which the scripture is given.

II Sam. 22:15 — Lightning *routed* (confused) the enemy — the lightning was sent out when He *uttered His voice*.

Ex. 19:16 — On the third day there was thunder, lightning flashes, thick clouds upon the mountain and a very loud trumpet sound so that all the people who were in the camp trembled. (On the third day the Lord was to come down in the sight of all people to Mt. Sinai so they might hear the words of the Lord as He spoke to Moses).

Ex. 20:18 — The people perceived the thunder (and) lightning flashes — the sound of the trumpet (this appeared so the people would fear God and *not sin*).

Job 28:26 — When He set a course for the thunder bolt — then He saw it (wisdom and understanding) He established it (wisdom and understanding) — searched it.

Job 36:30 — He spreads His lightning around Him — for by these He judges people (clouds, thundering, lightning).

Job 36:32 — He covers *His* hands with lightning (light) and commands it to strike the mark, its noise declares His presence.

Job 37:2 — He thunders His voice. Rumblings go out from His mouth and His *lightning* to the ends of the earth. **After it**, a voice roars. He thunders with His majestic voice. He does **not restrain** the **lightnings** when His voice is heard.

Job 37:11-13 — He *disperses* the cloud of His *lightning* and *it changes* direction, turning around by His guidance. That it may do whatever He commands it on the face of the inhabited earth. Whether for correction or for His world or for loving kindness, He causes it to happen.

Job 37:15 — Do you know how God establishes them and makes the lightning of His cloud to shine?

Job 38:35-36 — Can you send forth lightnings that they may go and say to you,"Here we are?" Who has put wisdom in the inner most being or has given understanding to the mind?

Ps. 18:14-15 — He sent lightning flashes in abundance and routed them, *then* the channels of water appeared *and* the foundations of the world were laid bare.

Ps. 144:6-7 — Flash forth lightning and scatter them — stretch forth Thy *hand* from on high.

Ps. 77:18 — Thy lightnings lit up the world.

Ps. 97:4-6 — His lightning lit up the world, the earth saw and trembled, the mountains melted at the presence of the Lord. The heavens declare His righteousness. All the peoples have seen His glory.

Ezk. 1:13-14 — In the midst of the living beings there was something that looked like burning coals of fire, like torches darting back and forth — the fire was bright and lightning was flashing from the fire — And the living being ran to and fro like lightning. (Living beings are symbolic of the overcomers).

Dan. 10:6 — The Heavenly visitor had a face that had the appearance of lightning (countenance).

Ps. 135:7 — He makes lightning for the rain.

Zech. 9:14 — His arrow will go forth like lightning.

Nahum 2:4 — They dash to and fro like lightning flashes.

Matt. 24:27 — Just as lightning comes from the east and flashes toward the west, so shall the coming of the Son of Man be.

Matt. 28:3 — Angel that rolled away the stones, their appearance was like lightning.

Luke 10:18 — I was watching satan fall from heaven like lightning.

Luke 11:36 — If therefore your whole body is full of light, with no dark part in it, it shall be wholly illumined, as when the lamp illumines you with its rays.

Rev. 4:5 — And from the throne proceeded flashes of lightning.

Rev. 8:5 — The Angel took the censer and filled it with the fire of the altar and threw it to the earth; there followed peals of thunder, sounds and flashes of lightning, and an earthquake.

Rev. 11:19 — At the resurrection of this working temple of God which is in heaven was opened and the ark, His covenant appeared in His temple and there were flashes of lightning.

CONCLUSION AND REVELATION:

Heb. 4:12-13 — "For the word of God is living and active and sharper than any two-edged sword, and piercing as far as the division of soul and spirit, of both joints and marrow, and able to judge the thoughts and intentions of the heart. And there is no creature hidden from His sight, but all things are open and laid bare to the eyes of Him with whom we have to do."

Conclusion: Lightning is the anointed word of God going forth from the mouth of the saints.

Note: It took 2 weeks to receive this revelation. It took reading and rereading the scriptures. It took much meditation and waiting on the Lord. When the revelation came, it was life and gave much understanding and imparted much faith.

The Conclusion is this: As we speak the Word of God, it goes forth from our mouth like lightning. It strikes the mark. It routes the enemy. It judges the people. It accomplishes whatever God commands it. It lays bare the foundations of mens' hearts. When His word goes forth, the channels of living water appear. It lights up everything. Nothing can hide from its light. The demonic powers melt at its presence. Men tremble before it. All the people see His glory.

Job 36:32 — "He covers His hands (hands represent His ministers) with lightning (which is the anointed word) and commands it to strike the mark. Its noise declares His presence."

Job 37:27 — "He does not restrain the lightnings when His voice is heard."

When we speak the anointed word, God does *not* restrain its *impact*. It goes forth like unrestrained lightning.

Ez. 1:13-14 — "In the midst of the living beings there was something that looked like burning coals of fire, like torches darting back and forth among the living beings. The fire was bright, and lightning was flashing from the fire. And the living beings ran to and fro like bolts of lightning."

In this symbolic description of the overcomers, they run to and fro like lightning. They are filled with the anointed word of God. They are guided and led by that word. Their whole appearance has the look of that anointing. Their words flash forth under the anointing of God, like the lightning. Their very life, words and actions declare His presence.

This word picture gives a mental impression and a very deep revelation of what the anointed word does as it issues forth from the mouth of God's servants.

GLOSSARY

Abdomen - the place of God's throne

Achor - trouble

Alabaster vial - soul of the believer

Amana - integrity and truth

Apple tree - Jesus in the fulness of His love

Arm - strength (Prov. 31:17; Gen. 49:24; Isa. 51:9)

Armory - a storehouse for weapons

Awesome - a mixed feeling of reverence, fear and wonder, caused by something majestic and sublime and having the power to inspire intense fear

Baali - my master

Banner - friendship, victory

Barefeet - signifies a slave in the presence of his master; also sensitivity to the Spirit of God

Bath - rabbim - daughter of many

Beauty - holiness

Bed - a place of spiritual rest

Belly - the spirit of the believer (John 7:38-39)

Beryl - Located in the fourth row in the breastplate of the High Priest and the tenth stone, the eighth stone in the Holy City (4 = completion of the New Creation, 10 = fulness of testing, 8 = resurrection), thus signifying that through the fulness of testing the New Creation will be completed and will bring forth the resurrection. It is green in color signifying eternal, never-ending, resurrection life.

Bether - separation

Blackness of his locks - God's hiding place where He separates and hides Himself in His terrible holiness from the eyes of men (Ex. 19:20-21; Ps. 18:9-12)

Blue - the presence of the revealed God, the anointing

Breasts or breastplate - the inward qualities of faith and love, righteousness and judgment, revelation and perfection; the balance of the two (Ex. 28:30; Num. 27:21); also the ability to feed others spiritually

Breath - that which makes man a living being (Gen. 2:7)

Brother - those who do God's will (Matt. 12:48-50)

Bronze - judgment

Burnt offering - a fellowship offering signifying the entire surrender of the individual unto God — this was a free-will offering

Carmel - the mount where Elijah's mighty prayers were heard and answered by fire, signifying the ability and power to bring wayward people back to God

Cast metal sea - basin in Solomon's temple where the priests washed their hands before entering the Holy Place

Cedar - a type of the saints, the righteous man (Ps. 92:12-15)

Cleft rock - the crucifixion of Jesus (John 19:33-34; Ex. 17:6)

Chariot - a vehicle for swift movement in the earth, the prophetic anointing

Cheeks - humility and obedience

Cinnamon and the finest spices - represent a place

Crown, priestly - judgment, ability to judge righteous judgment

Crown, royal - dominion, ruling and reigning

Crown, victor's - victory, victoriously overcoming the world

Crystal - clear, transparent,pure, the renewed mind

Cypress tree - a funeral tree, found commonly growing in the graveyards of Judea, signifies death

Dance - victory over the enemy, expression of joy and rejoicing (Ex. 15:19-21; I Sam. 18:6-7; Jer. 31:4, 12-13)

Damascus - oldest city in the East which is noted for the natural highway from east to west ; it is this great highway that is of importance here

Darling - an expression used by David in the Psalms to represent his own soul or his life — Jesus uses this expression to say that His Bride is as His own soul and an extension of His life on earth

Den of lions - speaks of spiritual forces in the heavenlies

Diadem - a crown with over two or three fillets signifying dominion over two or three countries, hence many diadems is a reference to the dominion of the Messiah as the supreme ruler of the earth which is also signified by His name,King of Kings and Lord of Lords.

Dove's eyes - singleness of vision (doves can only focus on one thing at a time) spiritual insight

Drops of the night - the agony of Jesus in Gethsemane (historical)

East - the mind of Christ, or an openness toward God

Engedi - a place in the wilderness where David fled to hide

Ewes, newly shorn - the mind shorn of the wisdom of this world which causes it to be deceitful in size and form

Faith - leaning of the entire personality on God and His Word in absolute trust and confidence in His wisdom and goodness

Fawn - a female deer having the inner quality of a very sensitive spirit

Field - the world (Matt. 13:38)

Fig tree - Israel

Fish - men

Flocks of His companions - people who follow men of God

Flowers - the shortness of man's life (Job 14:1-2)

Footsteps of the flock - steps or acts of those followers of Jesus who through faith and patience inherit the promises of God (Heb.6:12; Heb. 13:7; I Peter 2:21)

Frankincense - fragrant spice, used in making the priestly incense, it represents the intercessory prayer life of the priest (Rev. 8:3-4) and praise (Isa. 60:6; Ps. 100:4)

Garden - soul of the believer, the beauty of the New Creation life within, his life in Christ

Garments - all outward attitudes, behavior and external appearances

Gate - the mind of man

Gazelle - Jesus in His resurrection life

Gold - the divine nature

Grain - sons of the Kingdom (Matt. 13:38)

Green - freshness, vigor, prosperity and that which is flourishing, eternal life

Hair - separation unto God

Hand - the will in action

Hart - Jesus in His resurrection life

Harvest time - the consummation of the age (Matt. 13:39)

Henna flowers - used by Jewish maidens for adornment, signifies being transformed into His image

Hermon - destruction

Hesbon - stronghold

Highway - holiness (Isa. 35:8)

Hill of frankincense - Calvary

Hips - symbol of strength (thigh)

Honey - the sweetness of God's Words, His wisdom (Prov. 24:13-14)

Horn of David - the power and glory of the Messianic Kingdom, horn also denotes *position*

Ishi - my husband

Ivory - the King's throne (I Kings 10:18)

Jacob - type of Jesus

Jasper - the appearance of the One sitting on God's throne, the twelth stone in the breastplate of the High Priest, first stone in the Holy City (12 = divine government, one = God), thus revealing to us that the One who sits upon the throne is God, the supreme ruler of the universe; the red glowing appearance of the stone represents the mark of Jesus' passion, having redeemed man by His own blood

Jewels - words of knowledge and wisdom (Prov. 20:15; Prov. 8:11)

Leah - represents believers with weak spiritual insight

Leaping upon the mountains - the resurrection power of the Lamb in His exaltation above the kingdoms of this world and their satanic strongholds

Lebanon - the glory of God and His majesty (Isa. 60:13; Isa. 35:2)

Legs - the revealed Word upon which the believer stands

Lightning - the anointed Word of God going forth from the legs of the believer

Lily - the Bride of Christ; also spiritual thoughts and words imparted to the spirit of man by God

Lily work or design - (as on the pillars of Solomon's temple) the words of the Lord, the familiarity of that still small voice worked within the spirit of the believer (Song 1:13; I Kings 7:19, 22)

Linen - the righteous acts of the saints (Rev. 19:8)

Lion - kingly authority, bold, fearless

Lips - the speech

Kedar - dark room or chamber

Mahanaim - lit. two companies, signifying the place where Jacob met the angels of God along the way and said, "This is the place where God encamps" thus naming it "Mahanaim."

Milk - the elementary principles of the Word of God for sustaining the young in the Lord

Mount Gilead - the mountain on which the sheep and goats grazed awaiting sacrifice in the temple

Mountain - kingdom

Mountains of leopards - speaks of the spiritual forces in the heavenlies

Mountains of spices - speaks of the kingdoms of this world becoming the kingdoms of our God

Moon - the Church; full moon — the Church in its purity free from worldliness or any spot or shadow that the earth would cast upon it

Mother - those who do God's will (Matt. 12:48-50)

Mother's house - the system of grace (Gal. 4:26)

Mouth - the means by which one expresses that which fills the heart (Matt. 12:34)

Myrrh - an embalming spice, preserves; used in the anointing oil, speaks of healing, used for perfume and for beautifying as it helps smooth wrinkles; *myrrh and aloes* signify suffering love (John 19:38-40; Romans 5:8)

Nard - the fragrance of the Bride's love and appreciation for the Bridegroom

Neck - the will

Necklace - that spiritual quality of obedience that adorns the will (neck) of those who hear and do the word of God (Prov. 1:8-9)

Noon - the perfect light of the day, the sun in full strength

North wind - negative circumstances that the Spirit of God brings into your life to cause spiritual growth

Nose - sense of smell, discernment

Oil - the Holy Spirit

Orchard of pomegranates - paradise of godly thoughts

Ornaments - original Hebrew means something like a crown, a golden braided wreath

Oxen - ministers of the gospel, those who give service to the Lord, the will being subjected to the Lord (I Tim. 5:18)

Palm tree - the righteous man (Ps. 92:12-15)

Parable - a story in which people, things, and happenings have a hidden or symbolic meaning

Peace offerings - a fellowship offering, sacrifices offered in communion with God, free will offering on behalf of those who desired a closer fellowship with God

Pierced ear - signifies those who through love for their master had chosen to be bonded to him as his slave for life

Pillar - the overcomer (Rev. 3:12)

Pillar of smoke - the mark of God's presence and the power of the Holy Spirit

Pillar of stone - used to mark the place where God spoke with man face to face (Gen. 28:12-18, 22)

Plumb line - used to measure God's people

Pool - water that is clear and still, signifying a life of great peace and very deep calm

Pomegranates - a fruit, their seeds are crystal seeds tinged with red, they signify pure and godly thoughts

Powders of the merchant - selling all for the Kingdom of God (Matt. 13:45-46)

Precious stones - the wisdom and knowledge of God

Purple - kingly authority

Red - the blood of Jesus

Rod - authority to rule

Rock - Jesus

Ruby - a red stone, signifying the blood of Jesus

Sapphire - a blue stone signifying the anointing as well as the presence of the revealed God

Sardius stone - the appearance of the One sitting on God's throne, the first stone in the breastplate of the high priest and the sixth stone of the Holy City (one = God, 6 = man), thus revealing that the One who sits in the midst of the throne is both God and man (Rev. 4:2-3); its red glowing appearance signifies the marks of His passion, having shed His blood for the redemption of mankind

Scarlet thread - redemption

Senir - coat of mail

Seven spirits (or seven eyes) of God (Isa. 11:2-3)

Sharon - a plain in Judea, the rose is a rambling rose, or some ordinary flower common to the area

Shepherd's tents - five-fold ministry (Song 1:8; Eph. 4:11-13)

Shield - faith (Eph. 6:16)

Shulamite - person of peace

Sister - those who do God's will (Matt. 12:48-50)

Silver - redemption

Snow - God's glory

Solomon - King of peace; speaks of Jesus as a type

Sons of the East - those who have a heart opened toward God (Gen. 29:1)

South winds - positive circumstances that the Spirit of God brings into your life for spiritual growth

Steep pathway (also, secret places of the stairs) - the call to ascend with the risen Christ

Stone heap - an altar on which sacrifice is made to God

Sun - Jesus (Ps. 84:11; Matt. 17:2)

Teeth - indicate the ability to appropriate food (the mind meditating on the Word)

Temples - the seat of man's thoughts

Thorns - the cursed earth (Gen. 3:18; Heb. 6:7-8) — they also speak of the cares of this life

Thummim- *perfections* found inside the breastplate of the High Priest and used to determine the Word of judgment from the Lord, signifies the perfect measurement by which the believer is being judged and also judging others

Tirzah - meaning *delight*

Tower - strength against the enemy (Ps. 61:3)

Traveling couch of Solomon - the resting place of the King of Peace

Turtle dove - type of the Spirit of God being poured out through the sacrifice of Jesus

Twins - balance (Job 11:5-6; Ecc. 7:18)

Urim - *lights* found inside the breastplate of the High Priest used in determining judgments, the supernatural revelation of the Word of God; by this revelation God makes known His counsel and His will (Ex. 28:30; Num. 27:21)

Veiled - hidden from the world (II Cor. 3:15-18)

Vine - the Church

Water - Word of God

Well - spirit of the believer

Wheat - source of bread, staff of life

Wheel - the spirit of man (Ezk. 1:20)

White - purity, righteousness

Wind - the Spirit of God

Wine - joy (Ps. 104:15) also Holy Spirit

Wool - the earthly life that the Lord has cursed, that which causes sweat (Ezk. 44:17-18; Gen. 3:17-19)

Zion - those who trust in the Lord (Ps. 125:1)

Zebulun - dweller, or dwelling (Gen. 30:20)

NUMBER KEY

0 — seed

1 — the number of God

2 — the matter is determined by God

3 — the fulness of God, divine perfection, completion

4 — completion of the New Creation

5 — grace

6 — the number of man

7 — completion, spiritual perfection (in regards to man)

8 — resurrection, new beginnings

9 — the end or conclusion of a matter, the number of finality, the number of divine judgment

10 — fulness of testing

12 — divine government

20 — expectancy

30 — consecration, maturity for ministry (Gen. 41:46; II Sam. 5:4; Luke 3:23)

40 — Probation, testing; closing in victory or judgment. (Num. 13:25; Num. 14:33; Matt. 4:2) Also deliverance, rest, and enlarged dominion (Judges 3:11; Judges 8:28; II Sam. 5:4; I Kings 11:42)

50 — the year of jubilee — everything returns to its rightful owner

200 — 40 x 5 — having been brought by God's grace into a place of deliverance, rest and enlarged dominion

300 — divine deliverance

10,000 — a seed in the image of God through the fulness of testing

Note: For a full and complete study of Bible numbers we recommend *Number in Scripture* by E. W. Bullinger.